IMAGES
of America

BRUNSWICK AND TOPSHAM

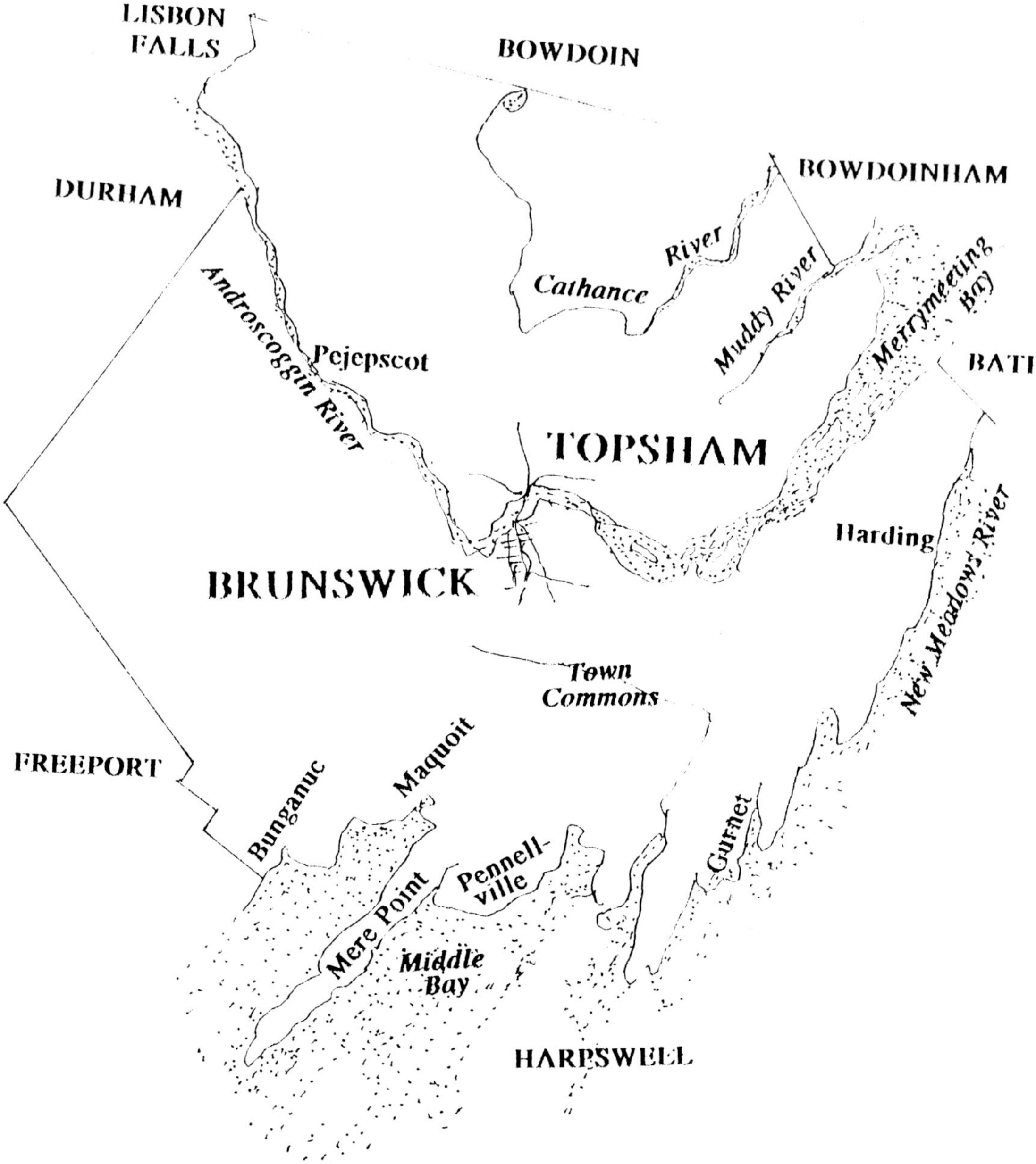

The Brunswick-Topsham region, showing the locations of sections mentioned in captions, as well as of the surrounding towns.

IMAGES
of America

BRUNSWICK AND TOPSHAM

Compiled by
Joyce K. Bibber

ARCADIA
PUBLISHING

ISBN 978-0-7385-8980-0

Published by Arcadia Publishing
Charleston, South Carolina

Printed in the United States of America

For all general information contact Arcadia Publishing at:
Telephone 843-853-2070
Fax 843-853-0044
E-mail sales@arcadiapublishing.com
For customer service and orders:
Toll-Free 1-888-313-2665

Visit us on the Internet at www.arcadiapublishing.com

Contents

Acknowledgments	6
Introduction	7
1. The River	11
2. Brunswick: Maine Street	29
3. The Mall	41
4. Topsham Village	45
5. Manufacturing	49
6. Agriculture	61
7. Topsham Fair	71
8. Transportation	75
9. Wartime	95
10. Getting Away From It All	97
11. Parades	105
12. Churches	113
13. Bowdoin	121
14. At Home	125
15. The Younger Generations	135
16. Other Activities	139

Acknowledgments

My fullest thanks go to Carol Hyde, who not only provided a place to stay, meals, and a telephone connection in Topsham, but located and introduced me to people with photos. Without her assistance, collecting these pictures would have been much more difficult. Among those helping with identifications were Lucienne Damours, Robert French, Richard Hyde, and the staffs of the Pejepscot Historical Society and the Maine Historical Society. Giving both data and ready access to their albums or collections were:

Anne Ackley (pages 25, 26, 27, 28, 33, 40, 57, 104u, 111, 112u, 118, 119, 120, 127, 140, 143); Viola Bibber (11, 12, 47, 82, 115, 133, 137); Robert Bisson family (65, 66, 67); Lee Chipman (68, 69, 70u); Andrew and Susie Dobransky (80u, 126, 137u, 142, 144); Kim and Greg Emerson (62u, 128); Sylvia Gaudet (128u); Myrtle Golding (62, 63, 74, 85, 102, 112); John and Marilyn Houston (20, 21, 22, 23, 24, 59, 60, 90); Town of Topsham (46); Percy and Virginia Hyde (61, 93, 94,138); Shirley Hyden (64, 86); Ruth Labbe (80c, 80, 126u, 135, 136, 137u); Richard Lord (10, 14, 15, 17, 19, 25, 36, 37, 38, 41, 53, 55, 58u, 71, 78, 79, 83u, 84u, 88, 91, 92, 98, 99u, 101u, 103, 104, 107, 109, 110, 117, 141); and the Maine Historic Preservation Commission (7, 10u, 13, 16, 18, 19u, 30, 31, 32, 34, 35, 38u, 39, 42, 43, 44, 49, 50, 51, 52, 54, 55u, 75, 76, 77, 81, 83u, 87, 97, 99, 100, 101, 102u, 105, 106, 108, 113, 114, 116, 117u, 121, 122, 123, 124, 125, 130, 131, 132, 134, 139, 140u). Earle Shettleworth, Jr., also provided the cover photo. A few photos are used by courtesy of the Pejepscot Historical Society (8-9, 29, 45, 47u, 48, 56, 58, 72, 73, 95, 96). Others came from the author's collection.

The Pejepscot Historical Society permitted the use of some of its photos.

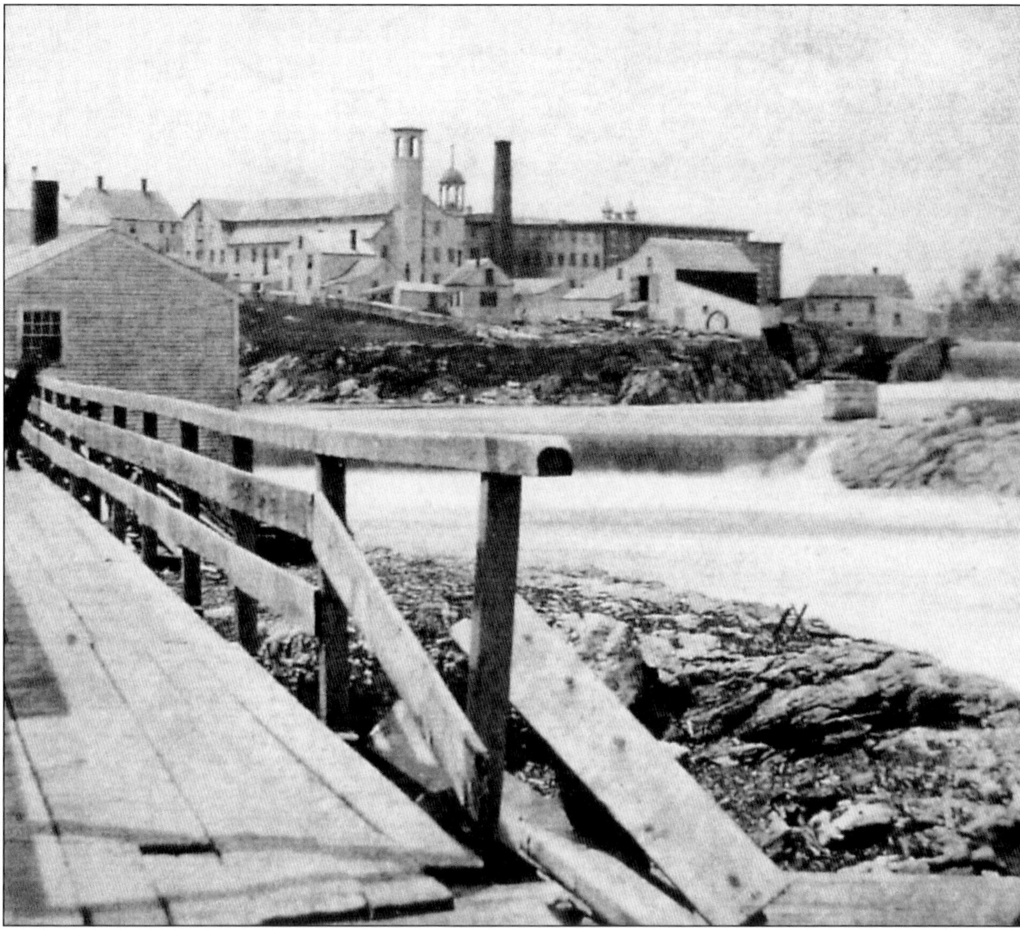

Introduction

There had been a few earlier claimants, but permanent English settlement of the towns of Brunswick and Topsham followed the Pejepscot Company's land grant of 1715. Brunswick, with both ocean and river frontage, had enough population to be incorporated as a town in 1739; Topsham gained that status in 1764. By the time cameras were available to record the scenes, Brunswick was a trading center and a college town, with the beginnings of a cotton mill, as well as an agricultural hinterland. Topsham was largely farmland and was developing an agricultural fairground. Its industry was in the form of small mills processing the harvests of local farms and forests.

The following pages present glimpses from approximately a century of development in the area, but are by no means an effort to tell the entire history of either town. Content has been shaped by the availability of pictures, some of which are one of a kind, while others better known, having been widely disseminated originally as photos, stereoptic cards (mostly 1870s) and post cards (largely early twentieth century.) Only a relatively few non-professionals used cameras locally before the 1920s or 1930s.

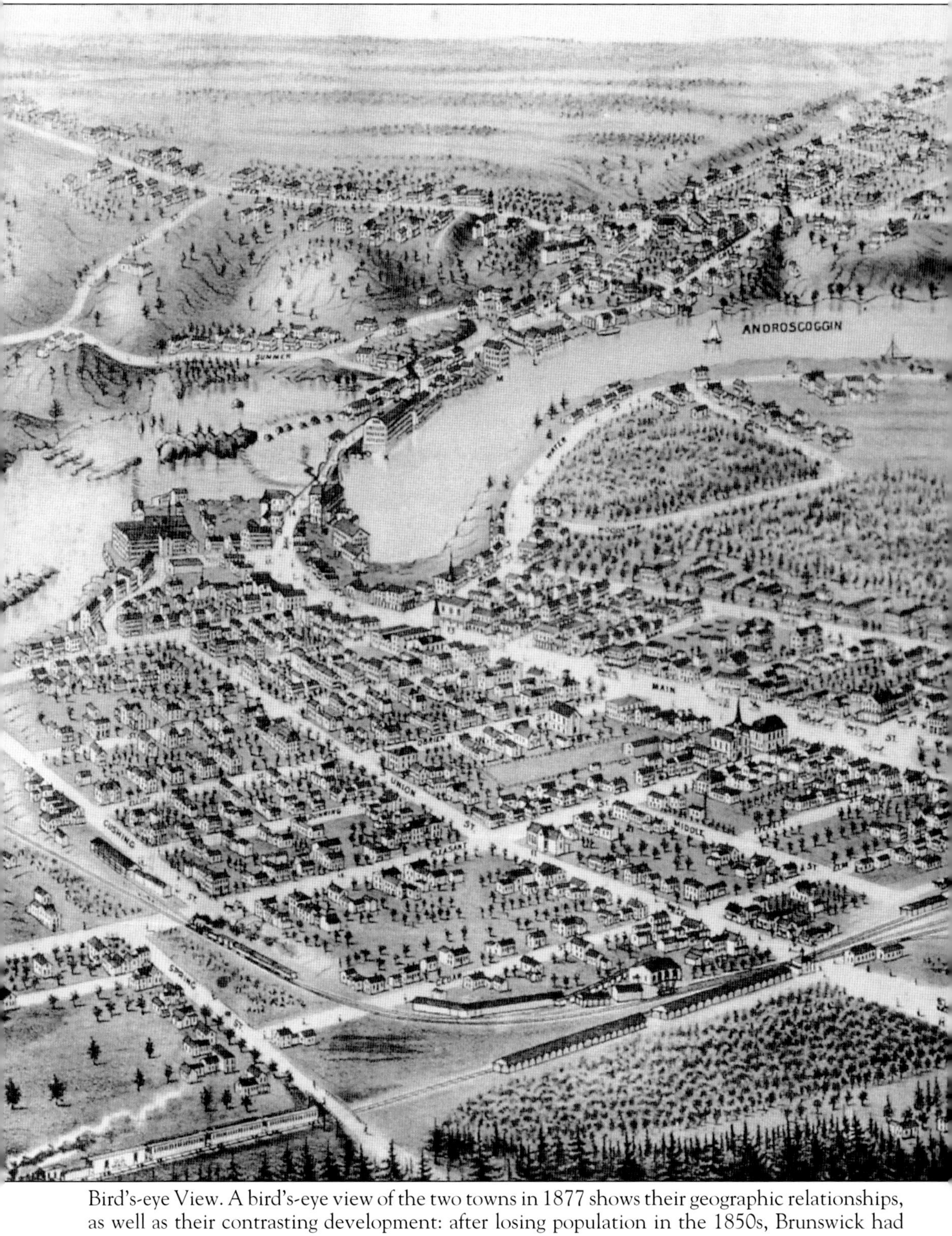

Bird's-eye View. A bird's-eye view of the two towns in 1877 shows their geographic relationships, as well as their contrasting development: after losing population in the 1850s, Brunswick had

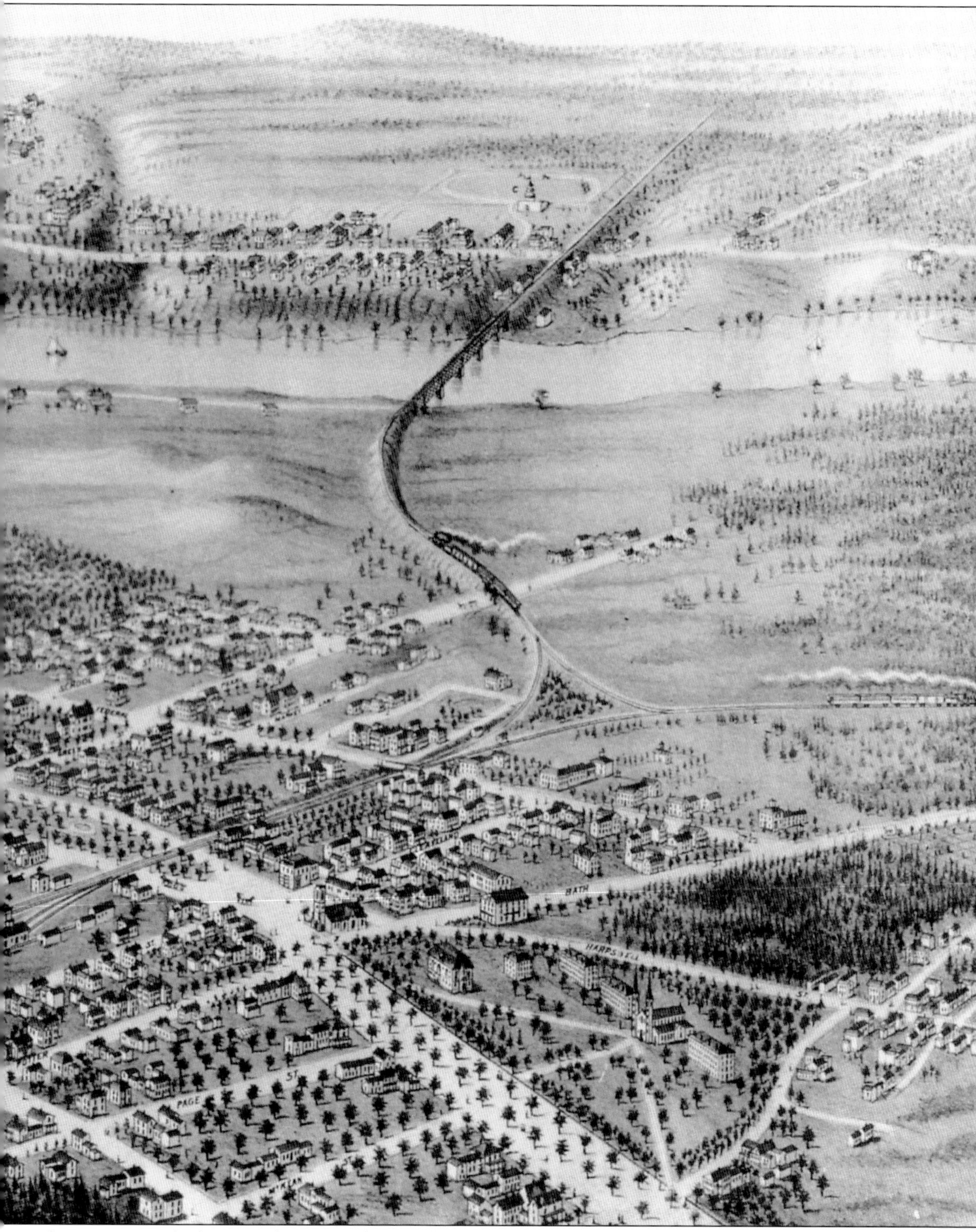

begun a period of tremendous growth. Topsham had between a third and a quarter of the number of residents and would not grow much until the 1890s.

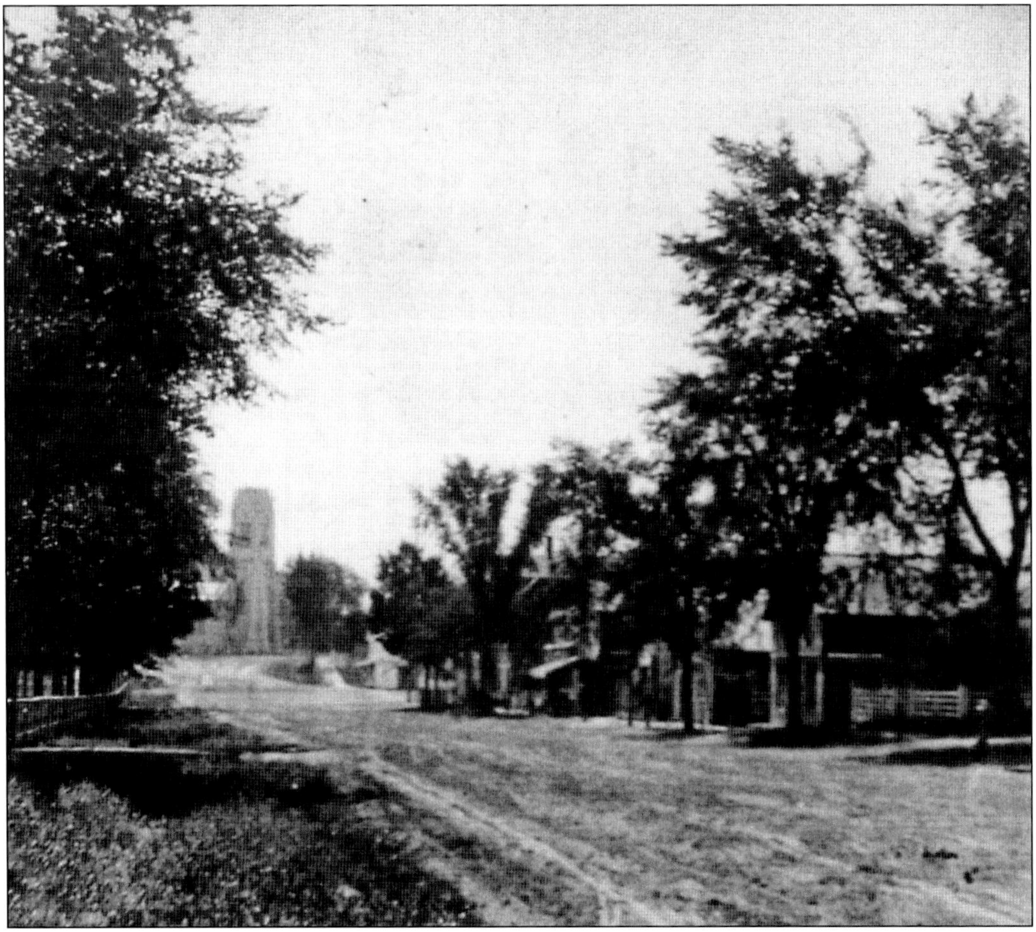

Upper Maine Street, Brunswick, in the 1870s.

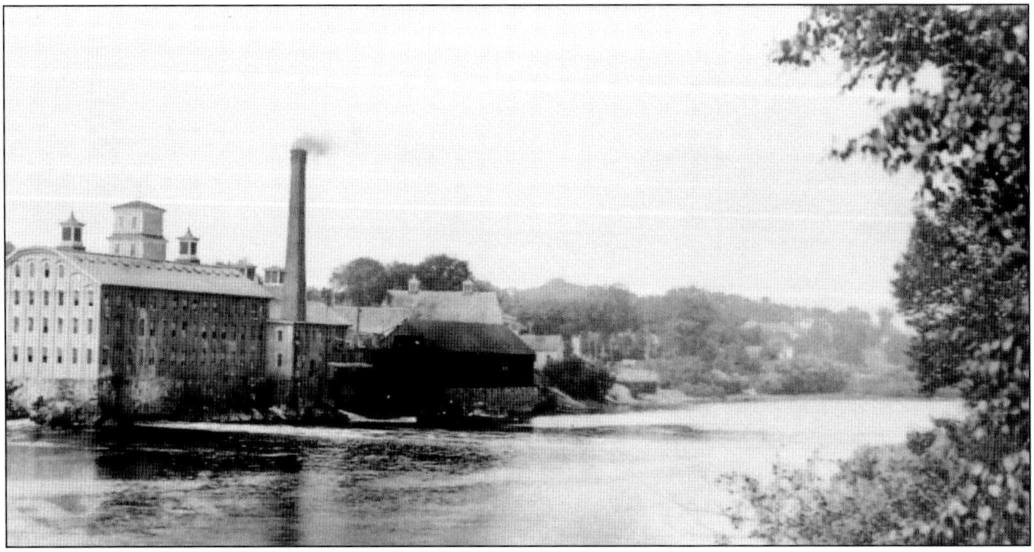

The paper mill, Topsham, *c*. 1900.

One

The River

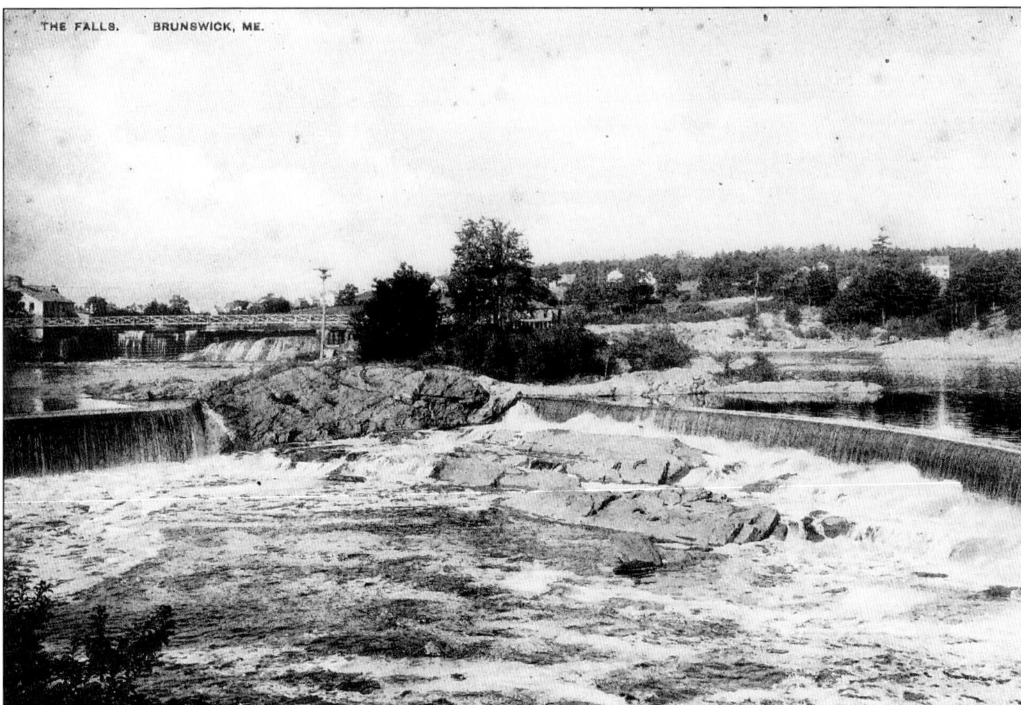

A river runs through.... The Androscoggin River, which forms the boundary between Brunswick and Topsham, was a contributor to settlement and to the development of both. Early lot lines were drawn by the proprietors in relation to waterfronts, as water routes brought people to the interior. Moreover, the two towns share the river's final set of rapids, which provided power for a variety of mills.

The falls were a favorite subject of photographers. A picture from the pre-1932 bridge showed the footbridge extending from the Cabot Mill to its power station, located on the Topsham side. Not a lot of water was flowing over the dam at the time.

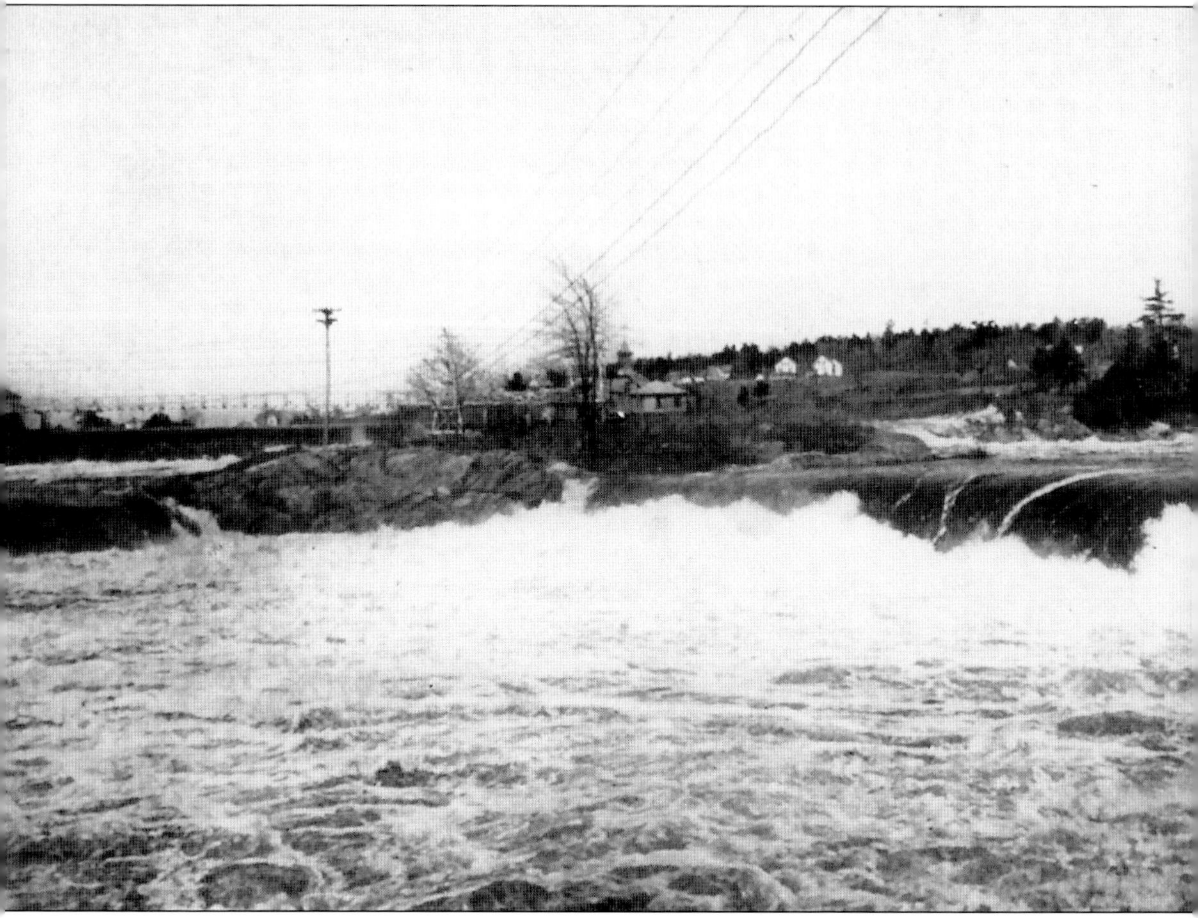

Every spring the river rose. Another view from almost the same spot shows a considerably greater volume of water.

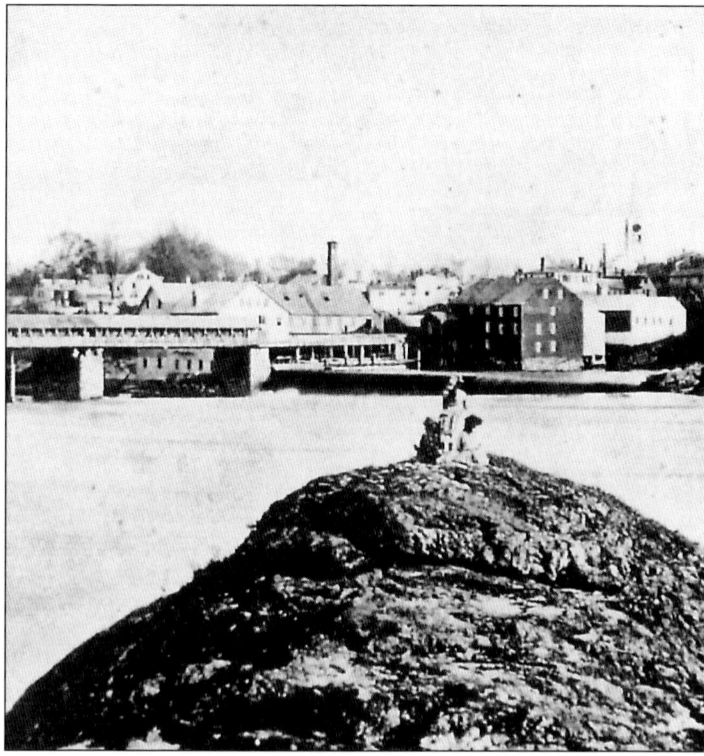

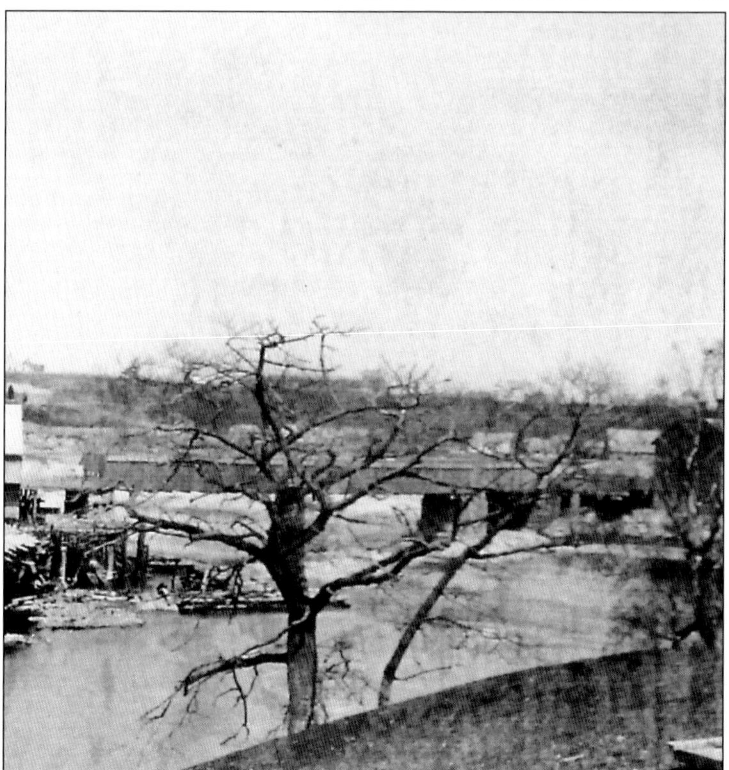

Bridges were needed and many were built; most early ones were destroyed by fire or flood. Three different bridges connected Brunswick's Maine Street and Topsham's Main Street during the era of photography. A high-sided toll bridge, built in 1842, extended to Topsham's Mill Island, from which shorter bridges led to the mainland. In 1871 the bridge became free; but it was reported a year and a half later that jokers on occasion convinced countrymen to pay them tolls.

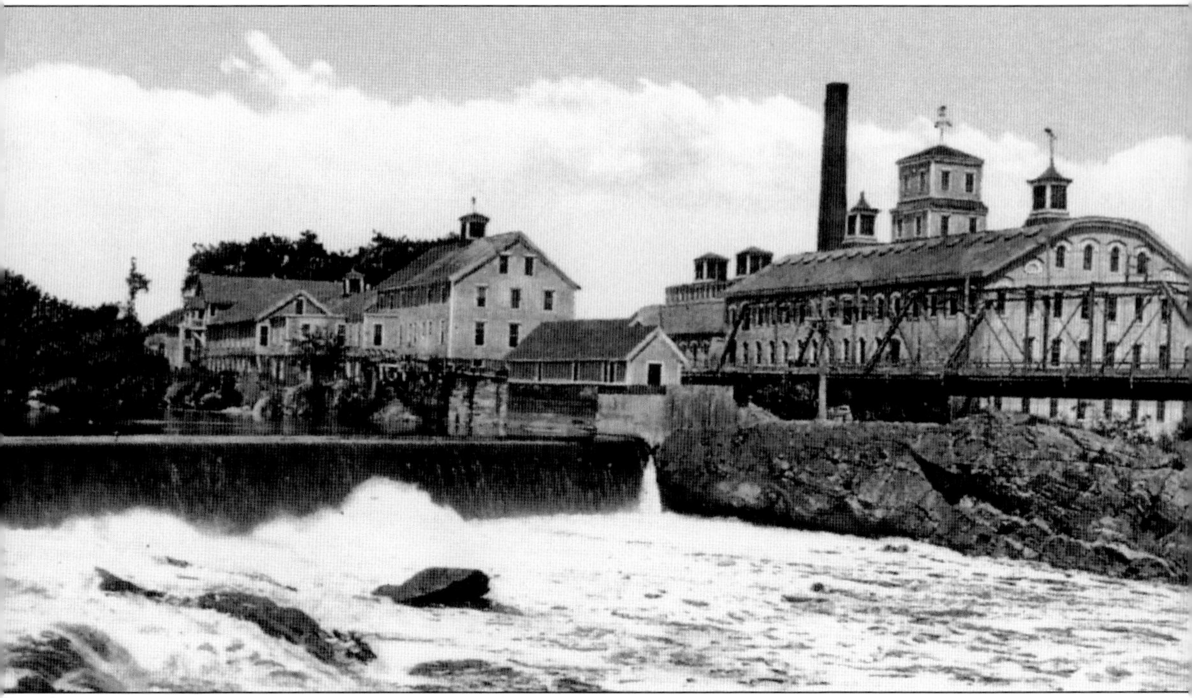

The span was then rebuilt as the "steel bridge," which remained in use until 1932. Paper mill buildings eventually stood on either side of the Topsham end.

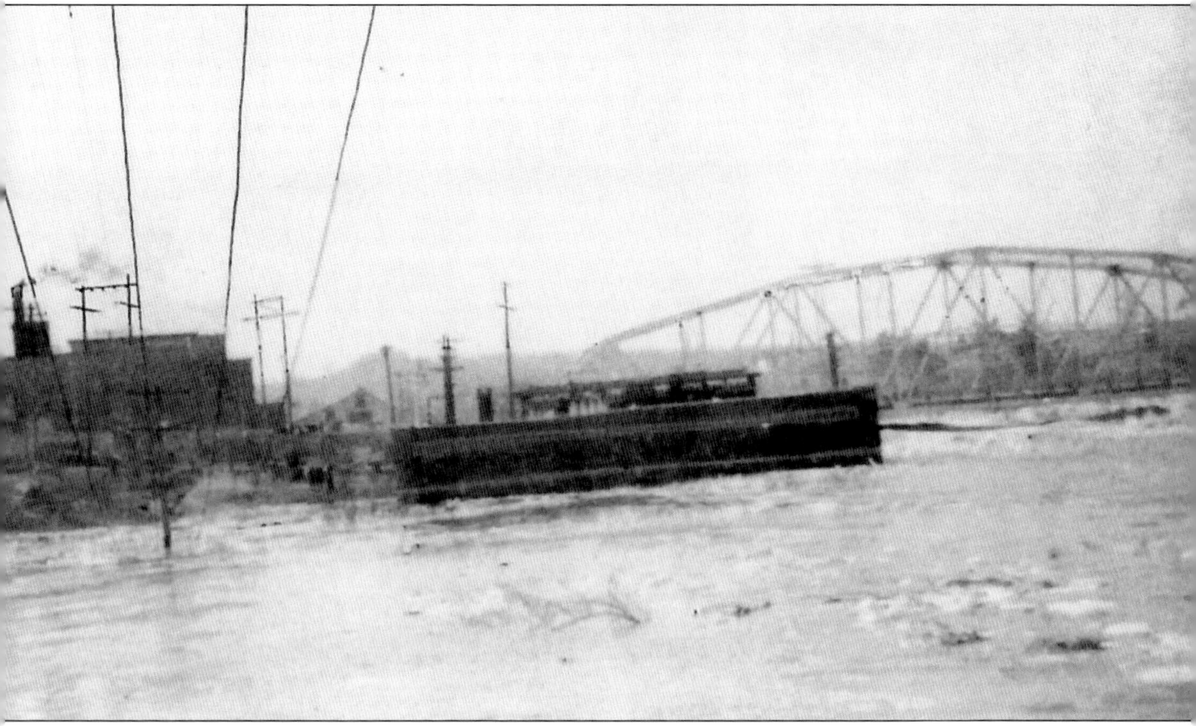

The Frank J. Wood bridge crossed slightly upriver from the previous ones, so that travellers no longer passed through what had become a mill yard. Shown here at the peak of the 1936 flood, it is still in use.

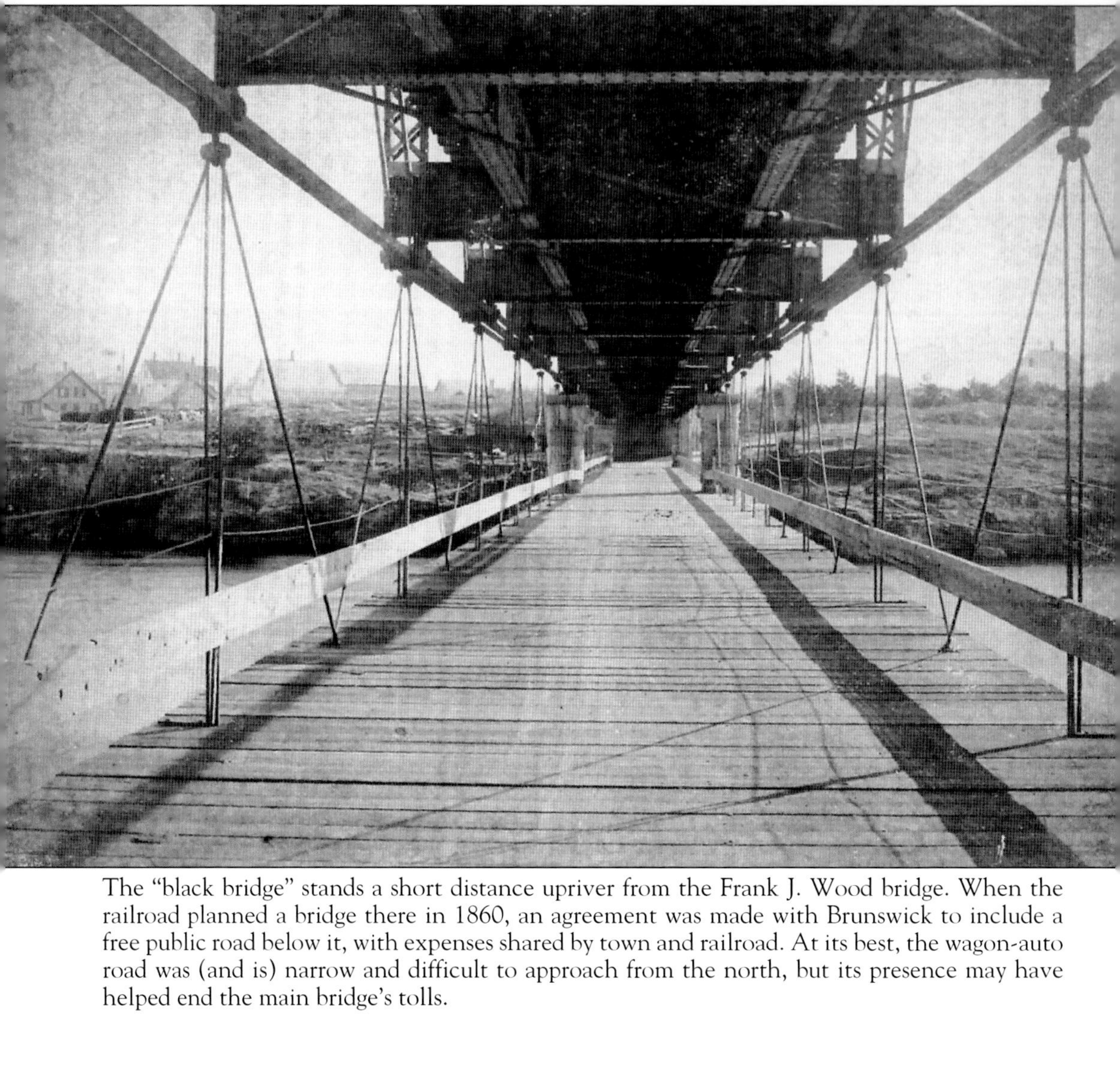

The "black bridge" stands a short distance upriver from the Frank J. Wood bridge. When the railroad planned a bridge there in 1860, an agreement was made with Brunswick to include a free public road below it, with expenses shared by town and railroad. At its best, the wagon-auto road was (and is) narrow and difficult to approach from the north, but its presence may have helped end the main bridge's tolls.

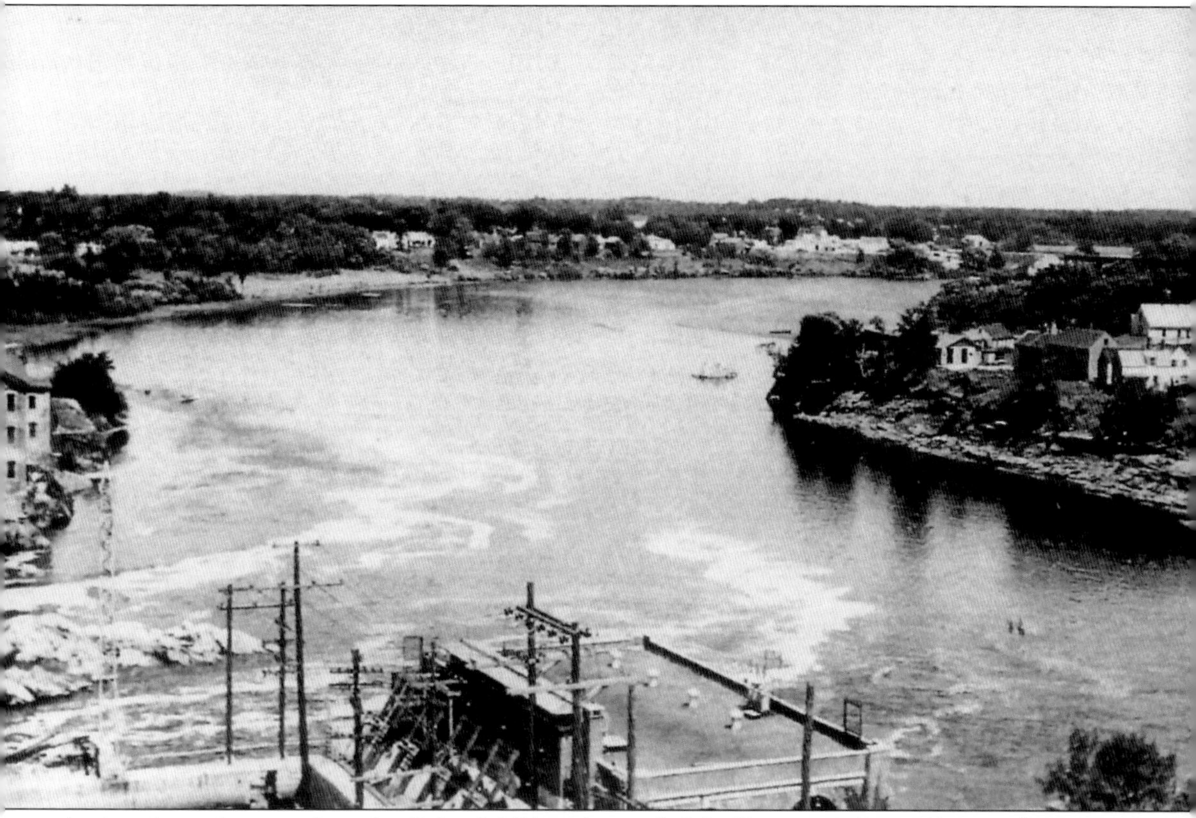

A view down the river from the Cabot Mill has the roof of the Brunswick Power Station (begun 1908) in the foreground; homes on Brunswick's Water Street are to the right, as is the lower railroad bridge.

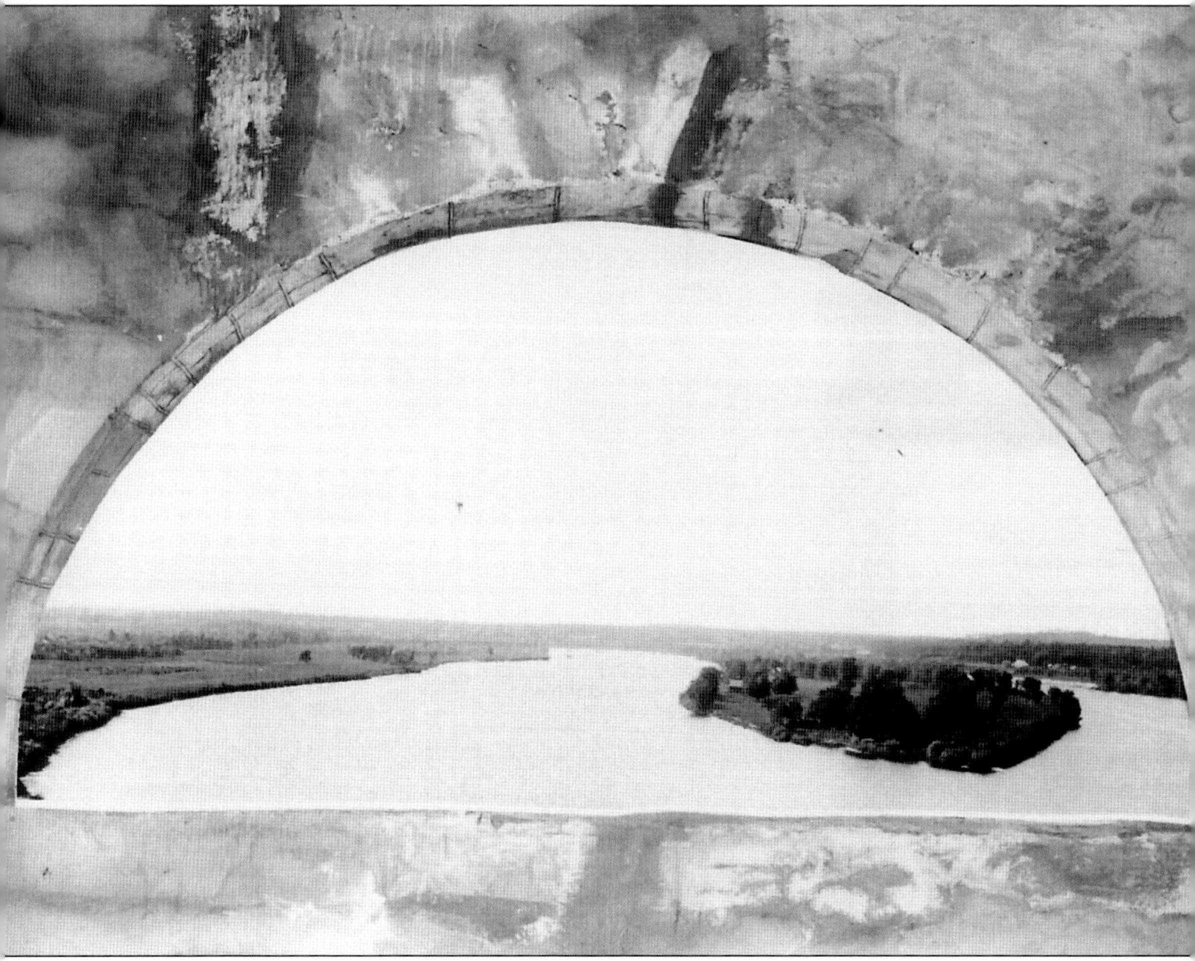

Below the falls the river flows gently eastward. This view of about 1898 looks back upriver from a "castle" in a pleasure park. Cow Island is in the foreground, with the lower railroad bridge barely visible at the river's bend.

Opposite: Sometimes the river rose too much: repairs had to be made on the upper railroad bridge in 1909.

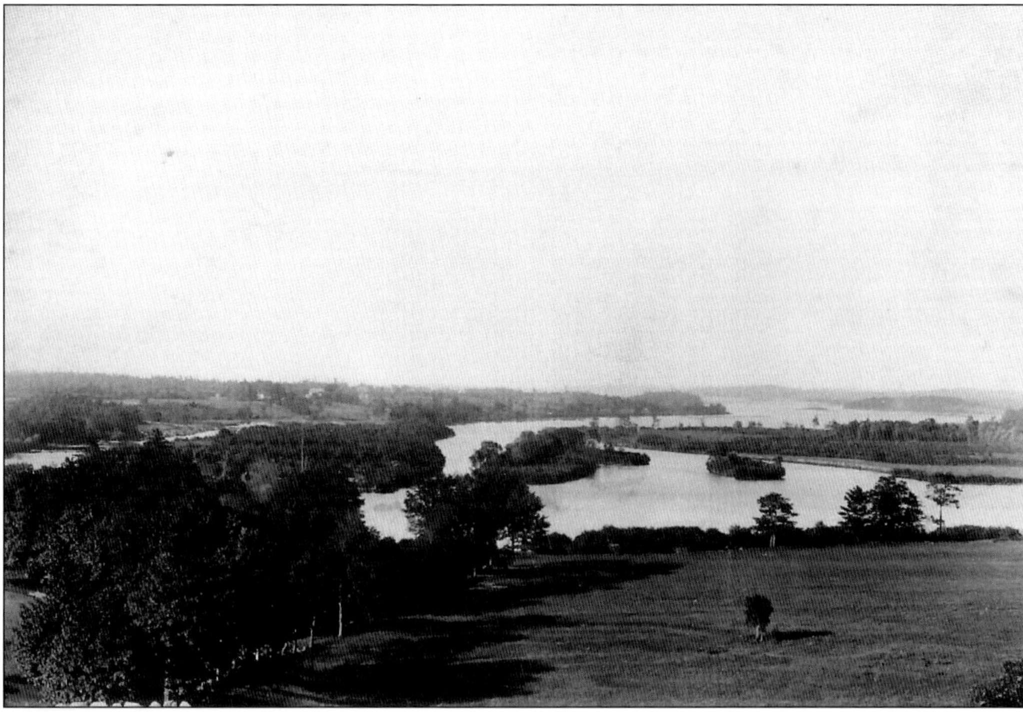

Downriver from the same spot, beyond more islands, lies Merrymeeting Bay, where the Androscoggin and the Kennebec Rivers join. A favorite waterfowl-hunting area in pre-settlement times, it remains so today.

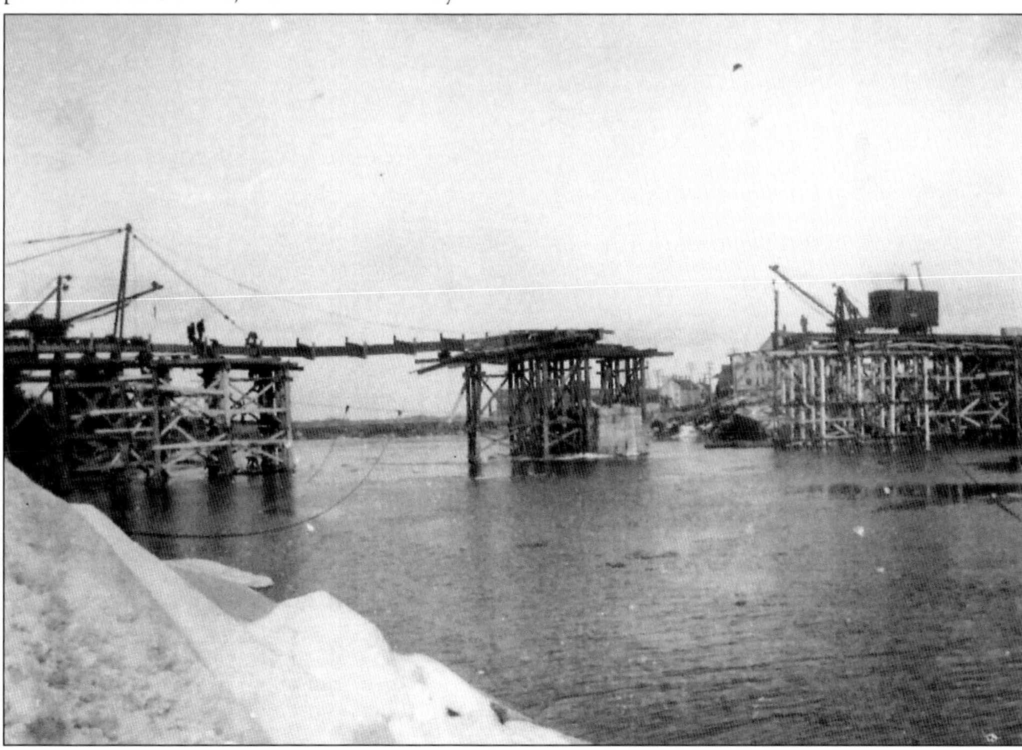

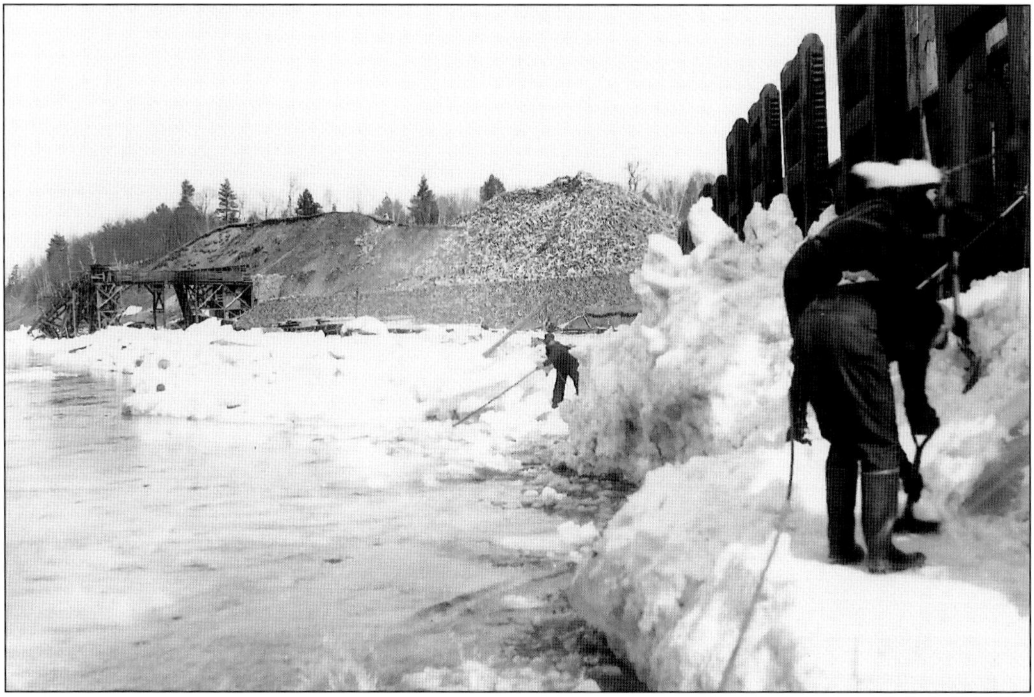

The March 1936 flood was the worst the town had known: twice water rose above all previous levels. Ice caused major problems. Workers at the Pejepscot Mill tried to remove massive ice blocks from the racks at the intake.

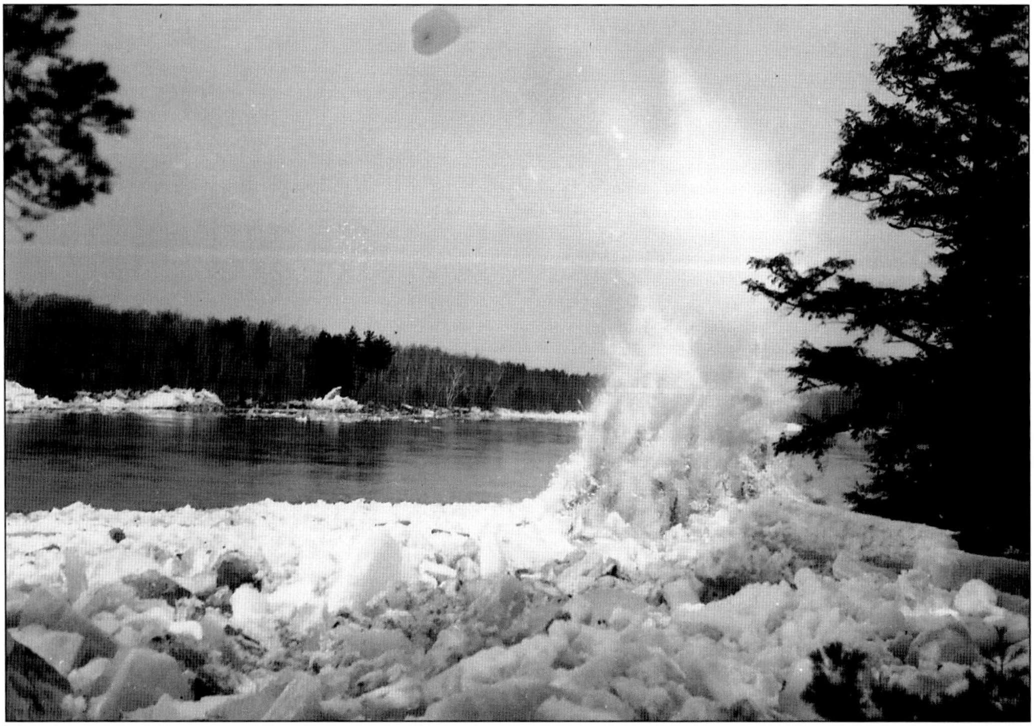

Ice jams on the river were blown up.

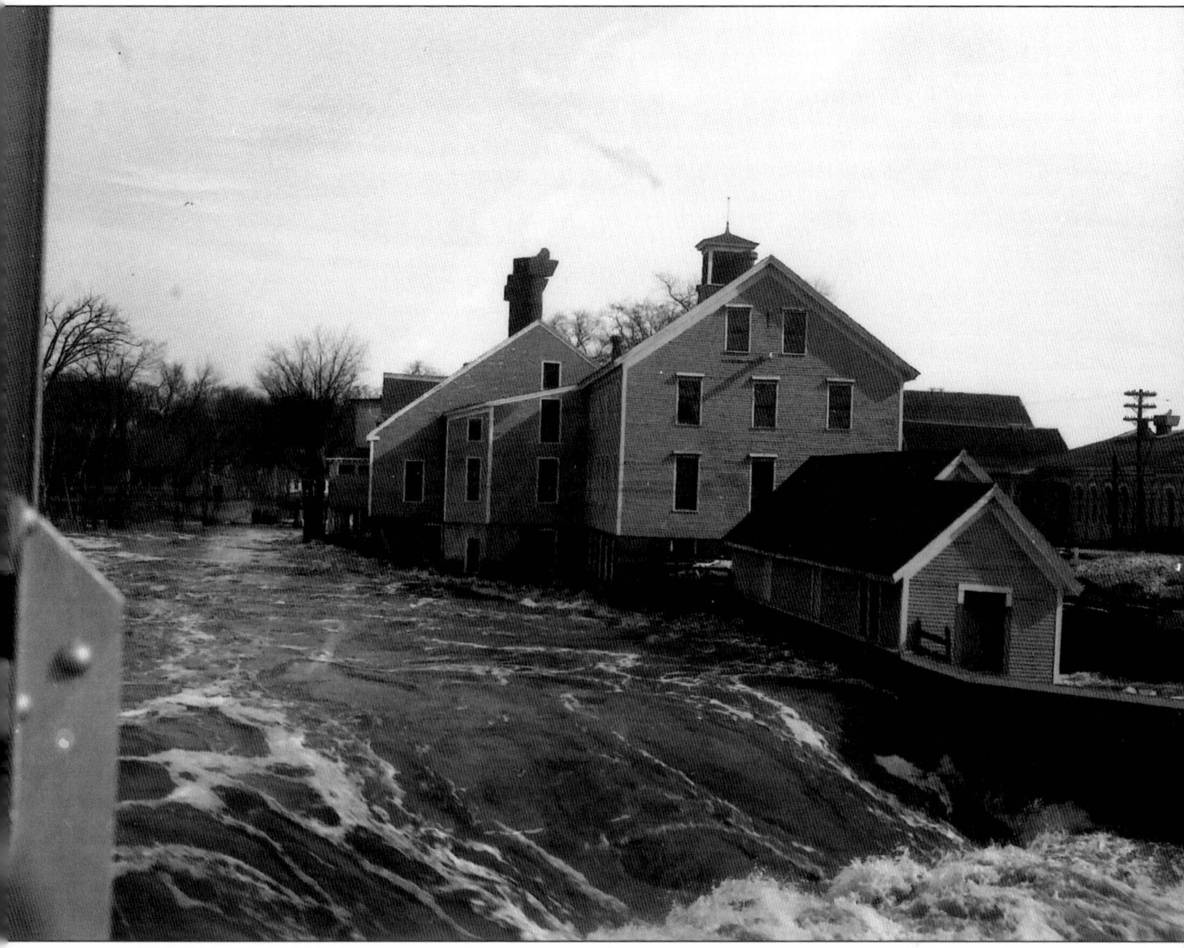

Water rose higher and higher at the Bowdoin Mill. Note the small building at the near end.

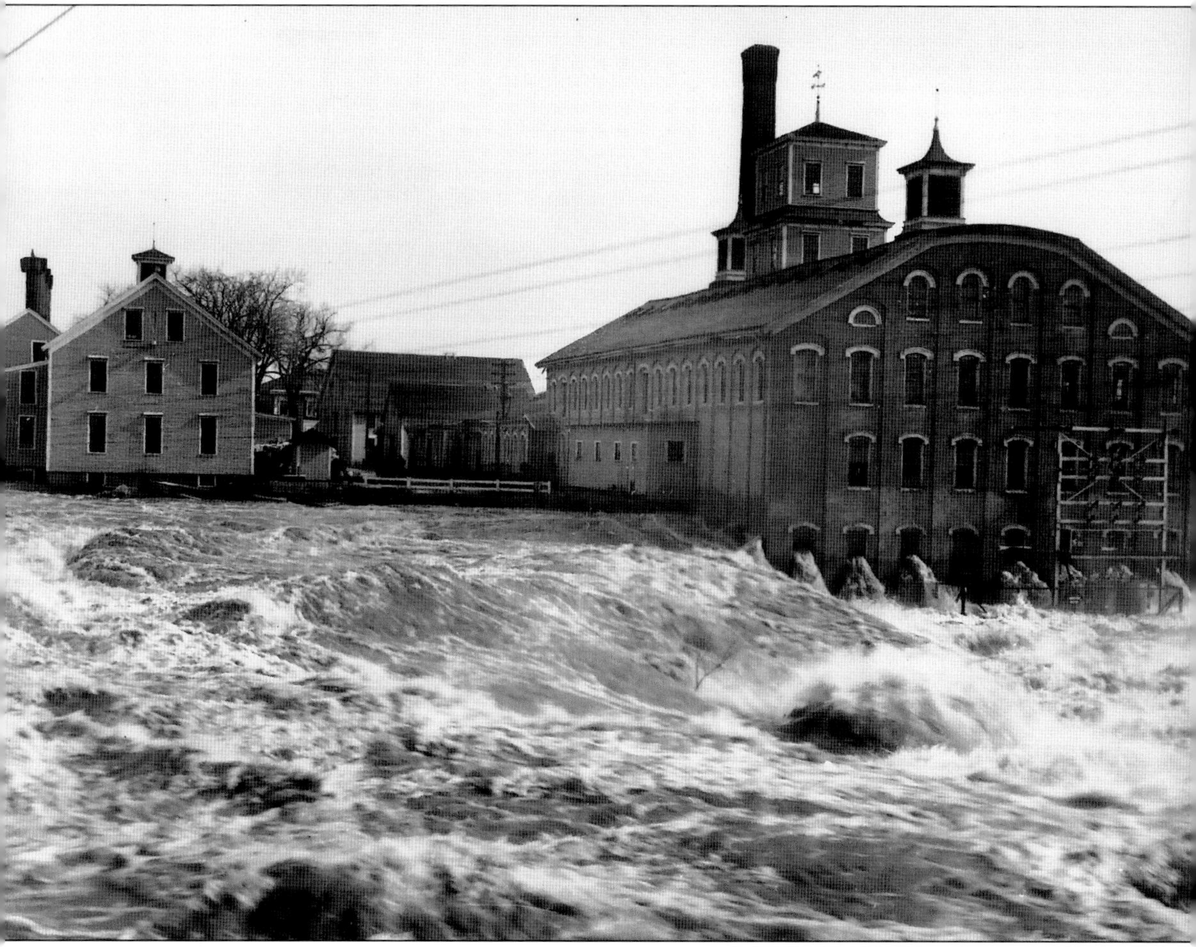

The building was no longer there a day or so later, by which time water poured from the windows of the mill's lower level.

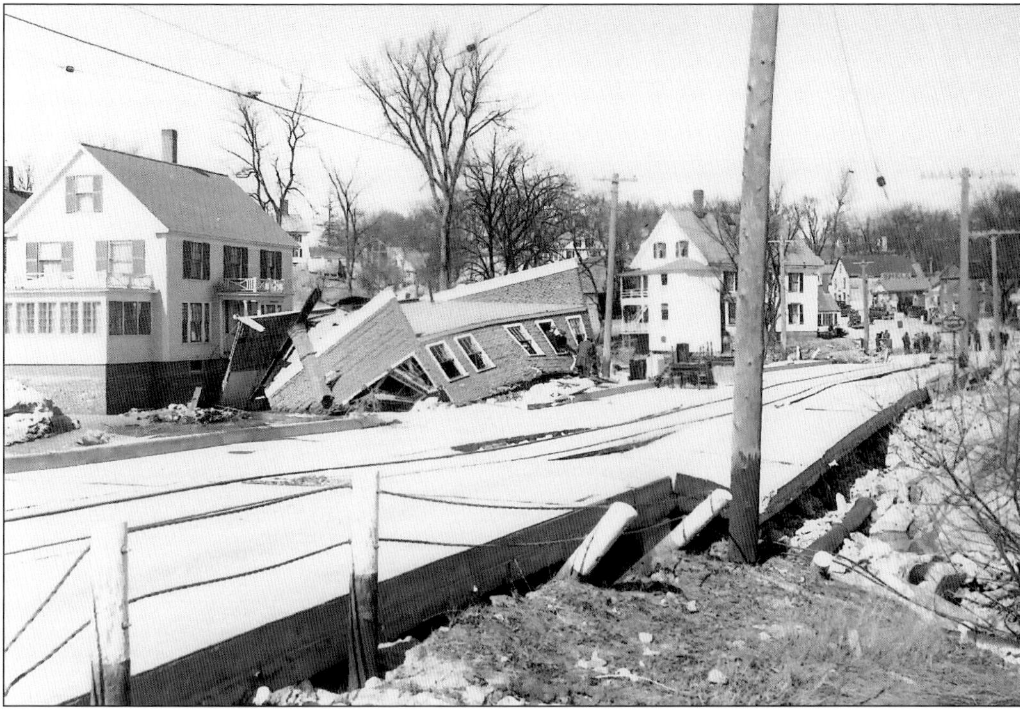

Across from the mill on Topsham's Main Street, Boucher's Diner was pushed onto what should have been the front lawn of his house. The four-year-old road was damaged at the spot where previous freshets had swept across the point.

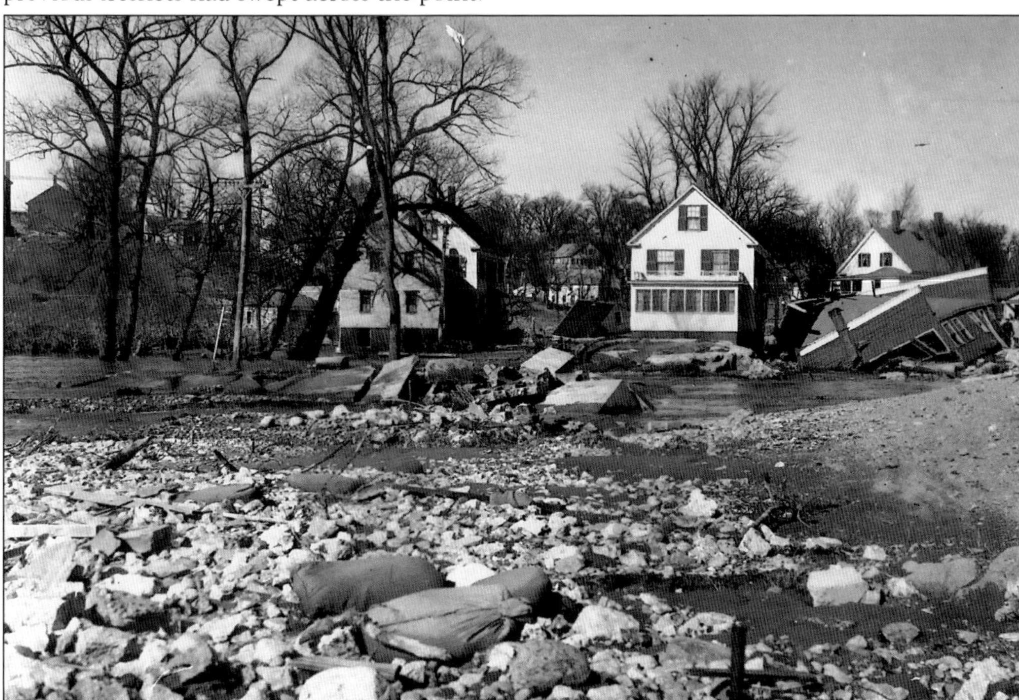

Another view shows the gully washed out behind the Boucher house.

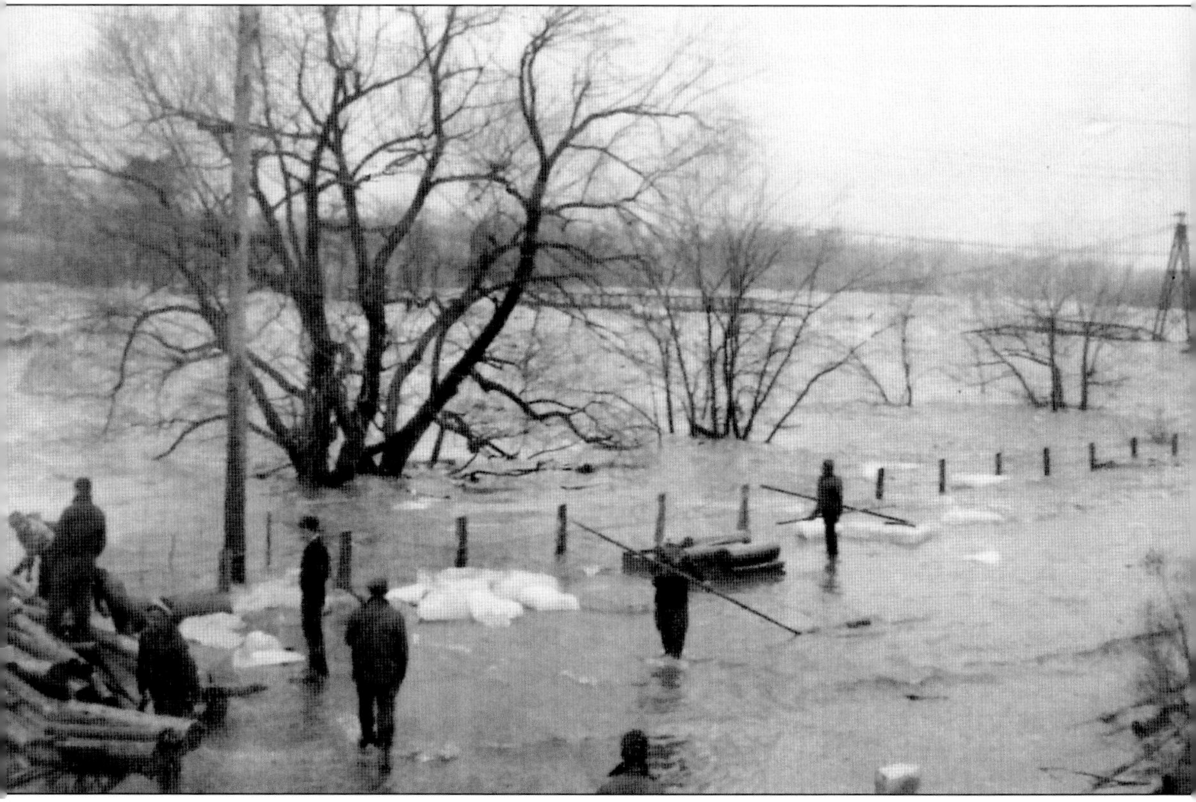

On Mill Street young people were rescuing pulpwood washed down from upriver. (The pulp mill later offered $3/cord "reward" to the rescuers in order to get the wood back.)

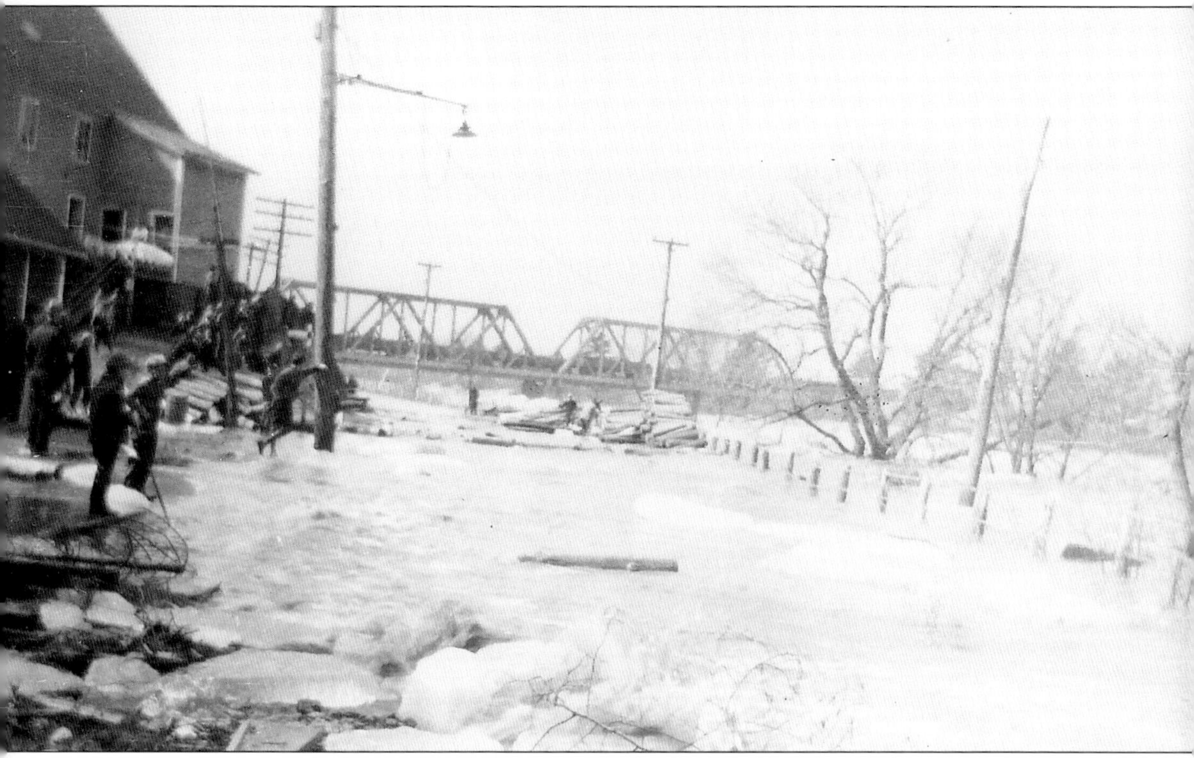

A view upriver along Mill Street, near Swett Street: notice that the railroad bridge in the background stood, weighted down by cars filled with sand, but that the auto bridge beneath it was gone.

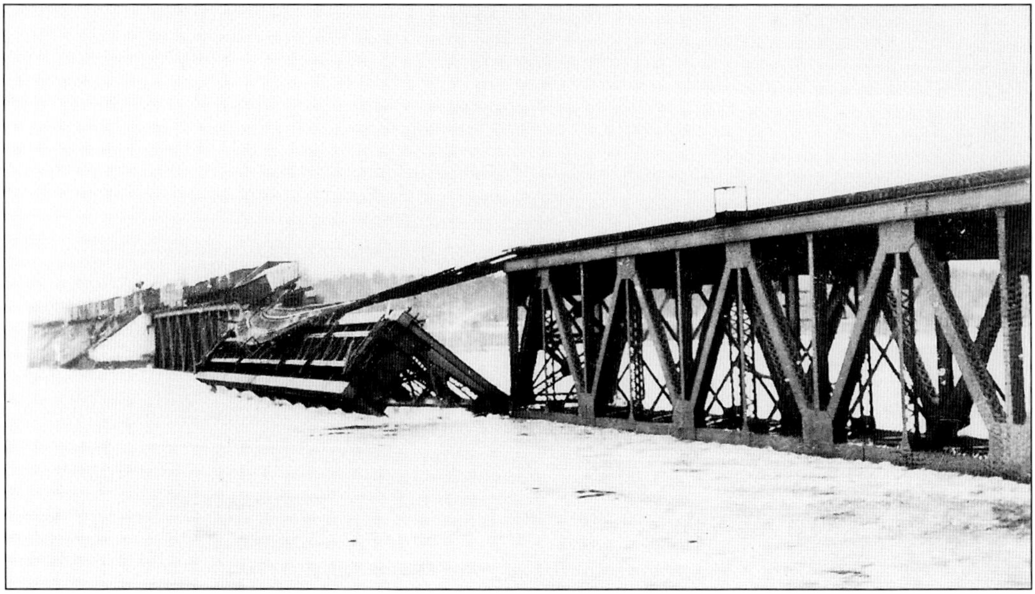

The lower railroad bridge, however, gave way to the battering of the ice cakes, and both bridge and weighted cars went down.

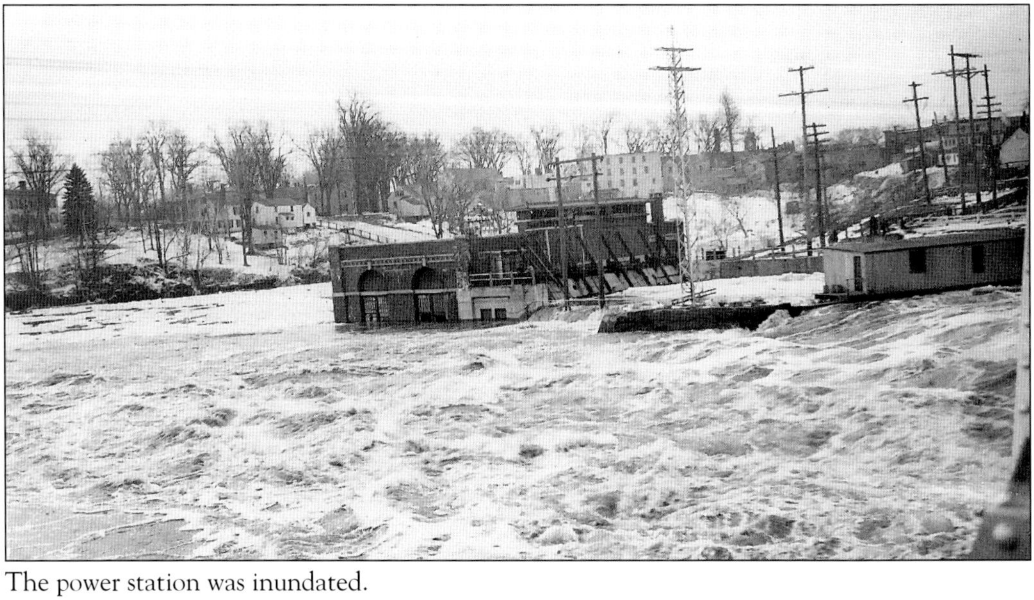

The power station was inundated.

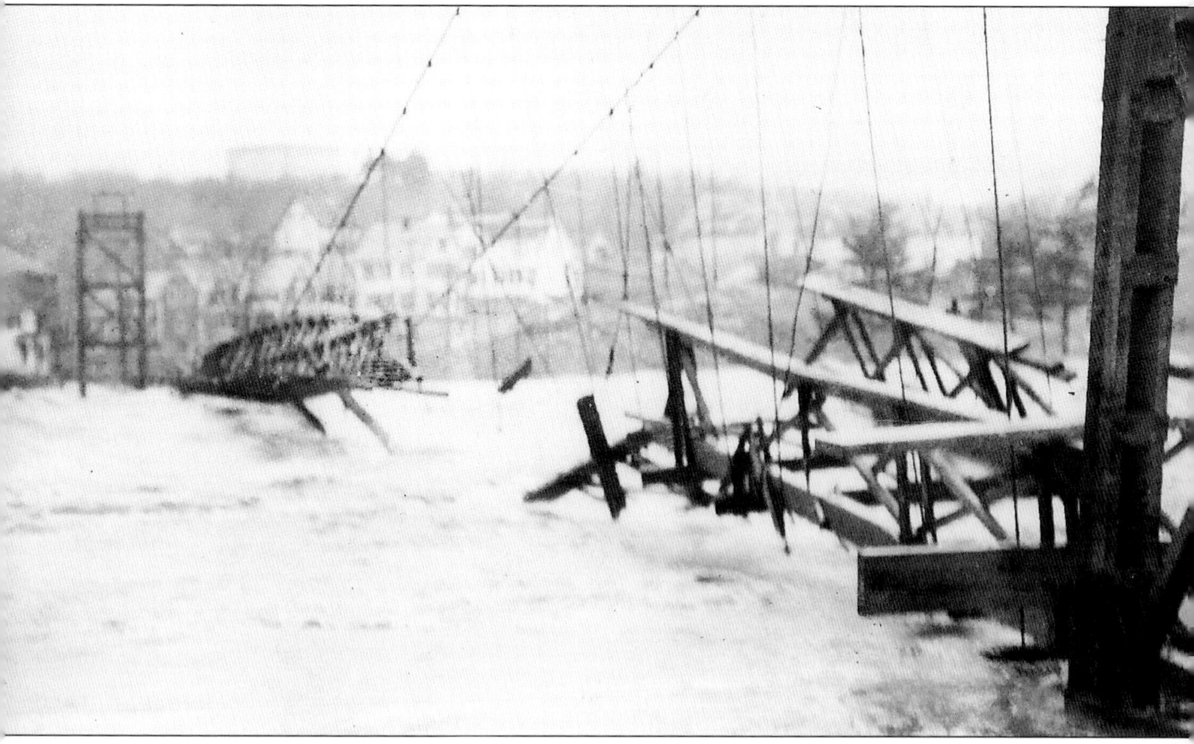

The swinging footbridge (built 1891) was also made useless, as the wooden floor and rails were swept away.

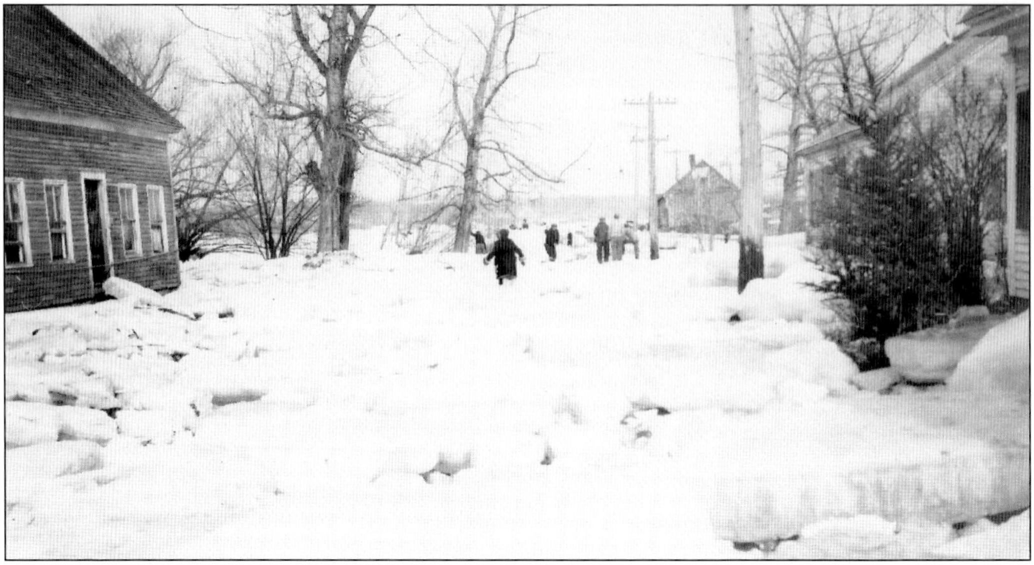

The greatest destruction to homes was on Water Street. One residence, numerous outbuildings, and an ice house were washed away, while many others were damaged by water and ice.

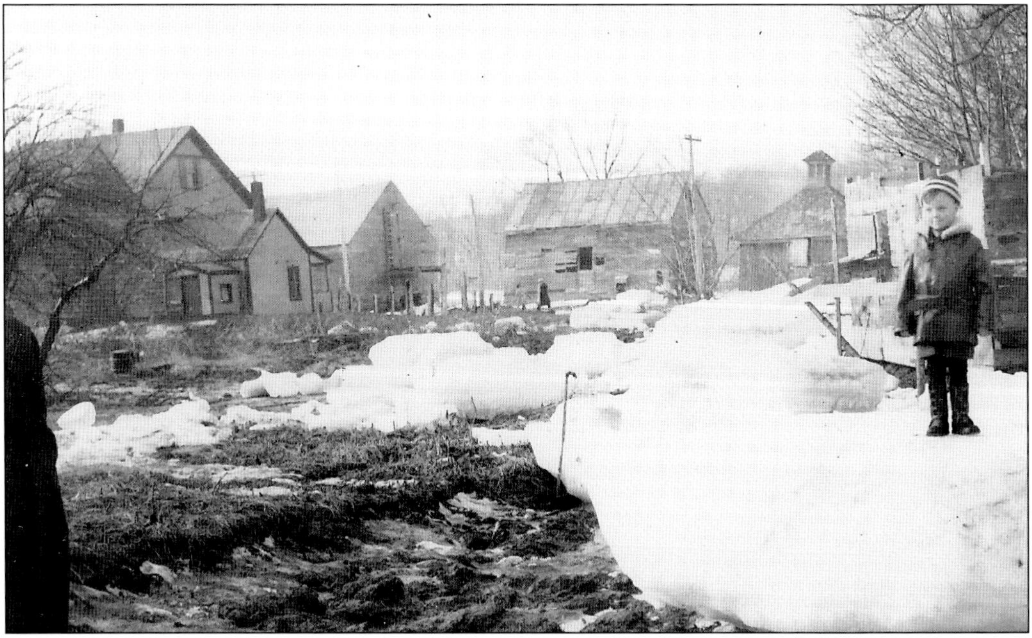

A small boy on an ice cake lends a human touch to the mess.

Two

Brunswick: Maine Street

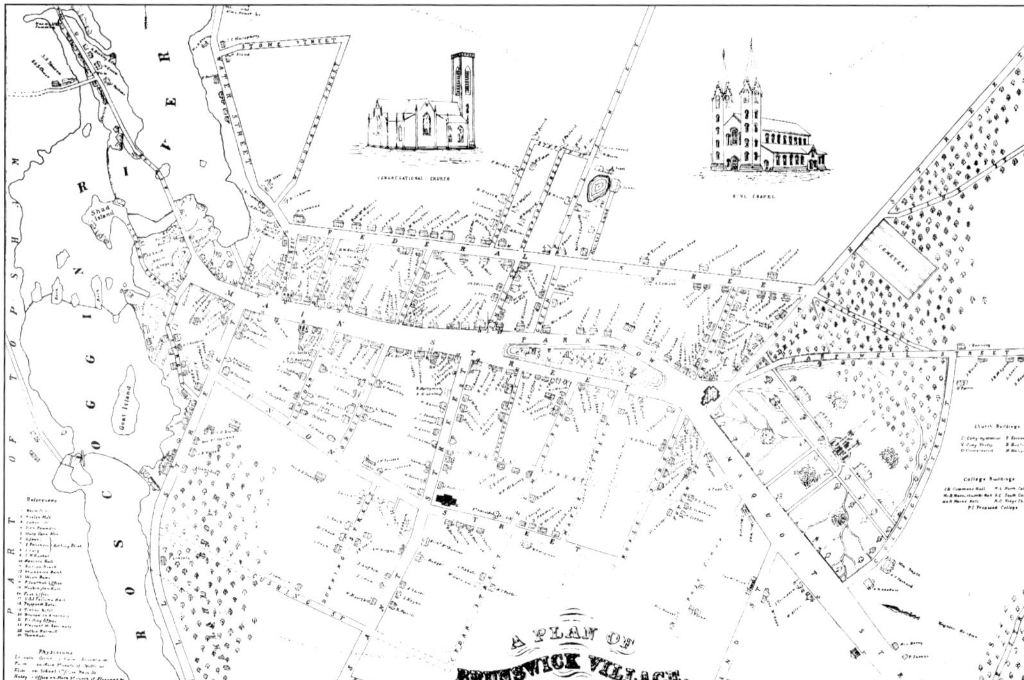

One of the earliest roads laid out in Brunswick was the Twelve-Rod Road; planned to be over 200 feet wide and to run between the falls of the Androscoggin and the ocean at Maquoit. It was never fully developed and lots on its sides were eventually sold off; Brunswick retains an abnormally wide central street in the half-mile or so south of the river, with the openness extended by the Mall and by similar open space next to Bowdoin College. In 1821, after statehood, the village section became Maine Street, although many people, including the engineer who drew this map, left off the final "e." Mr. Noyes either incorporated sketches from plans or made later changes in his map: the college chapel was in 1846 unfinished, while the Congregational Church was built with a spire.

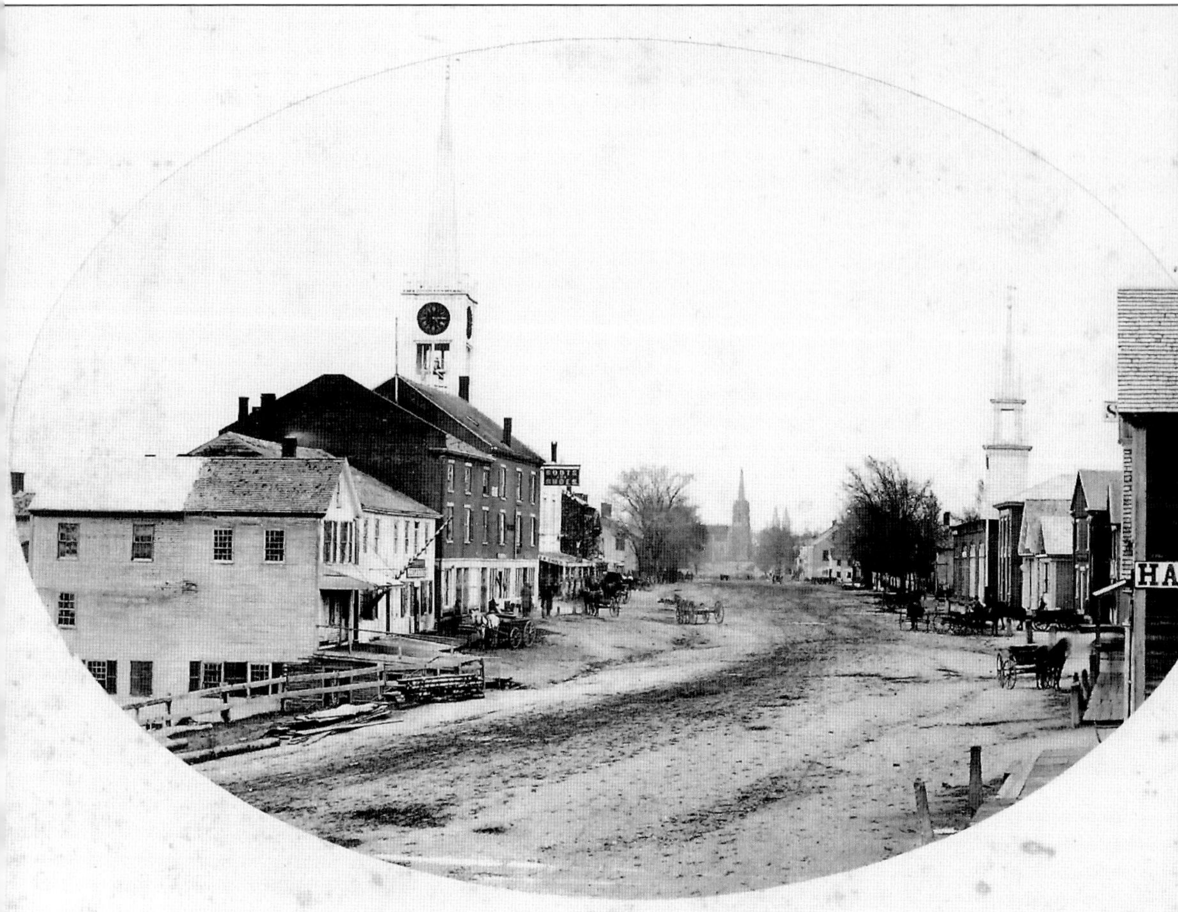

What may be the earliest photograph of the street, taken at the north end in the early 1860s, shows commercial development there. Much of the area lined by trees was still residential.

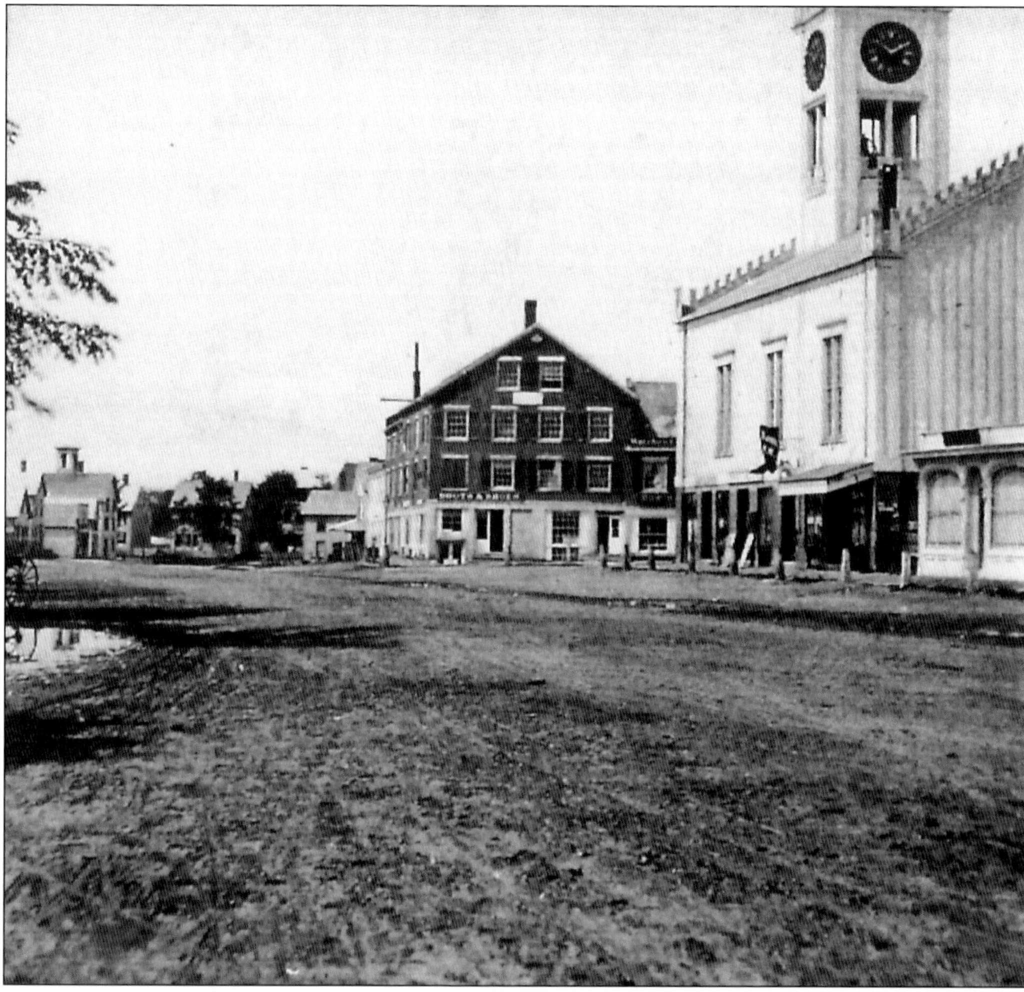

The 1837 brick buildings on the corner of Maine and Mason Streets are among the oldest business blocks in town.

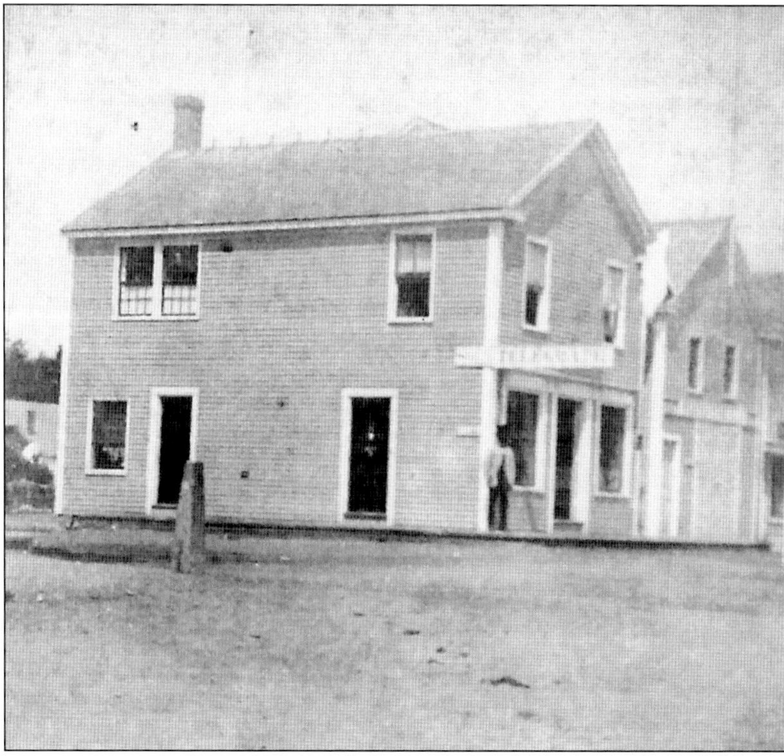

Farther up the street, the post office of the 1870s shared quarters with a telegraph office.

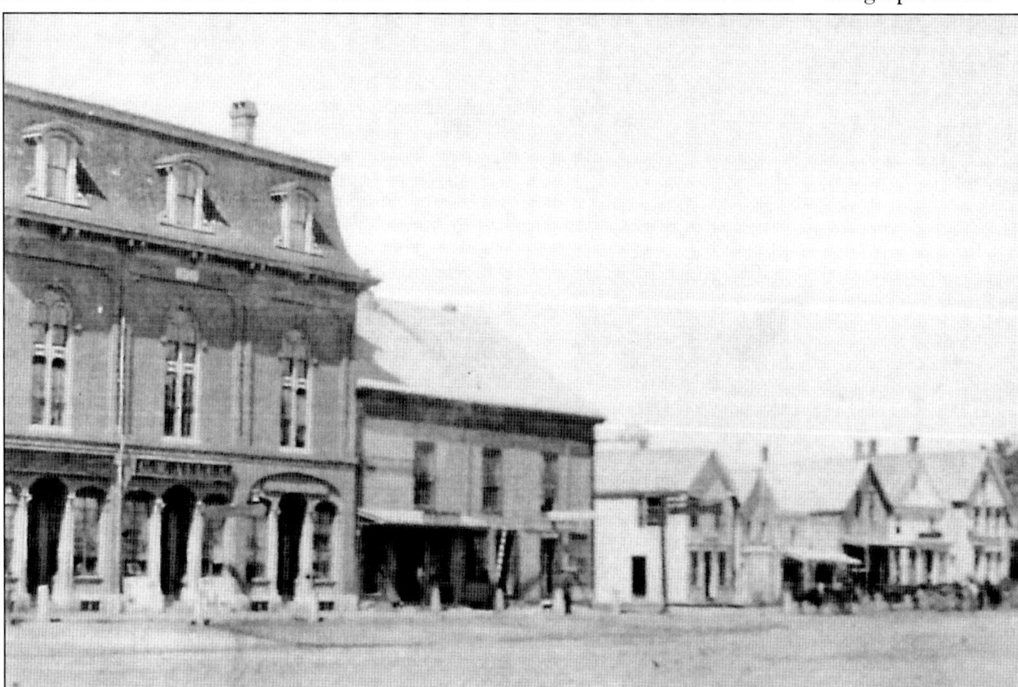

The post office in perspective: the Lemont Building, with three stores on the ground floor and a large hall above, is on the left. Built in 1870, it was the first large brick block in that section of town.

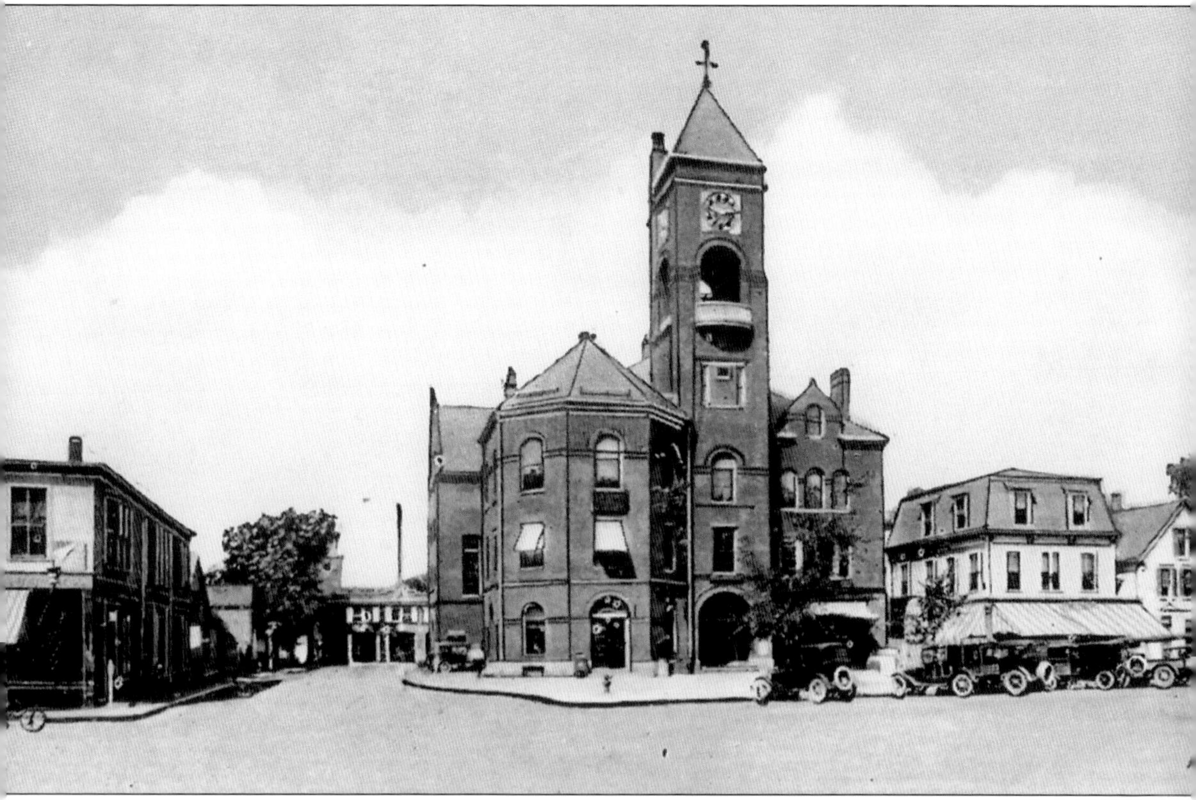

Over a decade later, in 1883-4, an impressive new brick town hall, designed by Frances Fassett, was erected on the post office lot. It had space inside for the post office, a courtroom, a jail, and a large hall with a stage for musical and theatrical performances as well as space for indoor sports. The tower's clock replaced the one destroyed with the Universalists' steeple that year.

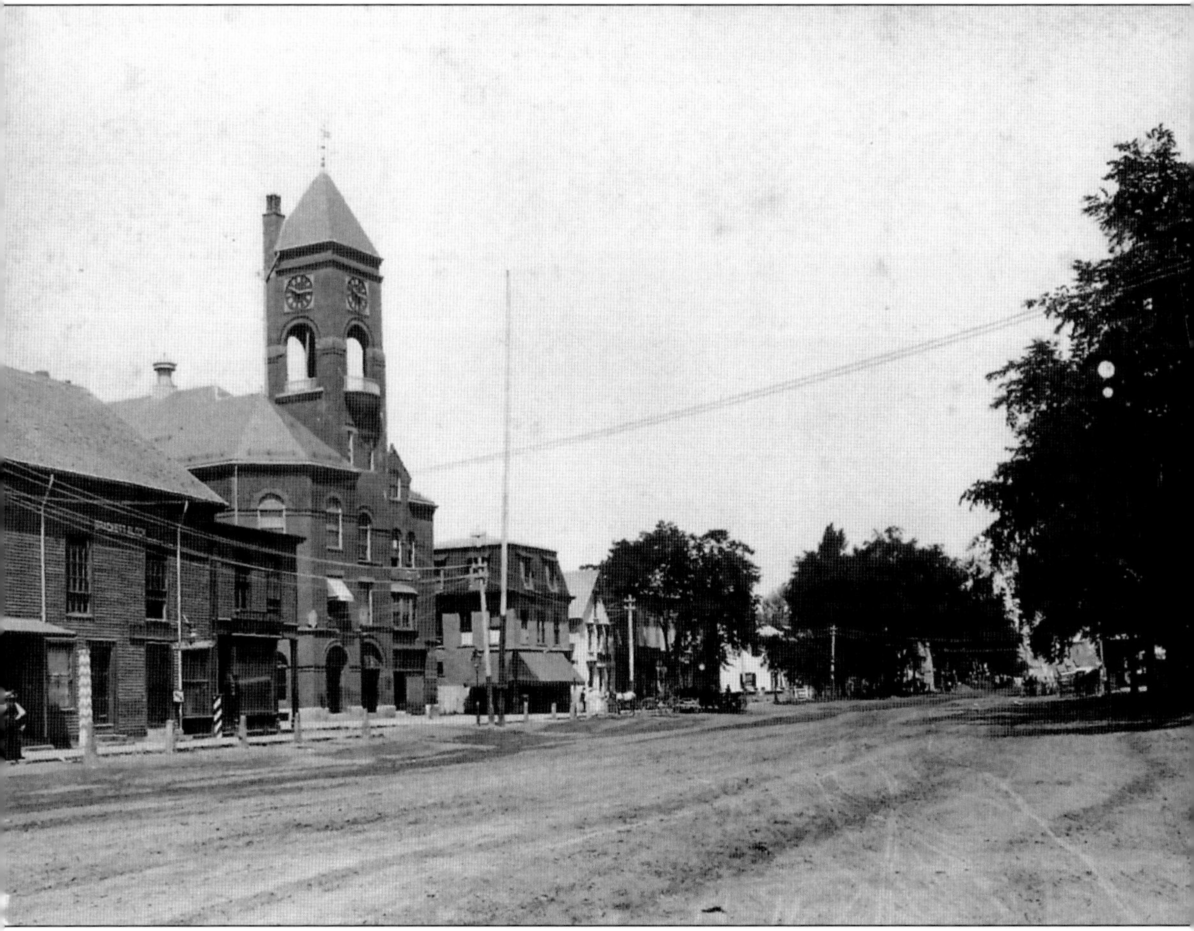

Growth in the area continued when the Brackett Block, across what was then Town Hall Place, and the store at the north of town hall were remodelled into modern mercantile and office spaces in 1885 and 1888.

Opposite: Four years after its construction, the Brunswick Town Hall was draped in flags and bunting to celebrate Brunswick's 150th birthday.

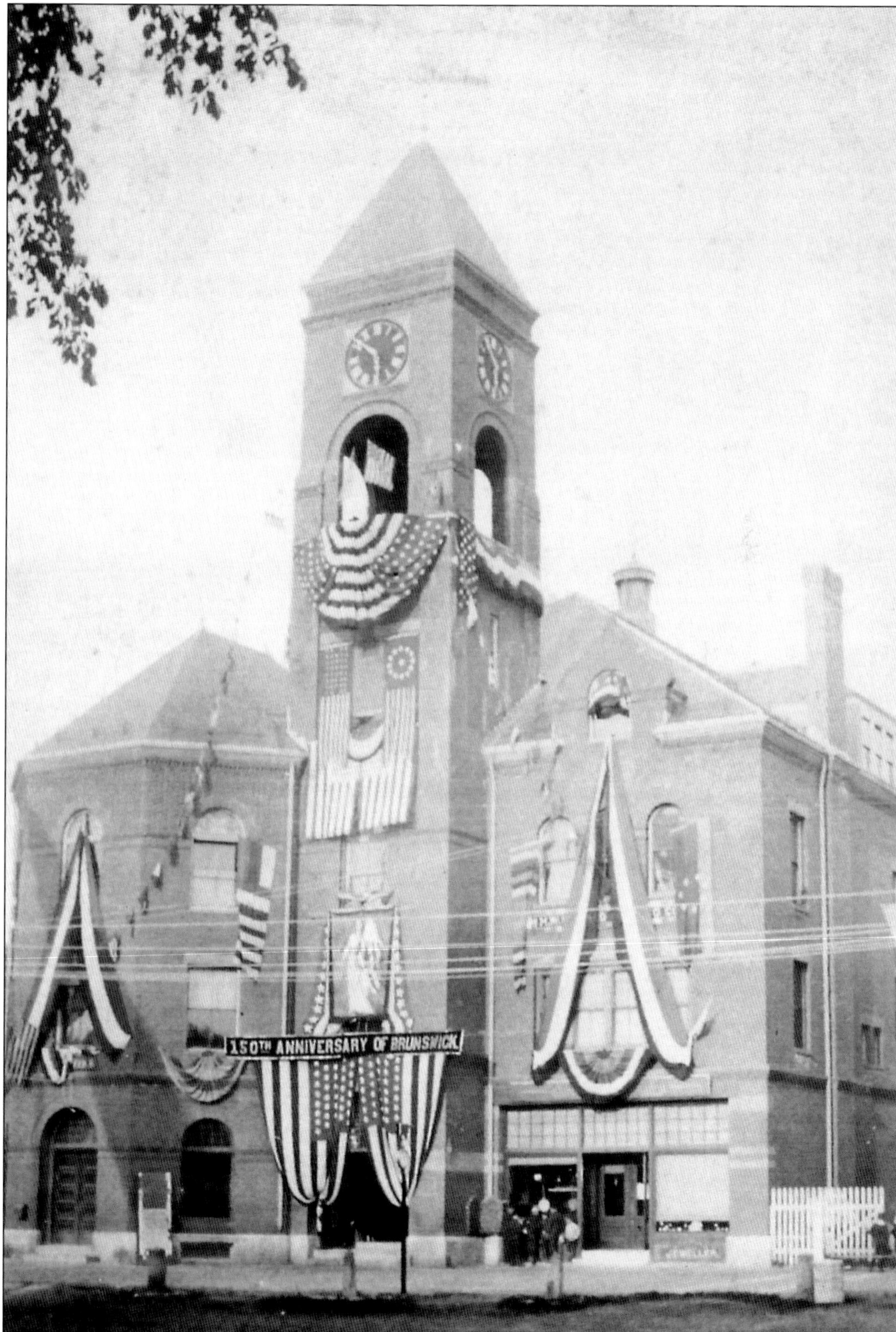
150TH ANNIVERSARY OF BRUNSWICK

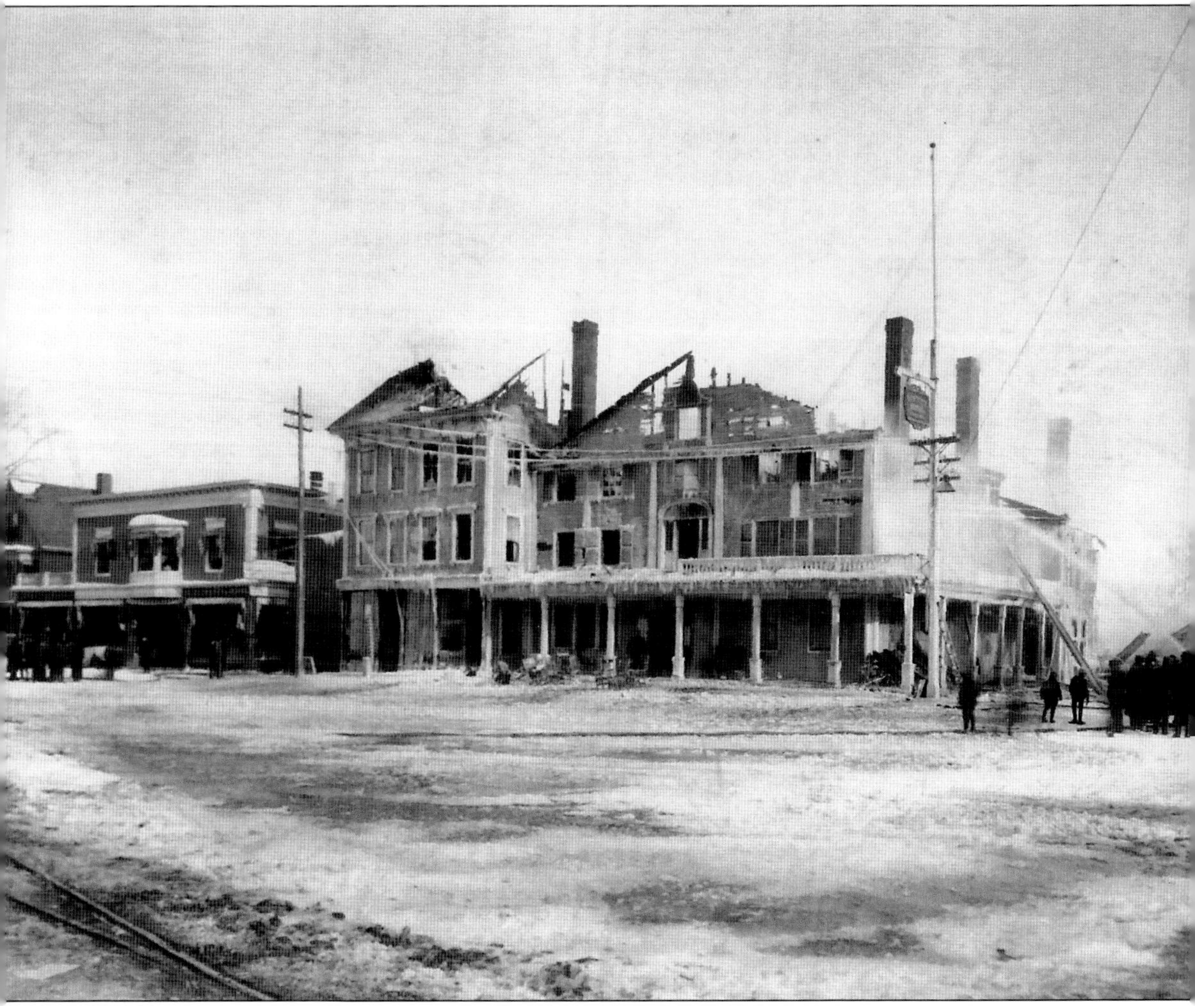

The east side of Maine Street at the time was anchored by a large old hotel, built in 1828 and enlarged in 1867. The Tontine Hotel, with extensive livery stables behind, had long been the town's major hostelry. However, by the time it burned in 1904, the facility was outdated and it was not rebuilt, the property being developed for an auto dealership and a movie theater.

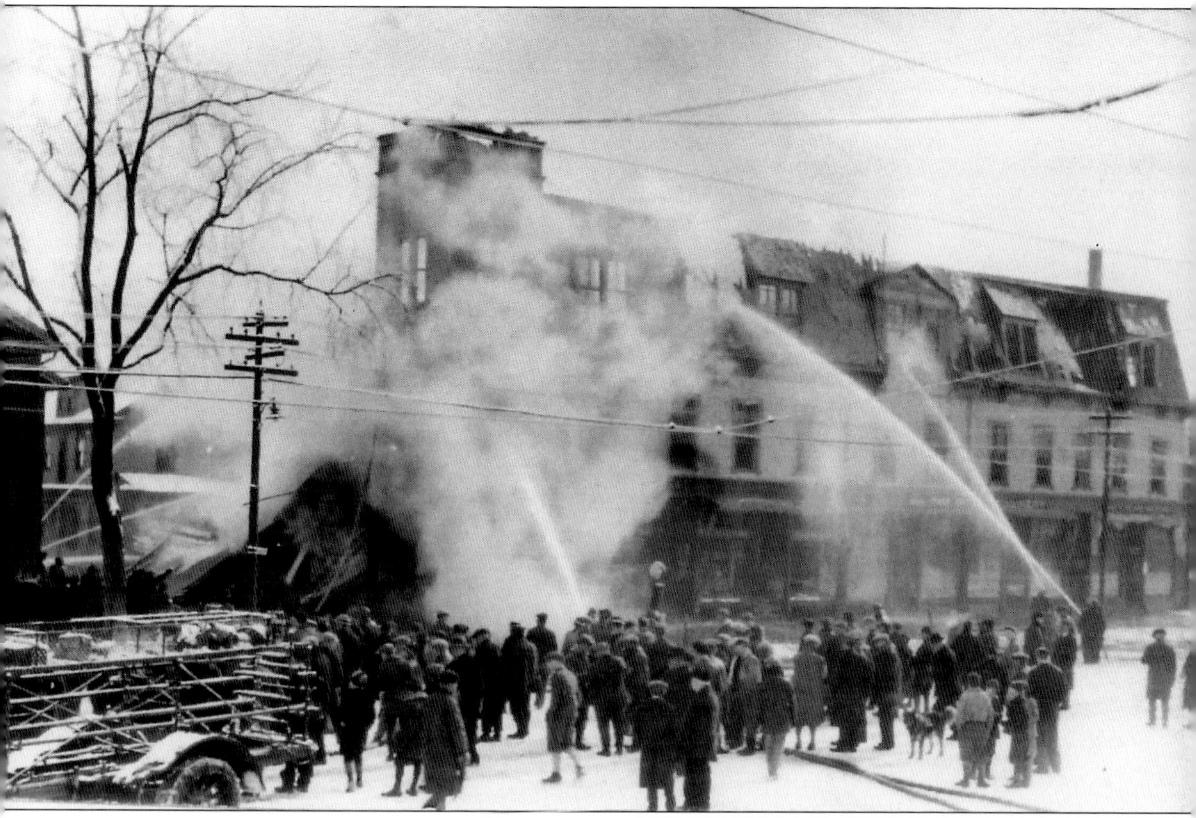

The Storer Block, a few blocks north of the Tontine, was built the year the town hall was completed; and planned by local architect Samuel Dunning it housed the Oddfellows' meeting hall on the upper story, offices, and five stores at street level. When it burned in 1926, the block's major occupant was the grocery of the Tondreau brothers, who replaced the wooden structure with a modern two-story brick one.

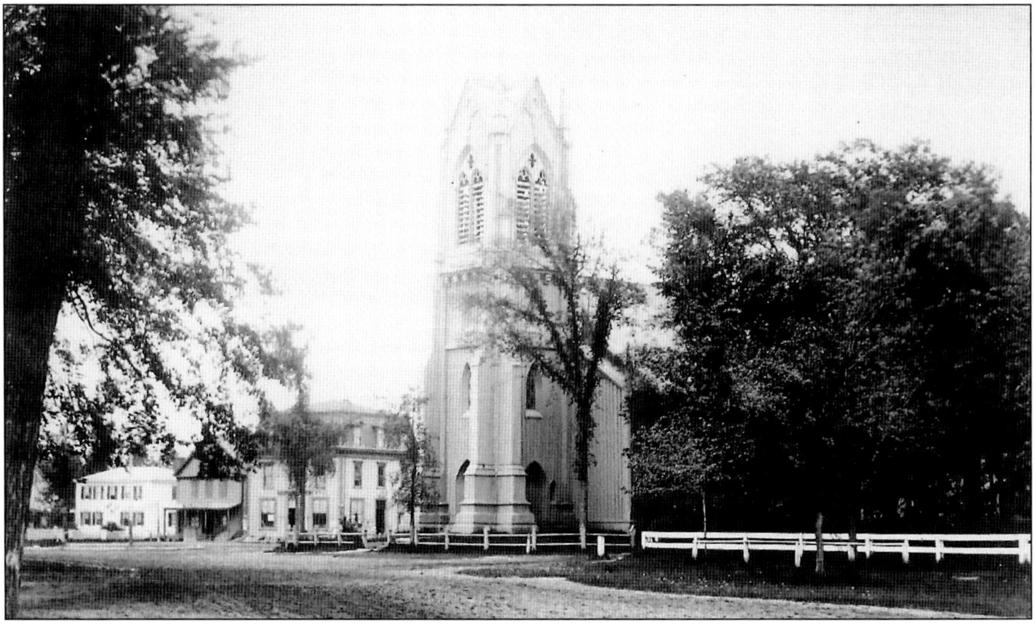

Upper Maine Street, near the college, also had commercial establishments. Nason's grocery can be seen on the east side of the street, north of the First Parish Church.

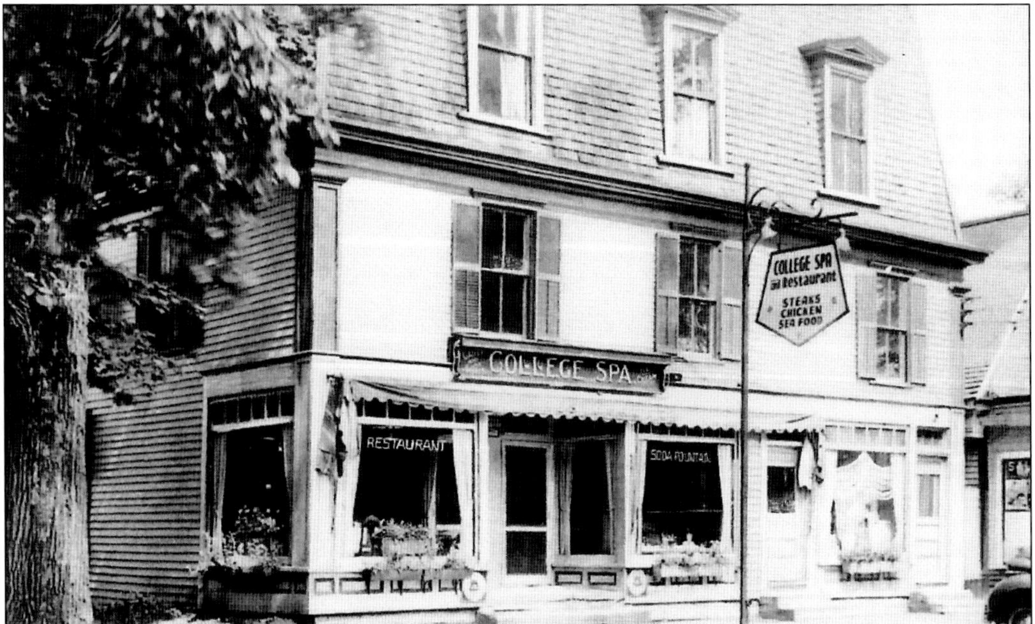

Across Maine street, a series of grocery stores occupied this building, which was remodelled to have a mansard facade in the late nineteenth century. The College Spa was there between about 1931-1950.

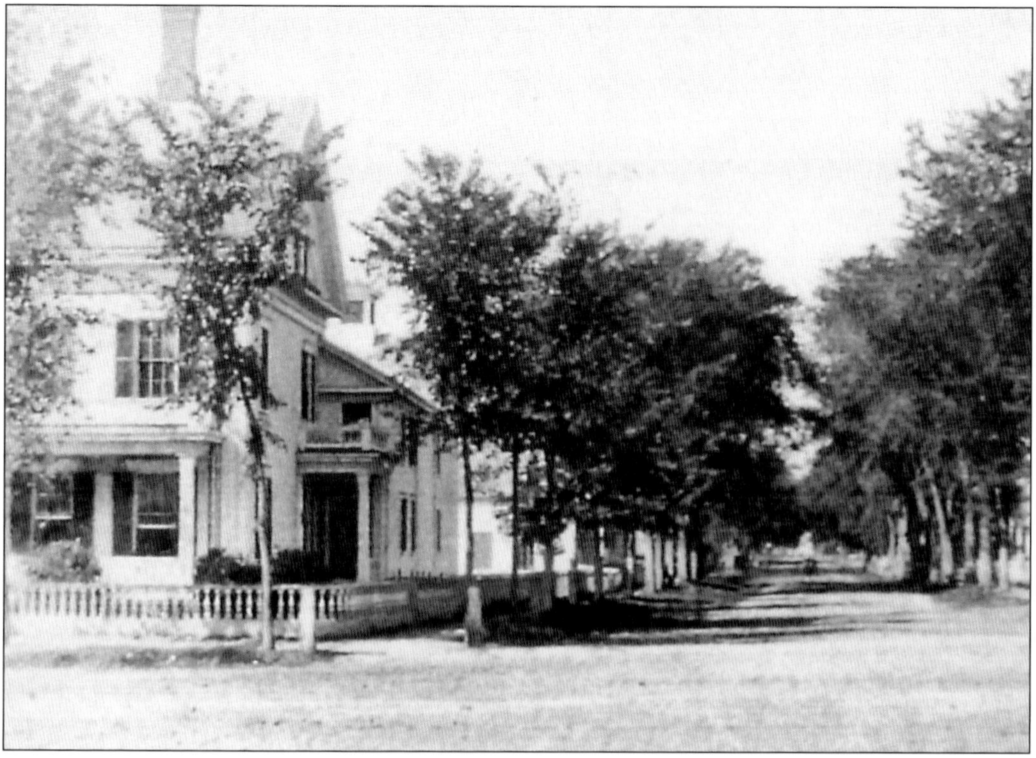

Private homes disappeared slowly from the commercial area. Among the last to go was the large house on the south corner of Pleasant Street, built in 1807, then remodelled in the early 1870s, just before this picture was taken. Some older people still recall visiting Dr. Elliott's office in the ell. The house was razed about 1950 to make way for a garage.

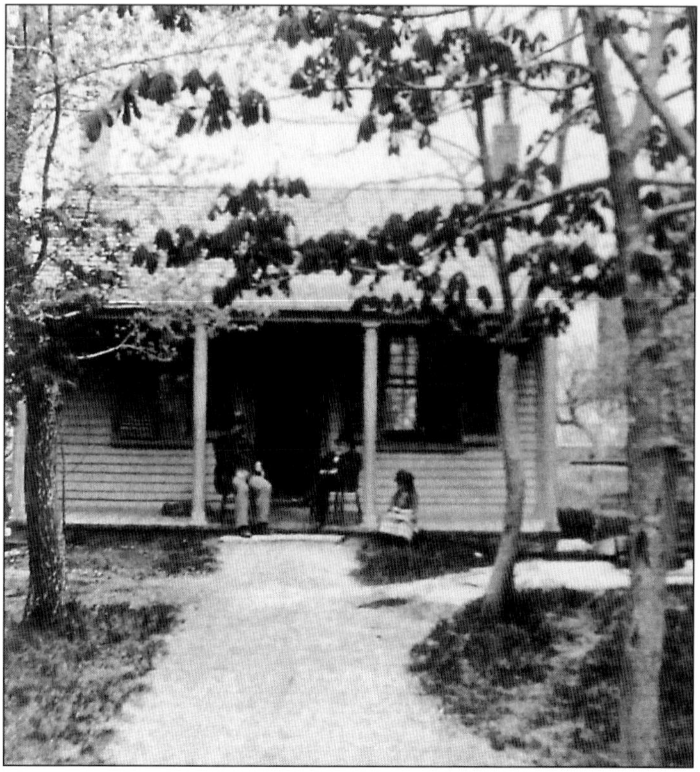

The home of Doctors Isaac and John Lincoln was also on Maine Street until 1896. John used this office beside it in the 1870s.

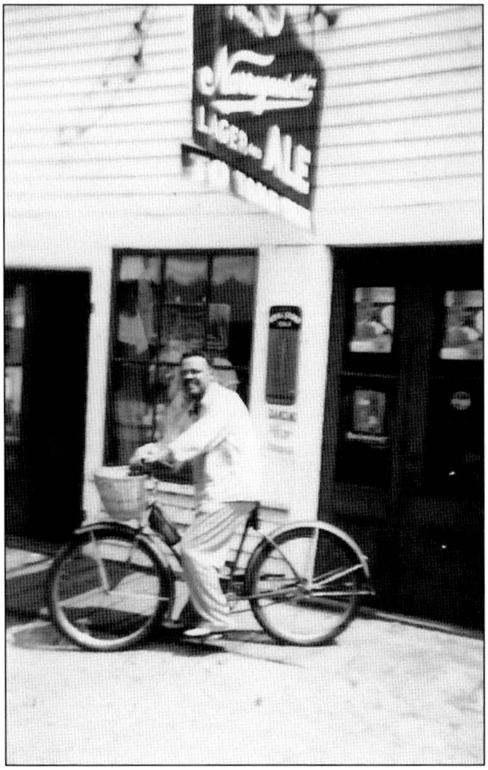

Stores were found on side streets, too: Lionel Gaudreau, here on a bicycle, had a variety store on Cushing Street in the 1940s.

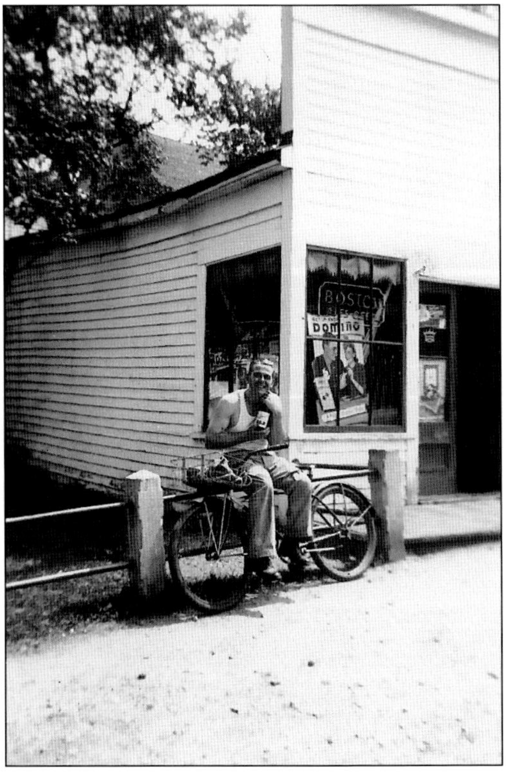

Michael Morin was one of the customers who crossed from Topsham to buy from a friend.

Three

The Mall

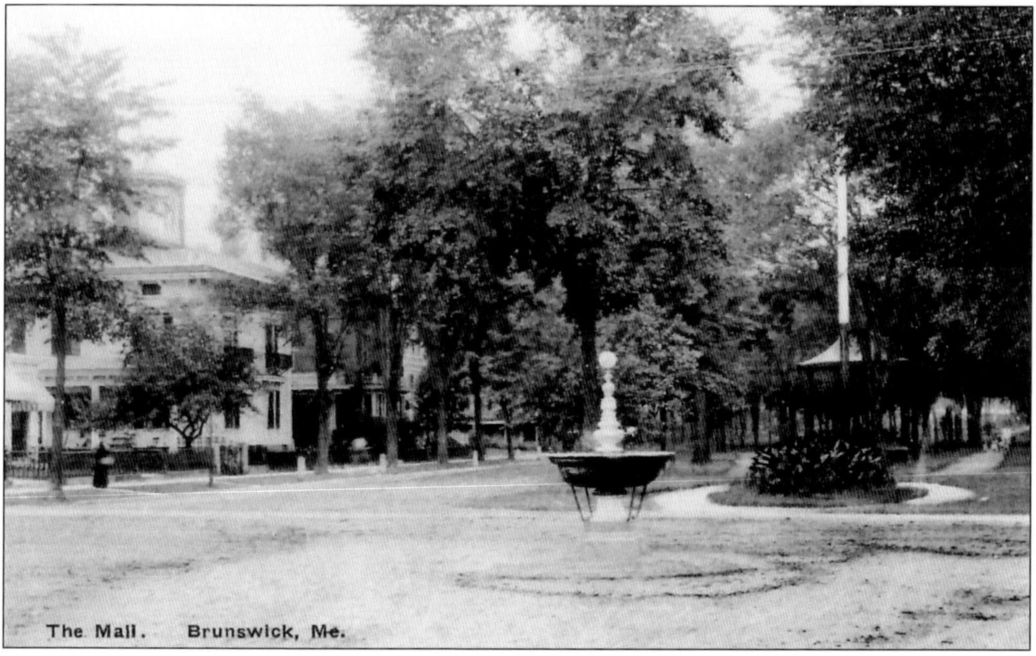

Between upper Maine Street and the wide lower section was the Mall, originally a bog to the east of which the street was first laid. This route later became Park Street. Volunteer work crews met to improve the area on successive July Fourths in 1826 and 1827. A town committee had trees planted and the Mall fenced in during the late 1830s to keep out the cattle which were daily driven along Maine Street. Paths were laid out, also; but little more was done. In 1880, the *Brunswick Telegraph*'s editor, having moved to Park Row, began to wage a campaign against the smelly and, he was sure, disease-ridden pond remaining there. His goal to get it filled in was accomplished within three years, and he then gloated over the increase in visitors to the site. Near the north end eventually stood a bandstand and flagpole, with a drinking fountain for animals at streetside.

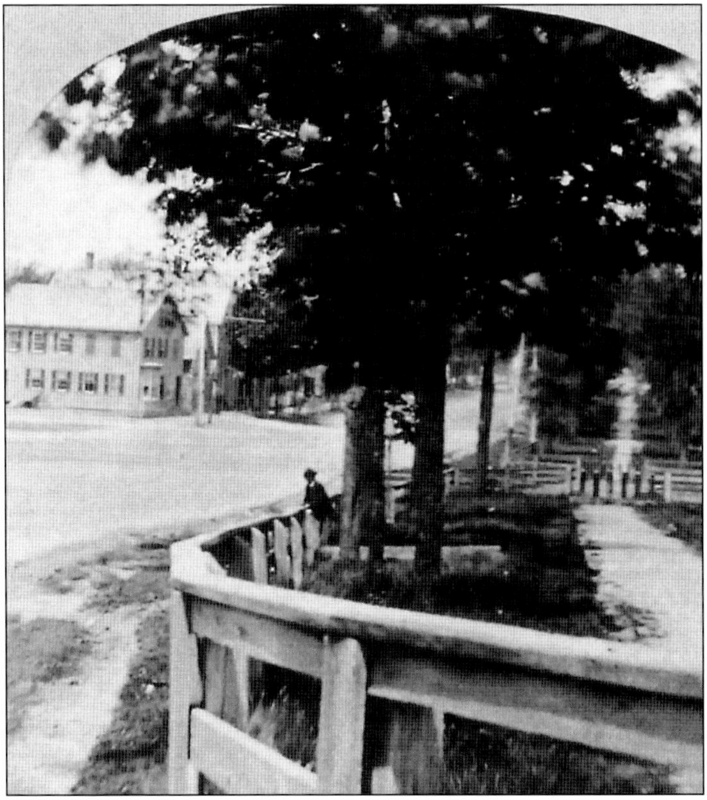

Two 1870s views along the sides of the Mall, looking north on Maine Street and Park Row, but fail to show the infamous frog pond. In each picture, the fencing accentuated the two sections, one above and, one below the railroad.

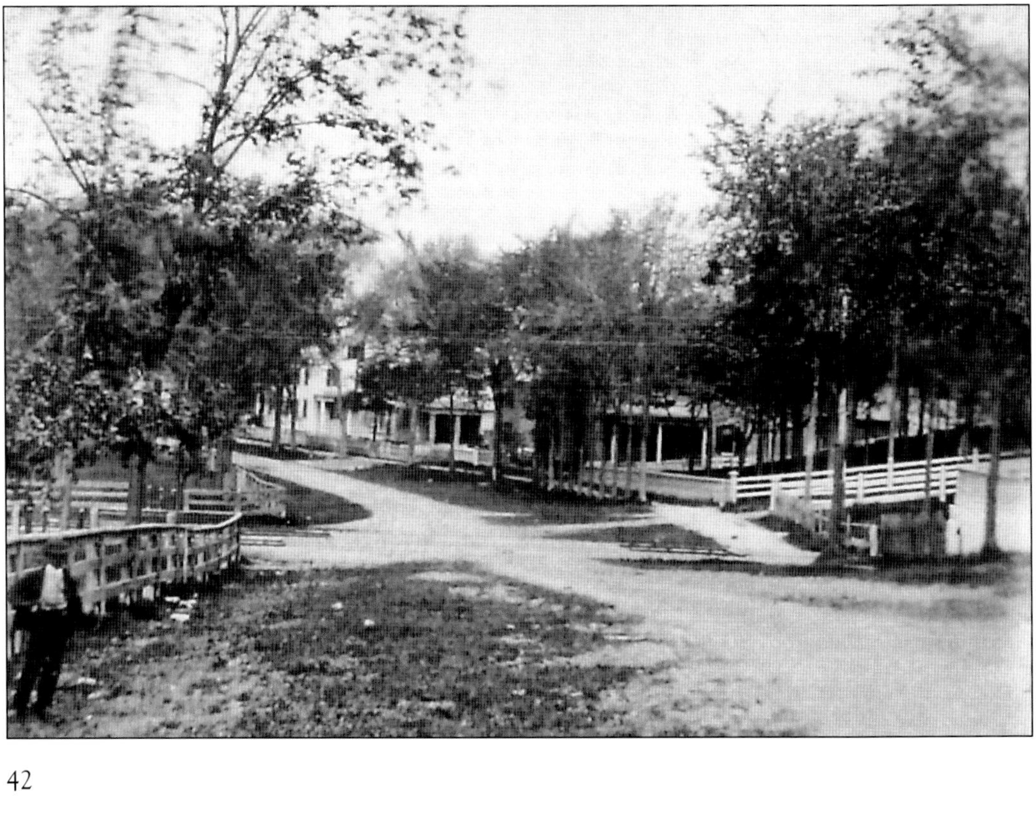

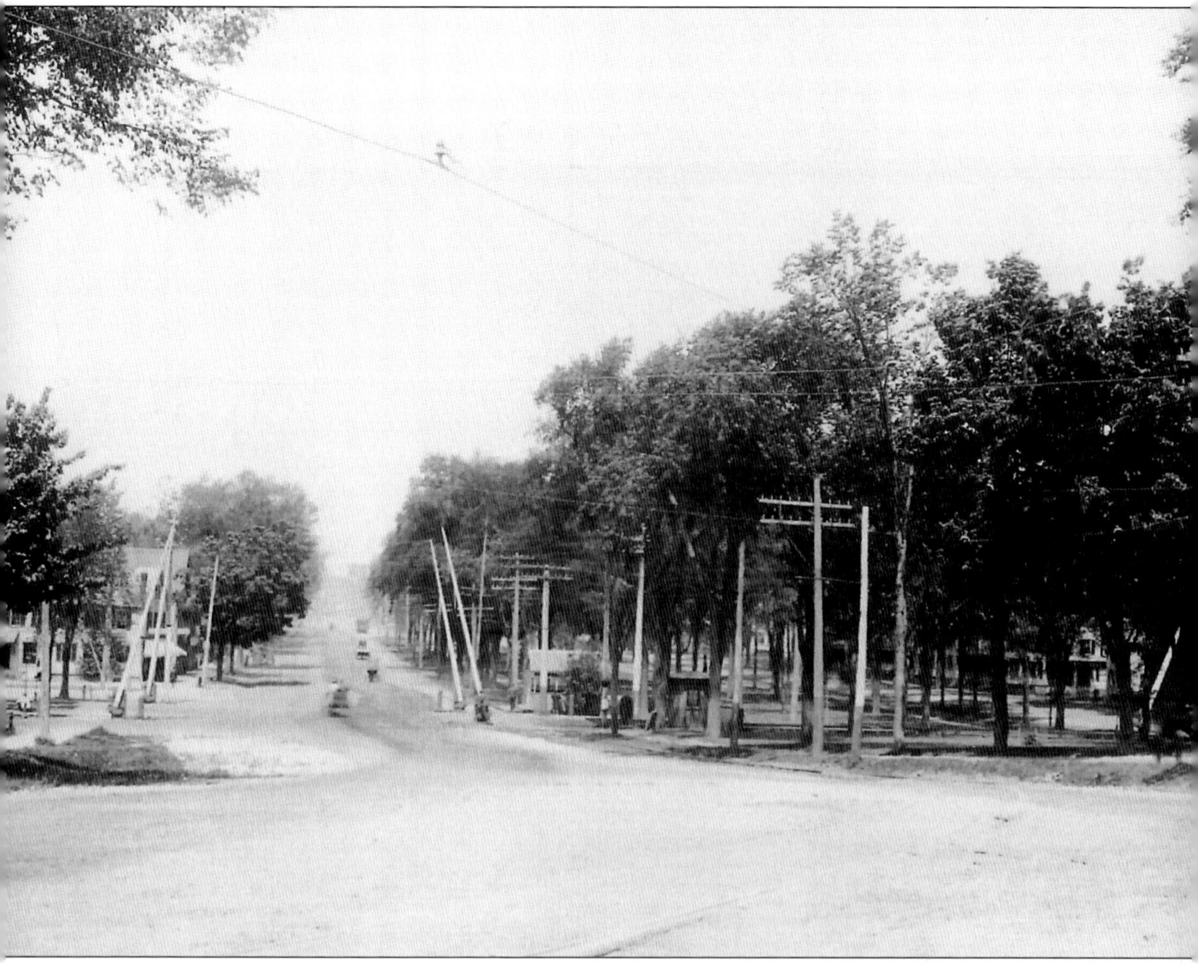

At the end of the century, the fences were gone; trolley tracks ran up the west side of the Mall and railroad safety gates were larger. Note the trolley car at the far end.

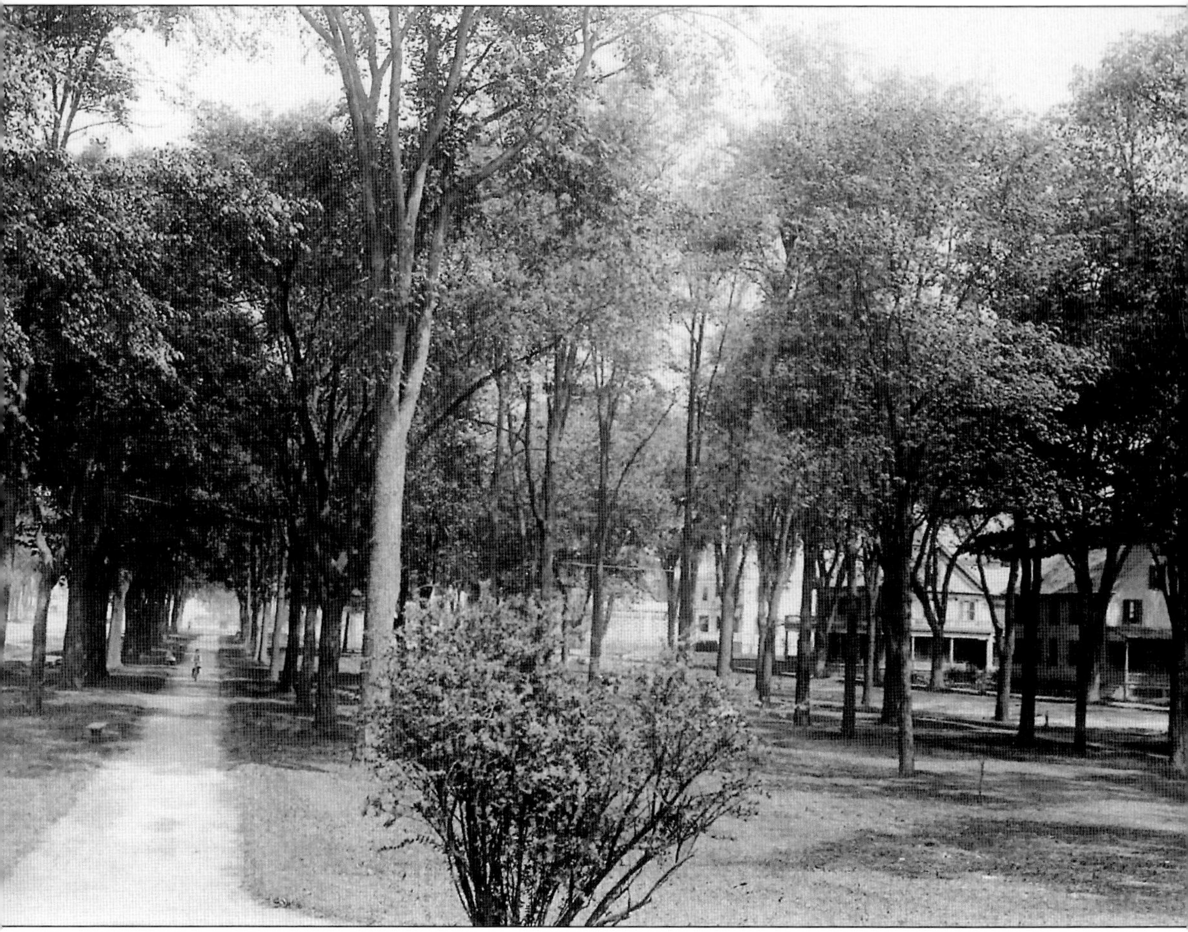

Elm trees had by then grown to shade not only the path, but much of what was by then a pleasant park.

Four

Topsham Village

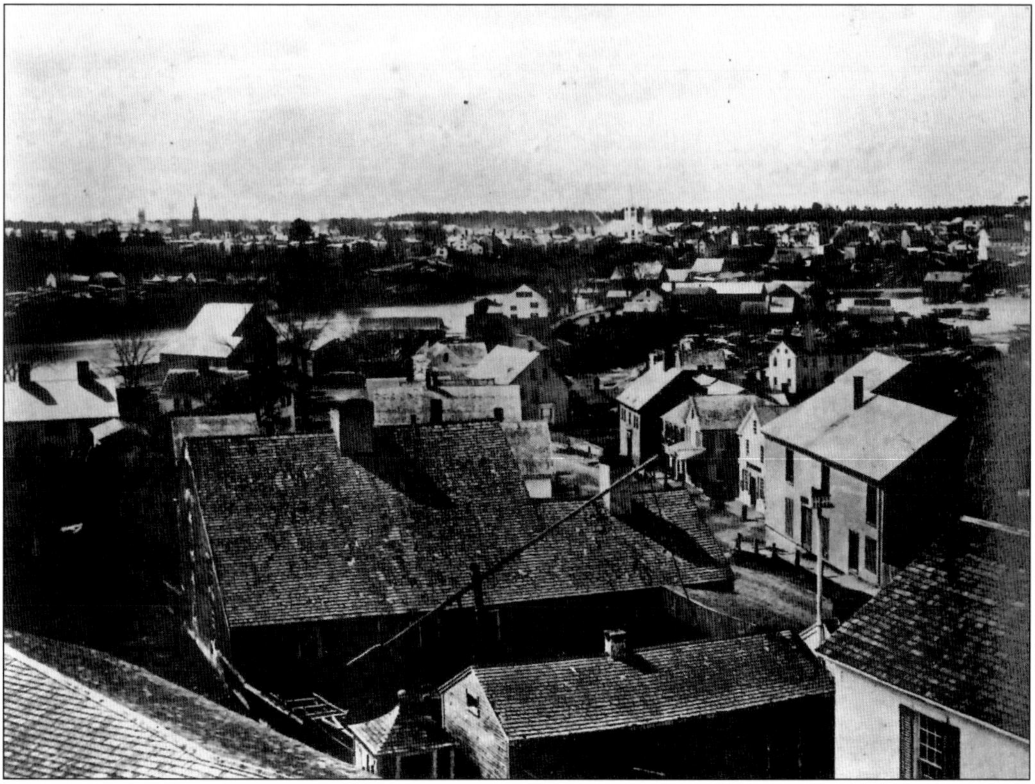

Hills rise from close to the river on its Topsham side, making the terrain less suited for extensive commercial development. A few stores and small businesses along Main Street can be seen in the lower right corner of this view taken south from the hill in the late 1850s. Just to the right of center Granny Hole Stream parts to form Mill Island, which then held a variety of small mills.

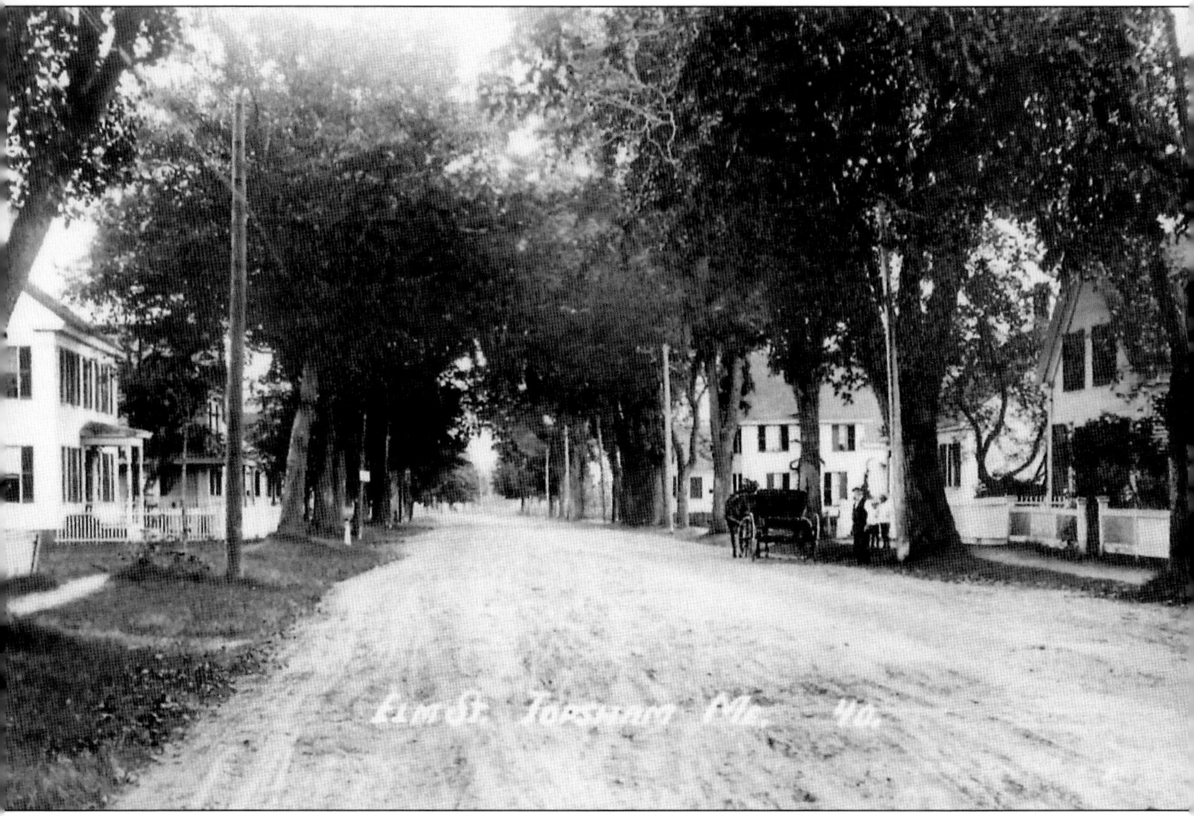

Topsham's most-developed streets were parallel to the river and remained largely residential but Elm Street, the village portion of the road to Bowdoinham, held churches, schools, and a series of town halls among the homes.

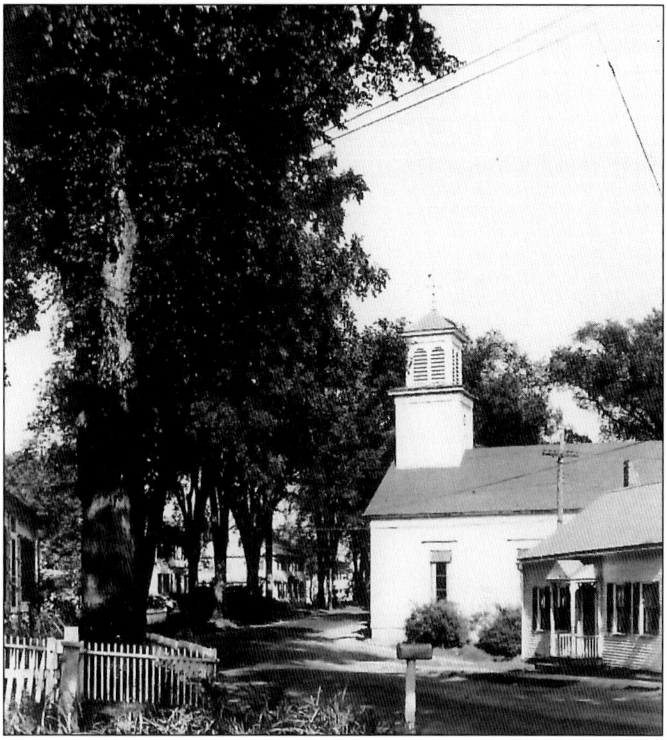

The building on the far corner of Elm and Green Streets, originally a Congregational church, served as the town hall before it burned in 1963.

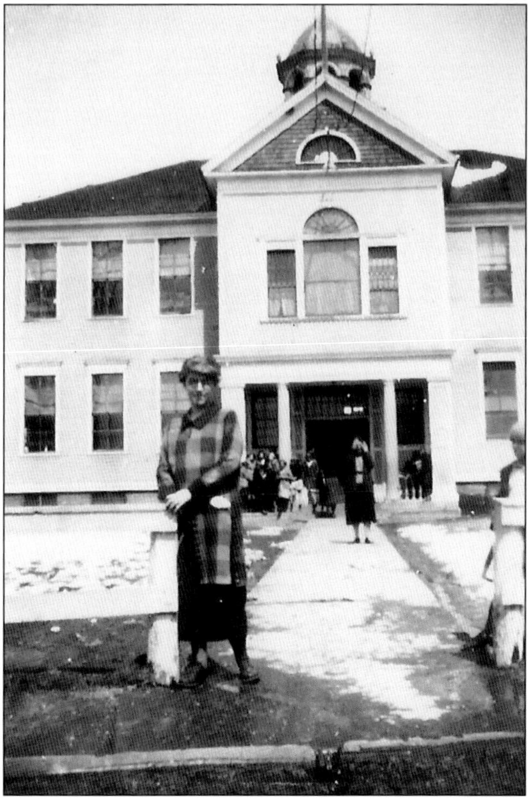

As one-room schoolhouses became outdated, the Topsham Village School, shown here in 1925, was built on Elm Street. In front stands Ethel Allen, teacher of the upper grades. Renamed the John A. Cone School in 1938, the building was the town's major educational facility until a more modern school was opened in 1954. After the existing town hall burned in 1963, the old schoolhouse was remodelled to serve as a new one.

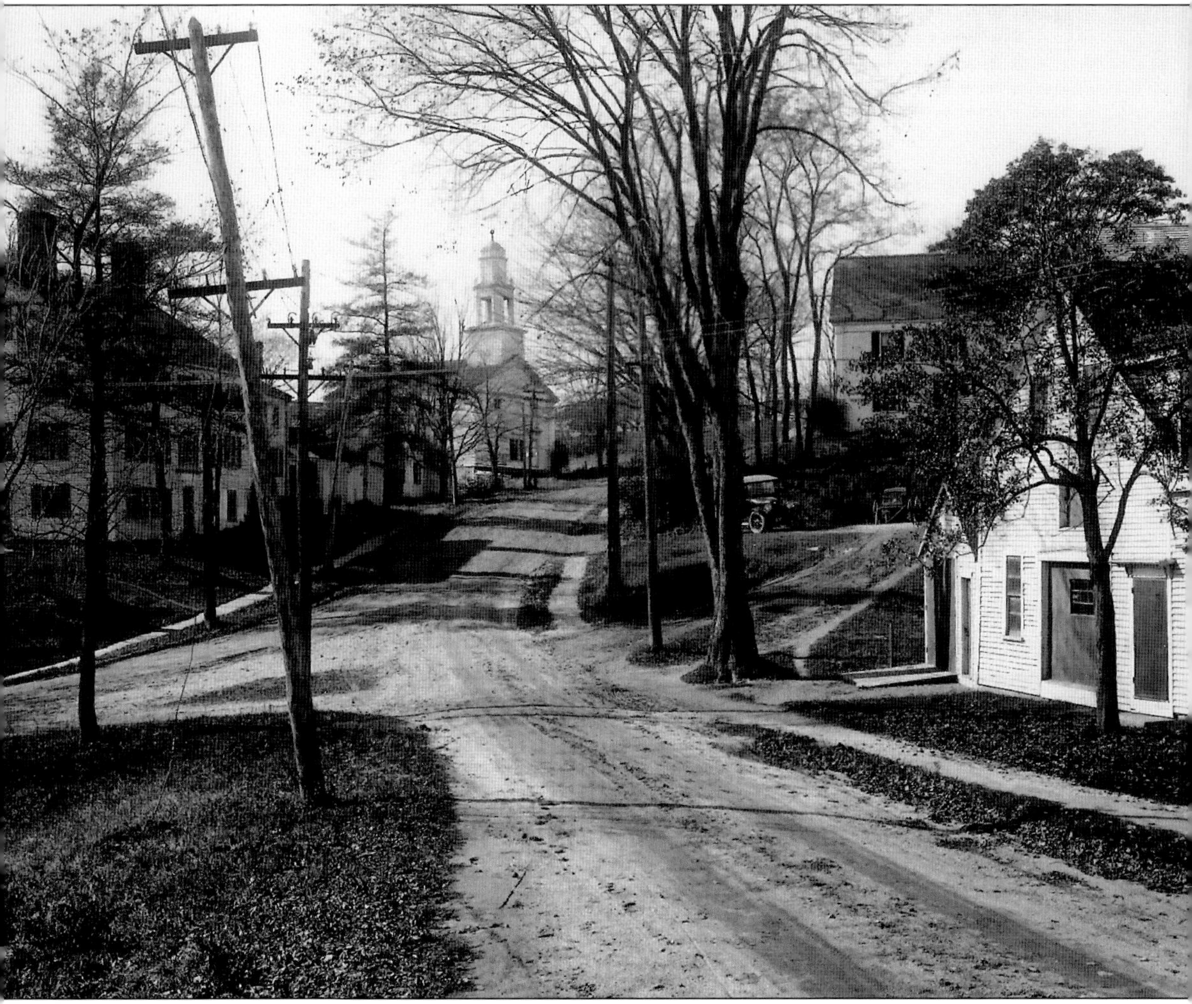

Winter Street was once the first section of the road to Lewiston. Businesses and churches occupied lots near Main Street. In the 1920s, Quint's Livery Stable operated on the right, but by then the Baptist Church on the hill beyond no longer met.

Four

Manufacturing

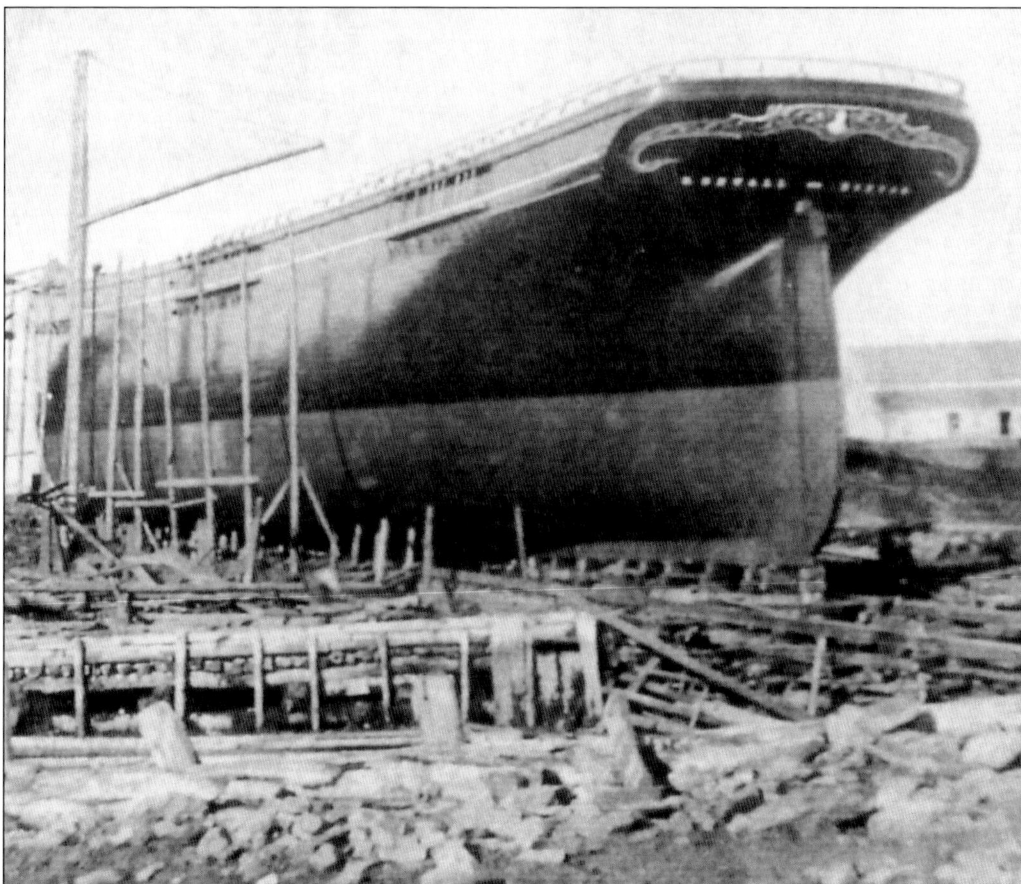

An important part of Brunswick's history included shipbuilding, and early yards operated on the river in Topsham as well. For over eighty years, beginning in the 1790s, vessels were launched at Pennellville, on Middle Bay. The 1874 ship *Benjamin Sewall* was the last (as well as the largest) vessel from there. Ship construction continued eleven more years at the Skolfield yard, to the east.

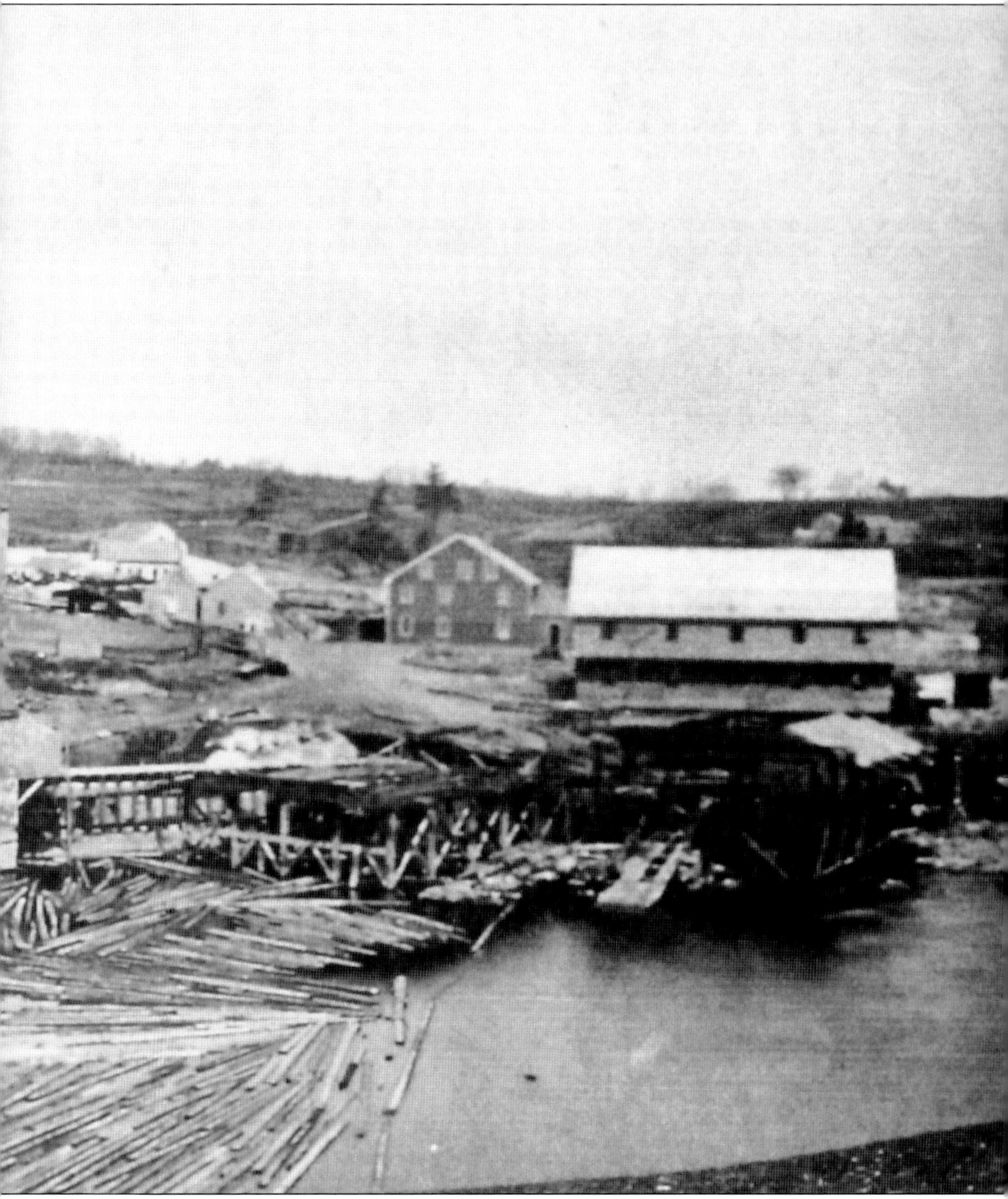

Saw and grist mills were established on both sides of the river. On lower Maine Street in Brunswick, seen from across the Cove in the 1870s, stood the Scribner Grist Mill (gable end toward the camera) and the Colby Sawmill. Logs in the river waited to be turned into boards. The background is Topsham's Winter Street Hill.

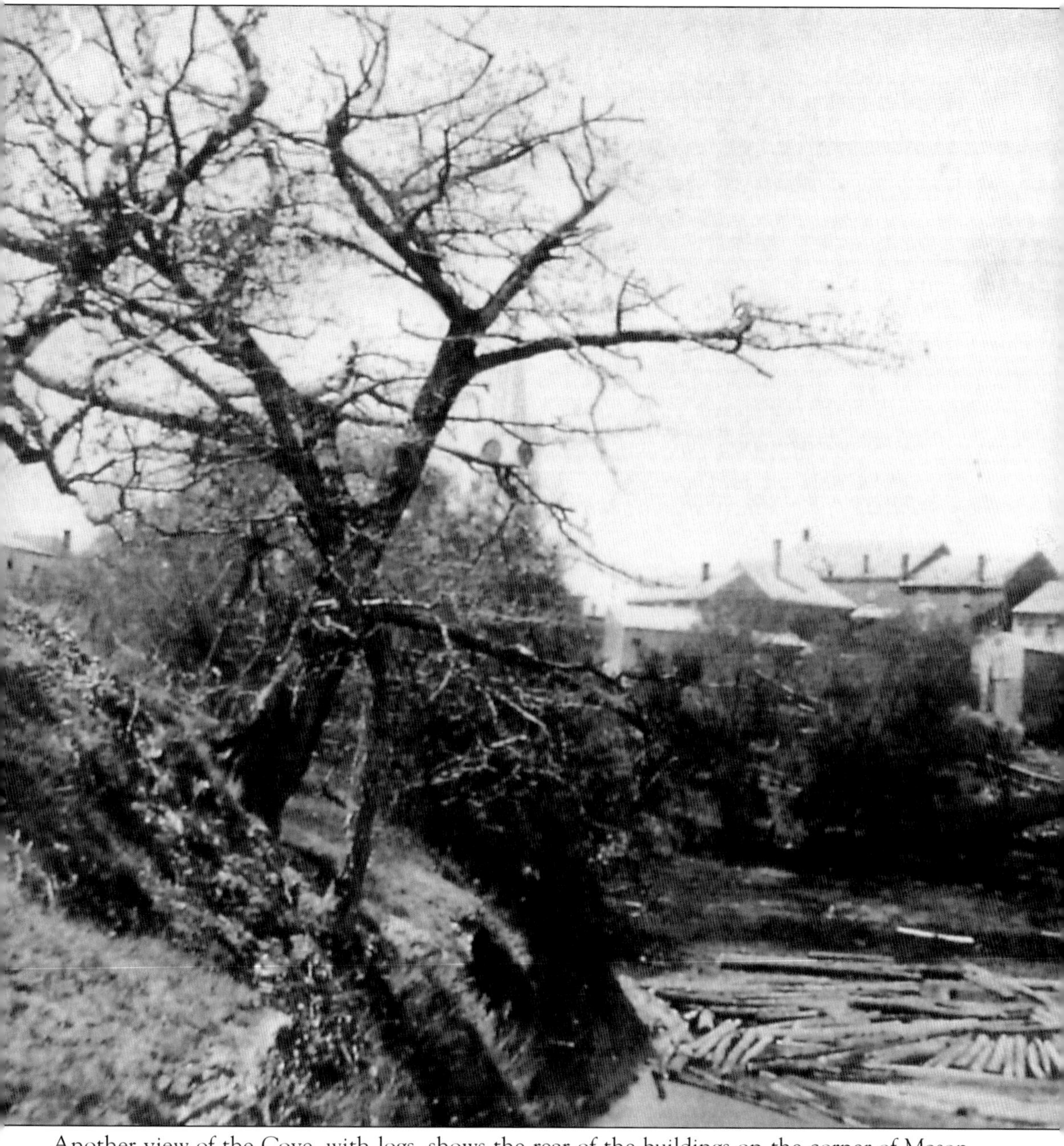

Another view of the Cove, with logs, shows the rear of the buildings on the corner of Mason and Maine Streets. What looks like a very tall building on the right had only two floors on the street side.

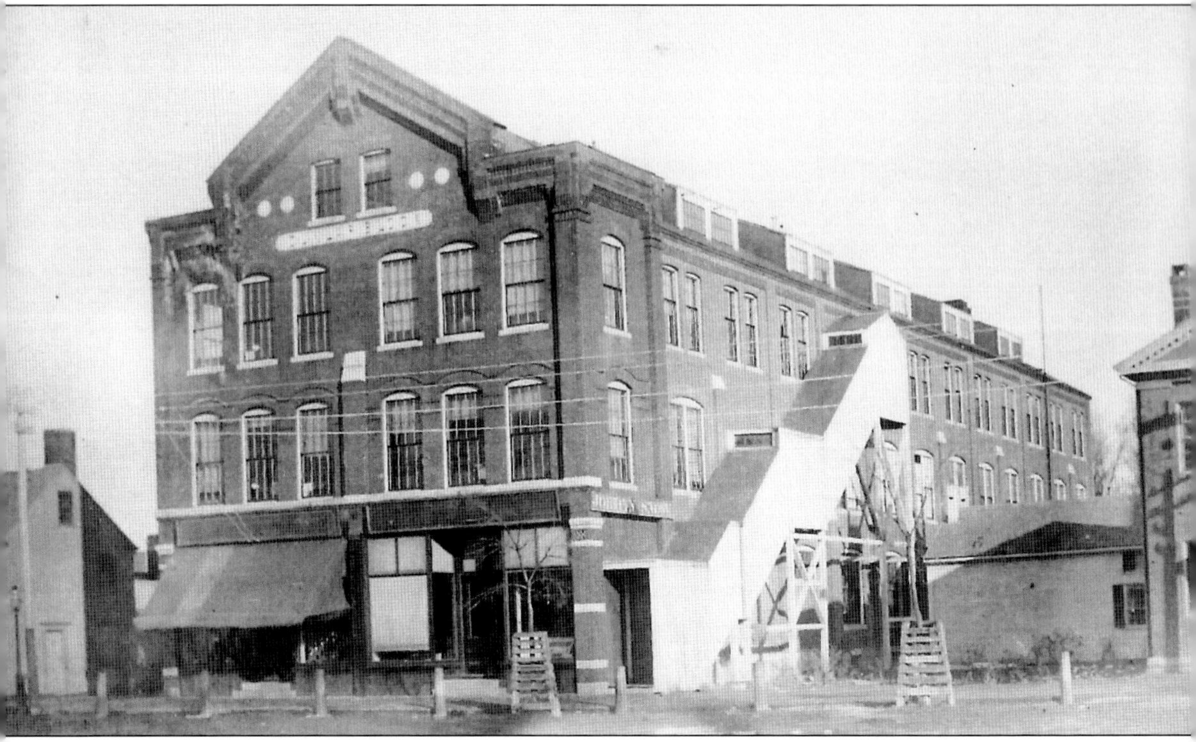

Among the smaller manufactories in the area was the box factory of Andrew Dennison, who had designed a machine to cut and score cardboard parts for boxes for a son's Boston jewelry store. In 1872 the Dennison Box Co. enlarged and moved into the Dunlap Block on Maine Street. In 1880 the building was rebuilt after a fire, and the Dennison Company maintained its Brunswick presence for decades. Later the space was occupied by the Brunswick Box Co. and by then the Baxter Box Co.

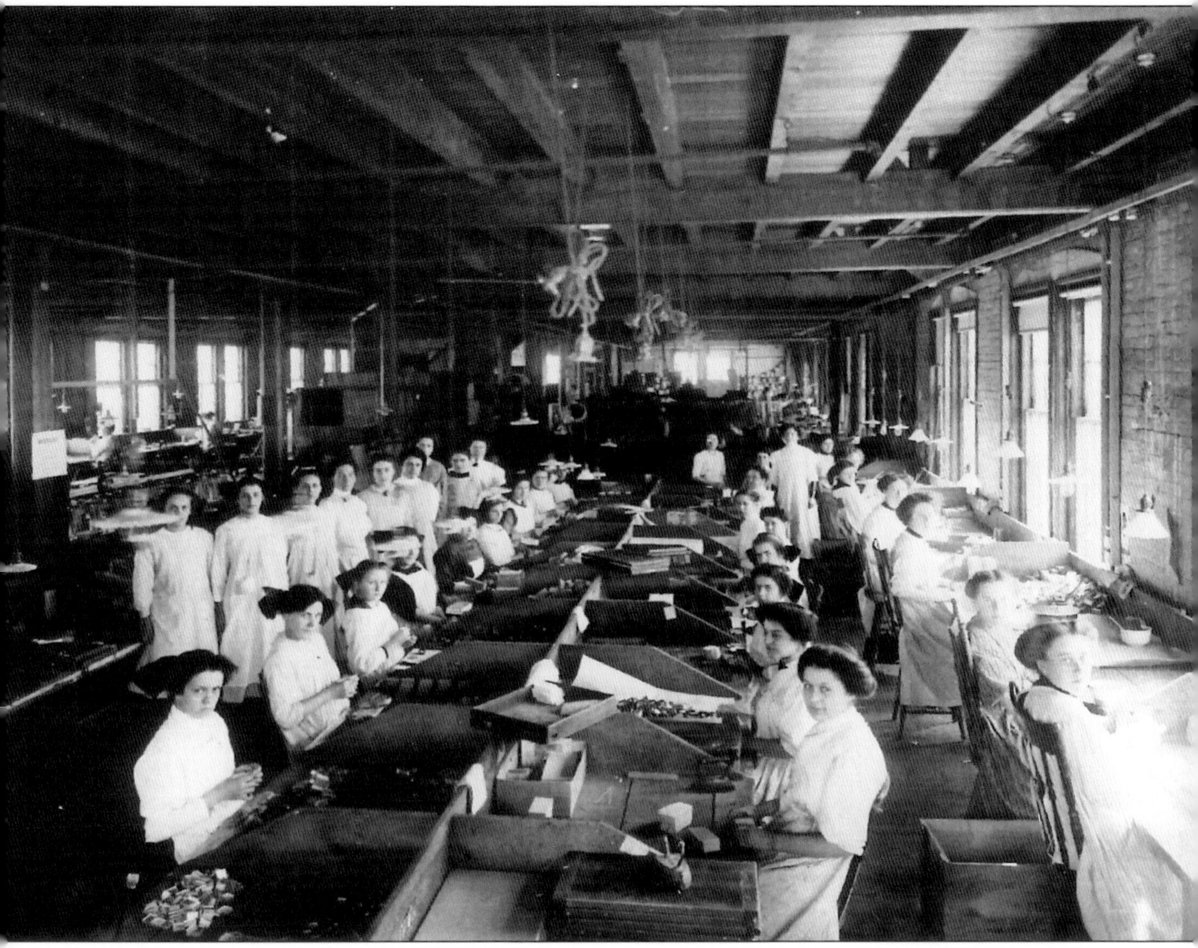

The work scene above was photographed after the town was electrified in 1887. Each worker had brushes and glue for assembling the boxes, and the height of the lights could be adjusted.

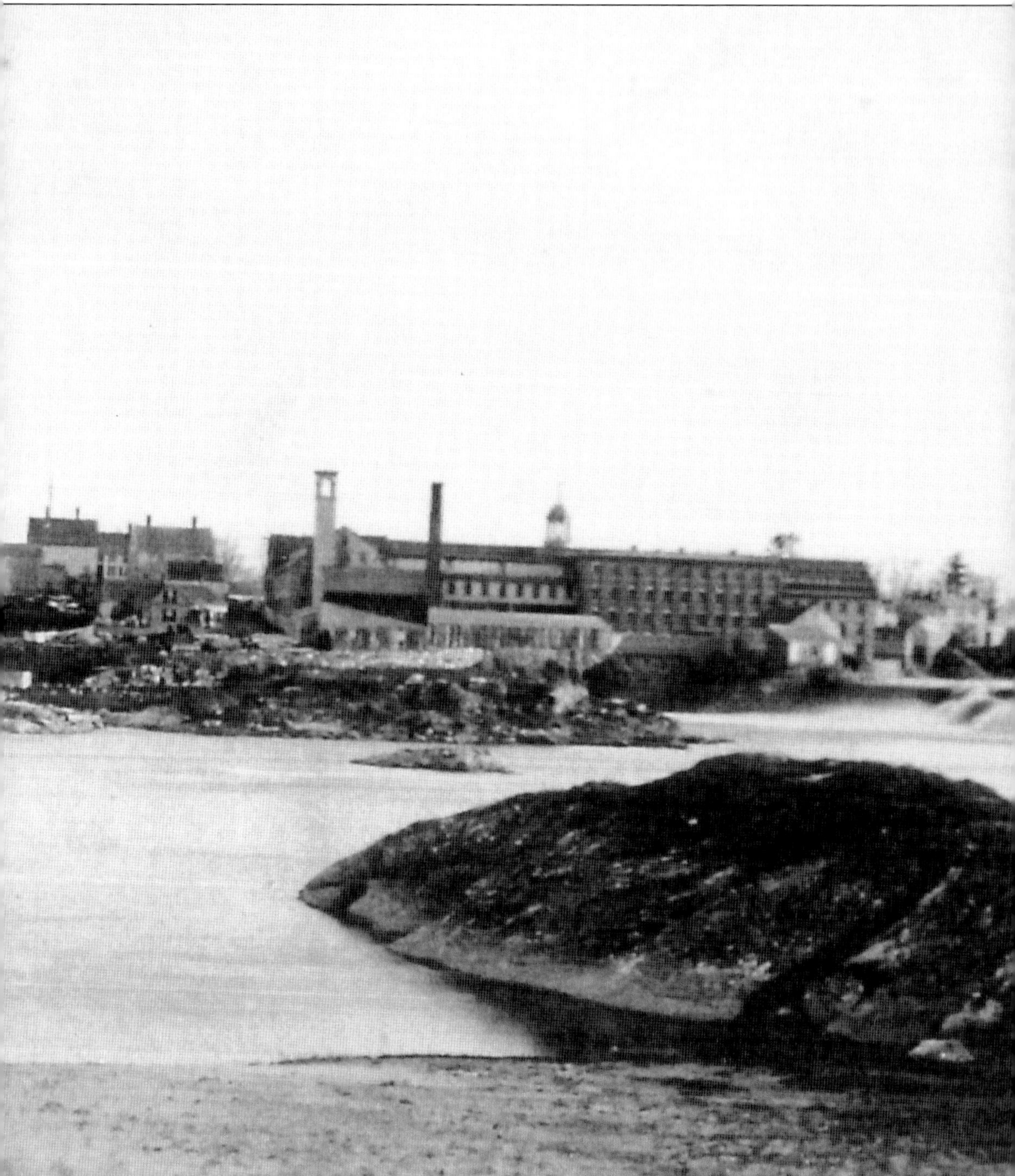

Bigger firms brought greater changes. The Cabot Manufacturing Company replaced earlier cotton mills and built a large factory, with more jobs available after the Civil War than the area had workers. The company built tenements nearby and recruited workers in Canada, bringing French-speaking Catholics into a town inhabited primarily by Protestants of British descent. For a while two separate societies existed.

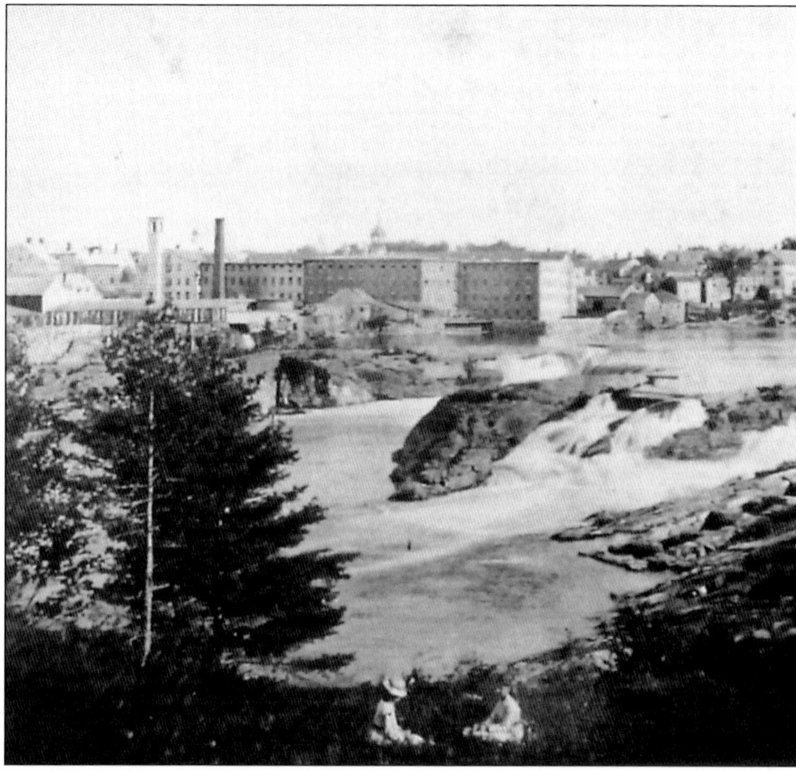

This scene could symbolize differences between the towns in the 1870s: women sitting in a park-like setting on the Topsham shore provide contrast with the cotton mill and tenements across the river. The picture was taken after the stone fishway was constructed around the upper falls in 1871.

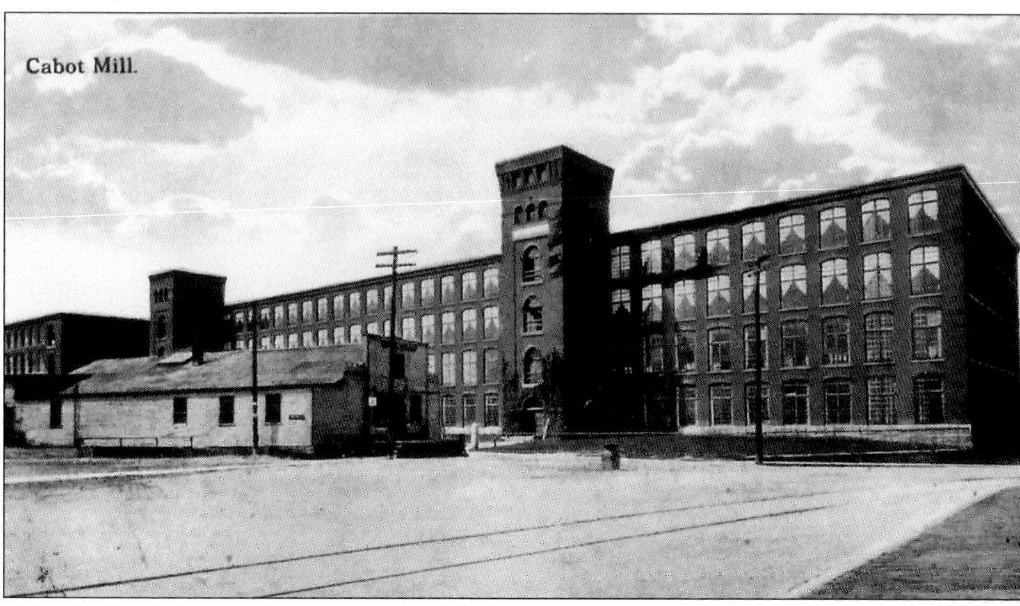

Cabot Mill after its 1895 enlargement necessitated relocating the end of Maine Street. In front is the company store.

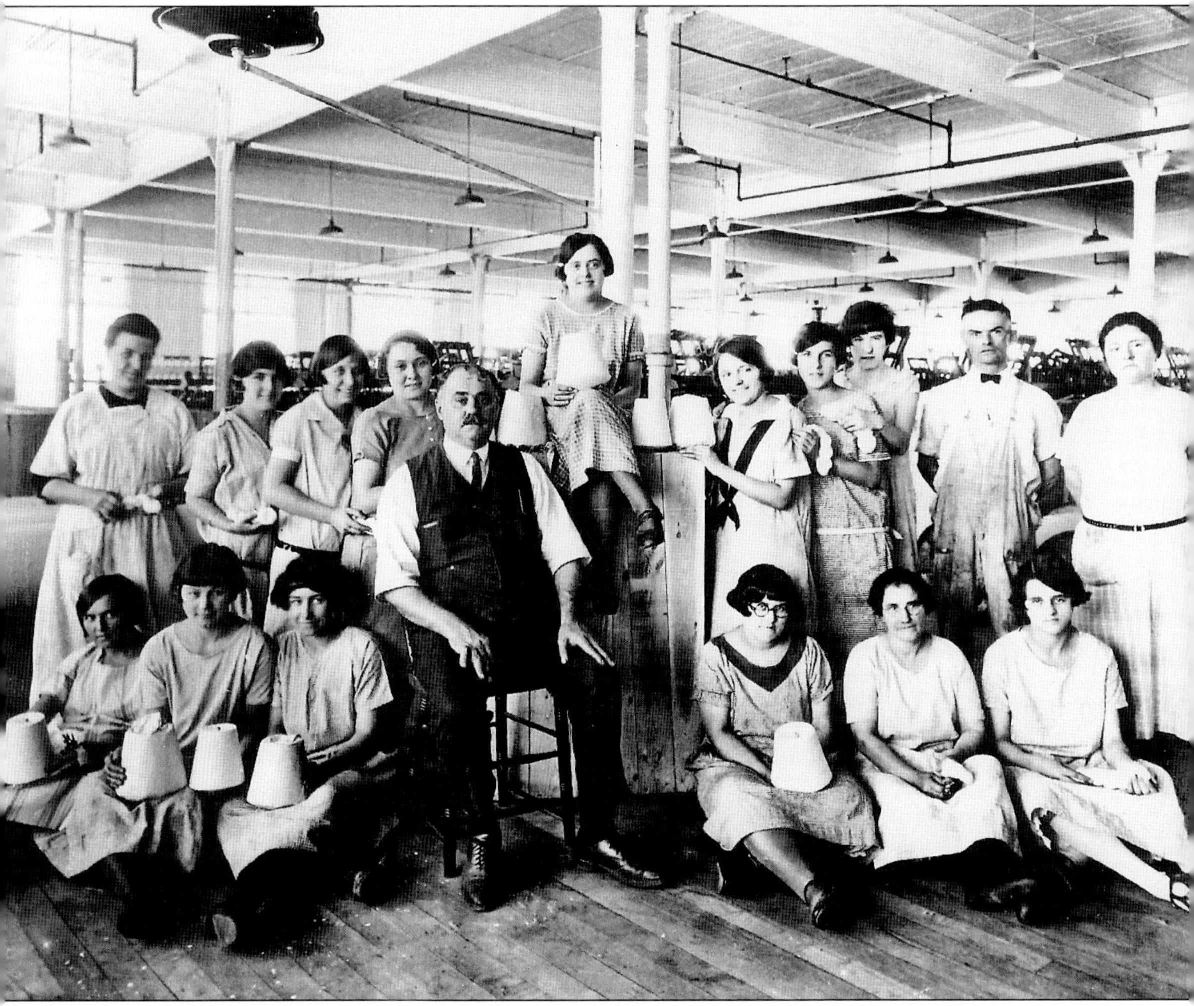

Joseph Lebeau was overseer and Honore Laprise his assistant in the mill's winding room about 1925. The women workers were all French, too. Identified are Cecile Tetreault and ? Bernier, to the left of Lebeau, then Jeanne Lebourdais, Lucienne Levesque, Claire Dehetre, unknown, Laprise, and Rose Marois, standing. Irma Fortin is seated on the right, with Agatha Paradis third from the right.

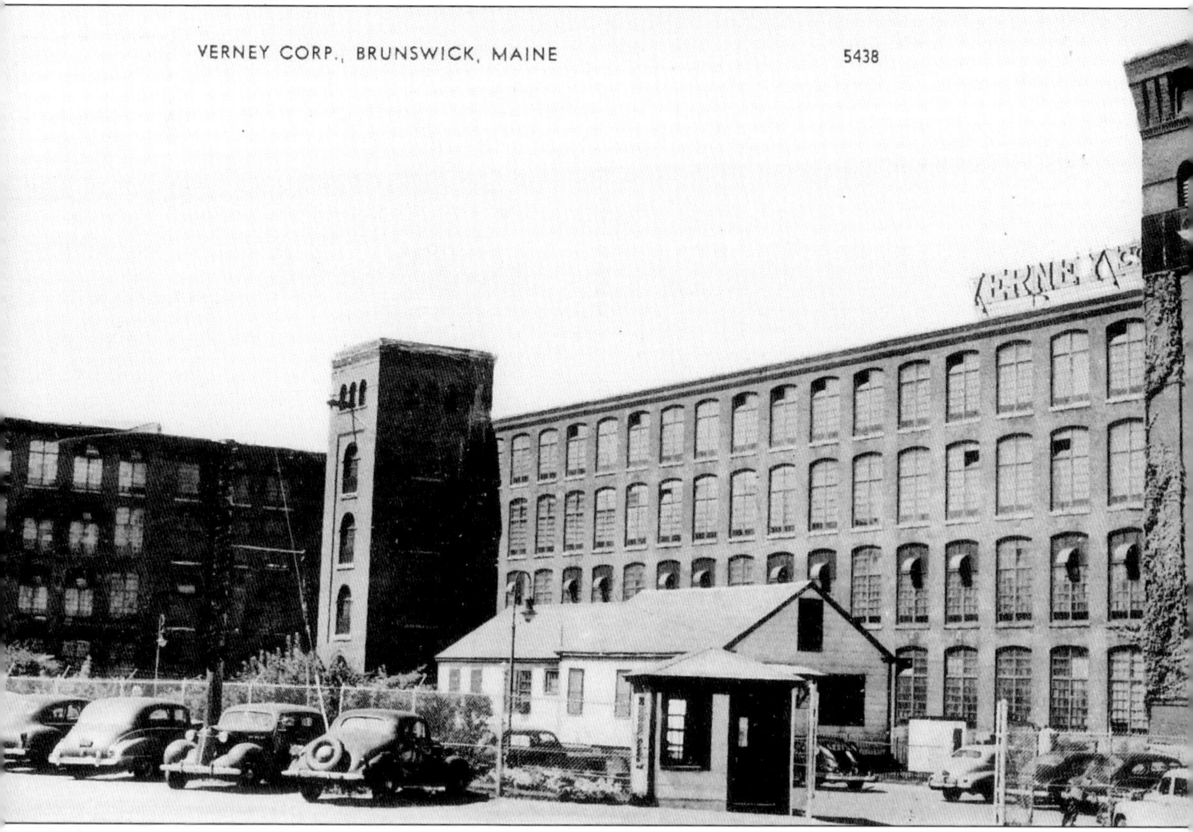

The Verney Corporation purchased the big Brunswick mill in 1942. The security booth at the gate was deemed necessary during World War II because the mill was producing material for military parachutes.

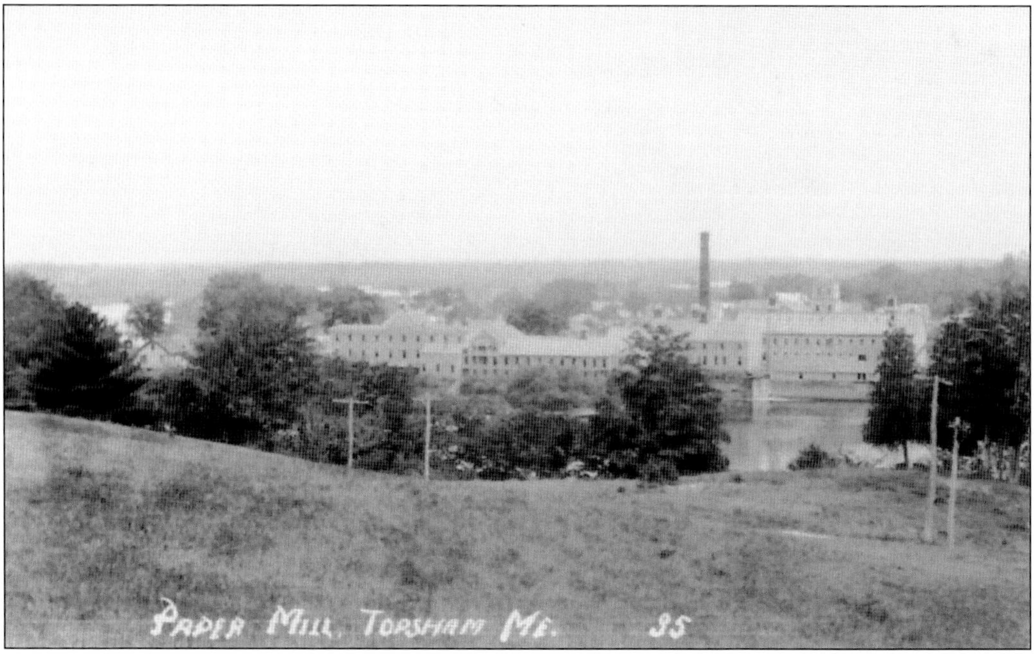

Topsham's Bowdoin Paper Mill, seen from the west and before the 1932 Frank Wood Bridge was built near its west side. The mill's first building was started in 1868, and the concern employed mostly local persons to turn out quality rag-based paper.

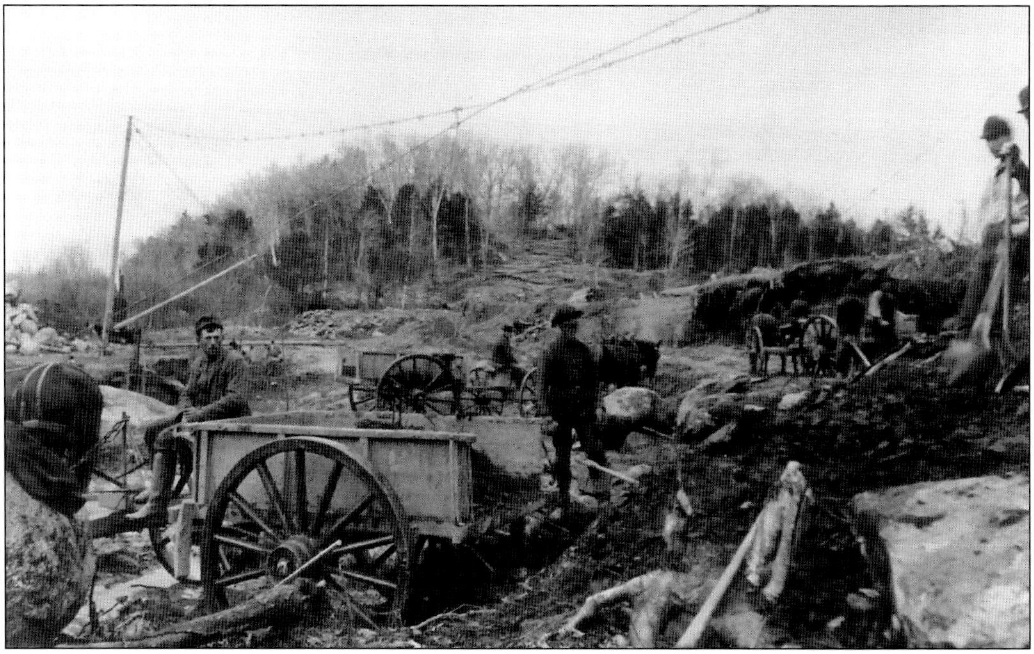
The company's new pulp paper mill was built at what became Pejepscot, excavation work beginning in April 1893, using picks, shovels, and horsecarts. The new location was distant from the villages and company housing was needed. Among the laborers who came to work and live there were many from the Slovakian section of the Austro-Hungarian Empire, bringing cultural diversity to Topsham.

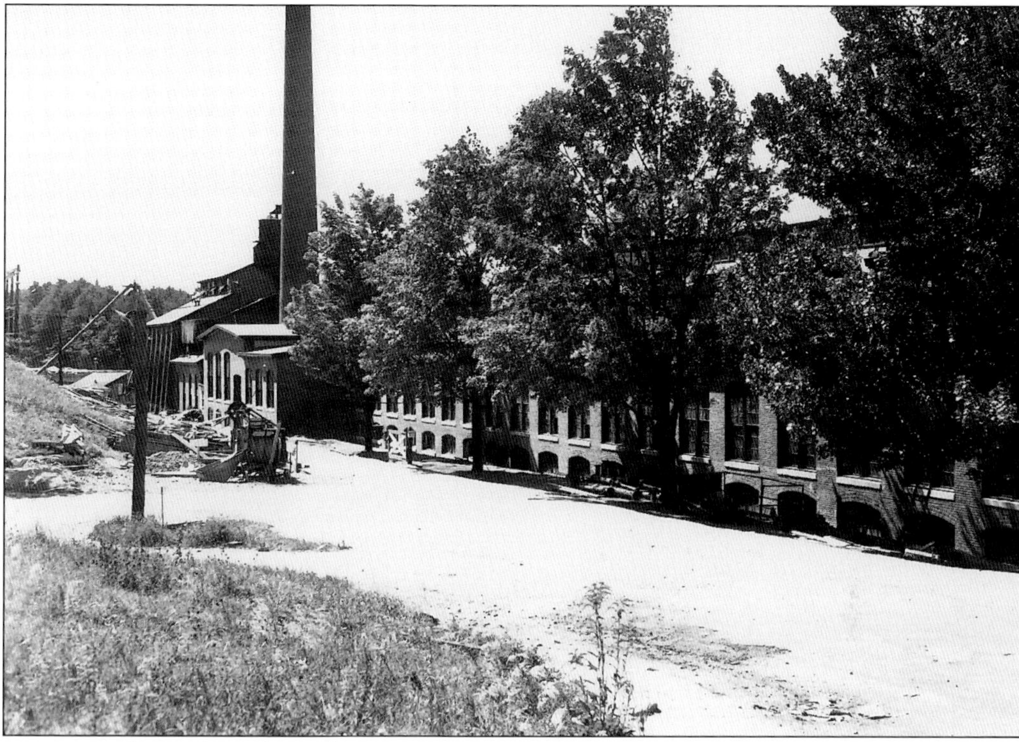

Company photos show the mill just as preparations were being made in 1941 for an enlargement to house the "No. 1 Machine," then still at the Bowdoin Mill facility.

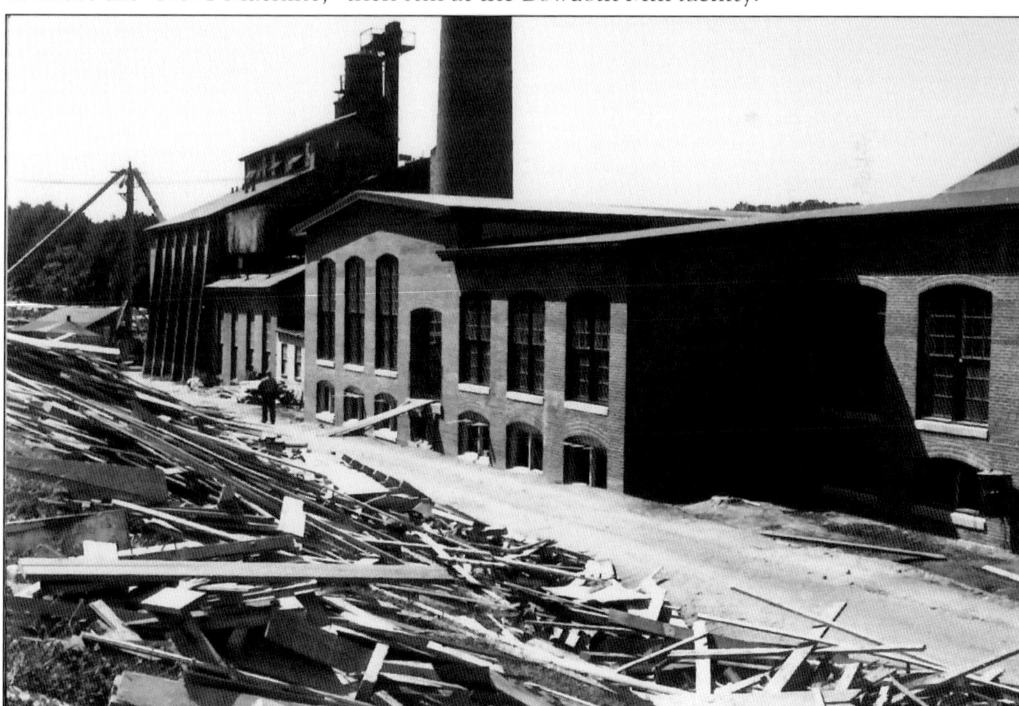

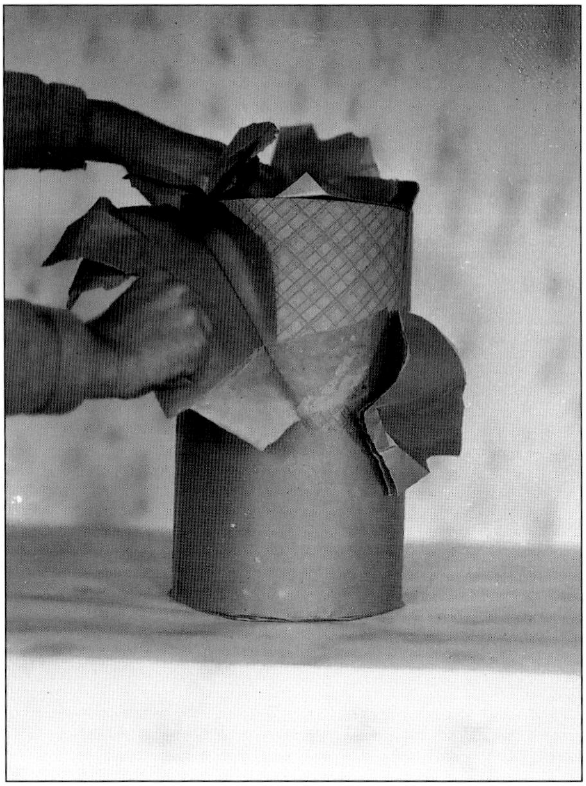

Numerous types and forms of paper came from the mill, including this fifteen-inch roll labelled "Scotch Plaid No. 556" from the 1940s.

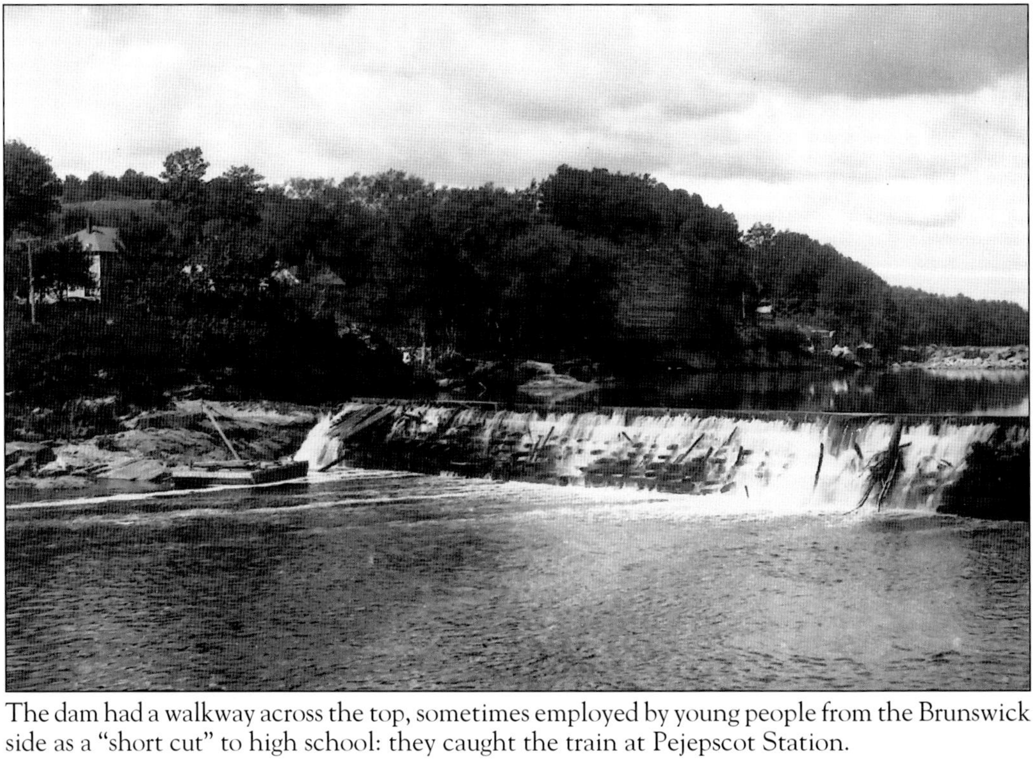

The dam had a walkway across the top, sometimes employed by young people from the Brunswick side as a "short cut" to high school: they caught the train at Pejepscot Station.

Four

Agriculture

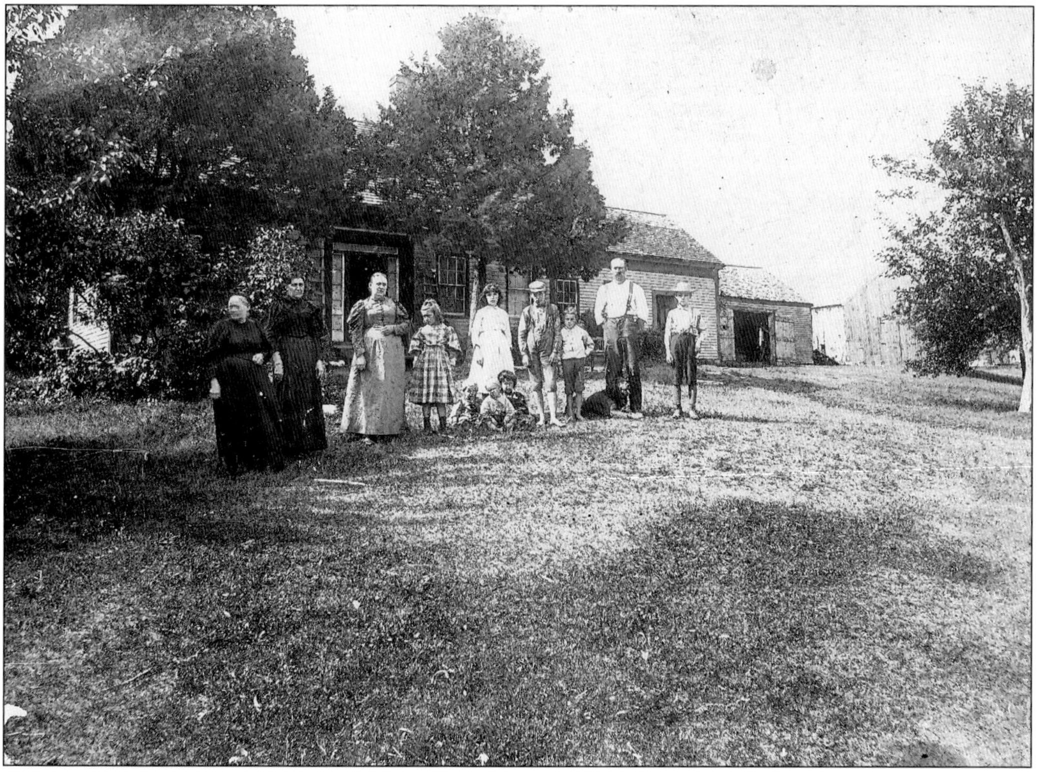

Although mills employed an increasing number of their populations, both towns had considerable land which continued to be used as family farms. Farming was proportionately more important in Topsham. A travelling photographer captured one family and its farmhouse for posterity. Julia and James Hyde (3rd and 8th) of the Foreside Road, Topsham, are standing: the others are with two of her sisters Lucy, Mildred, Percy, Lewis, and Robert. Seated on grass are Jude, John, and Mary Louise.

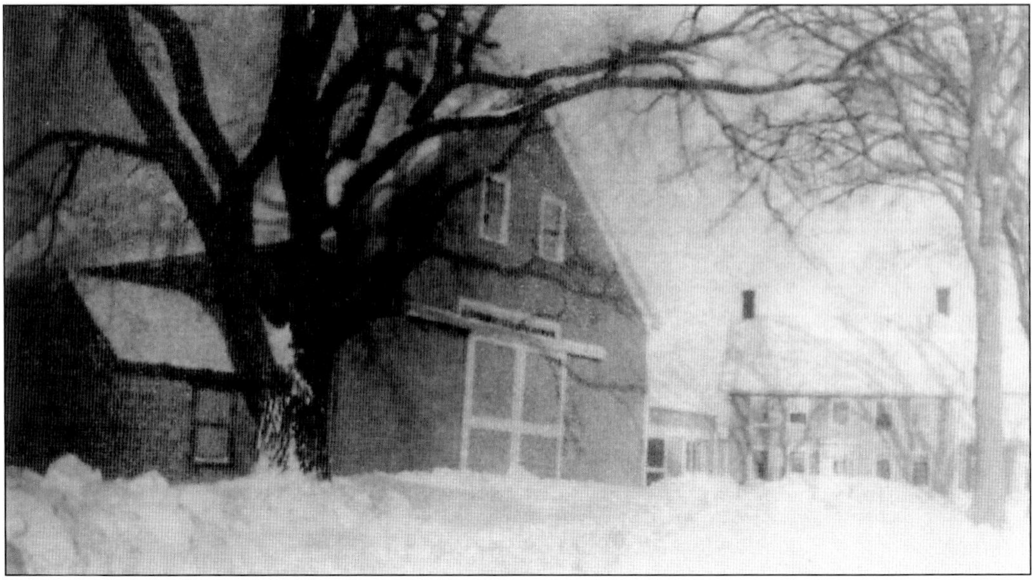

The Luce Farm on the Middlesex Road in the 1930s. (Area residents recall the huge barn as the location of Willey's Garage a few decades later.)

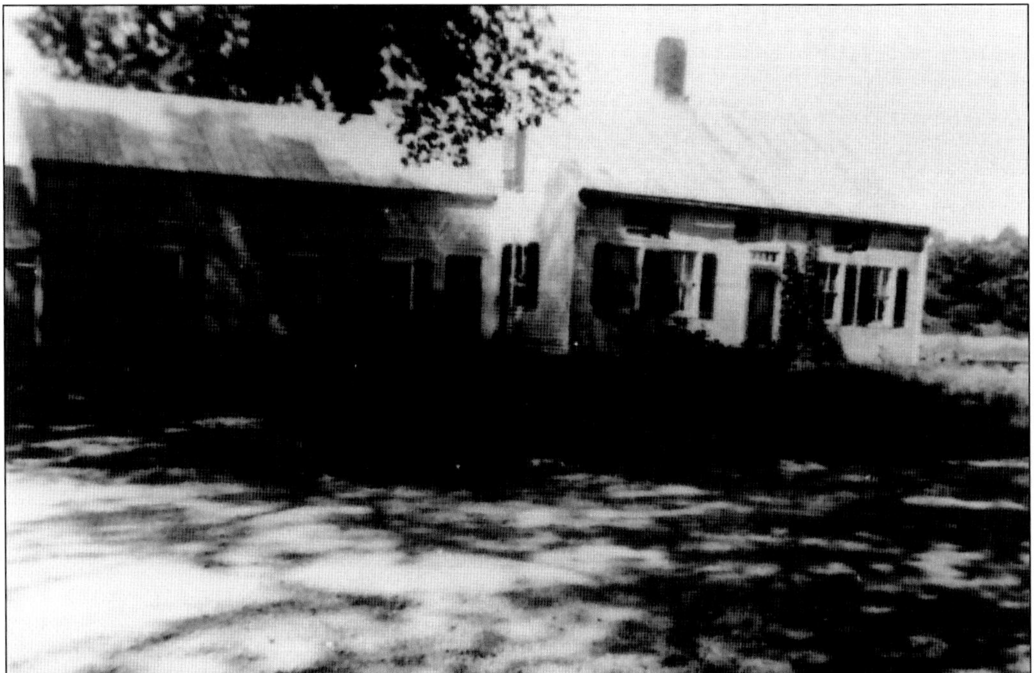

Agriculture was such a "natural" occupation that towns often bought farms to be worked on and lived in by the homeless and unemployed. Topsham purchased this property about 1860 and used it as a "poor farm" when needed.

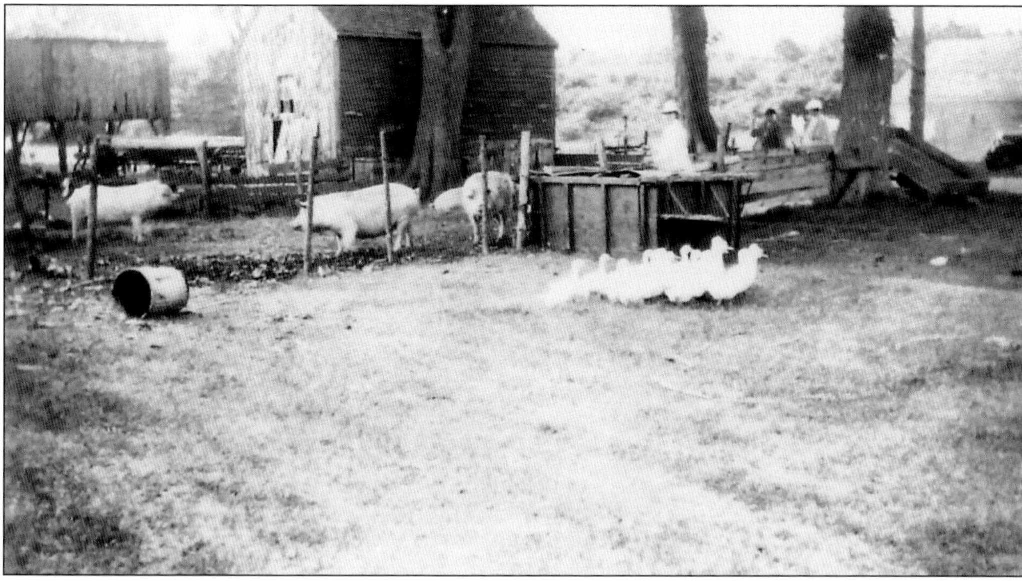

In the 1930s, a former "poor farm" was leased to the Lewis Hasty family, some of whose ducks and swine are shown here.

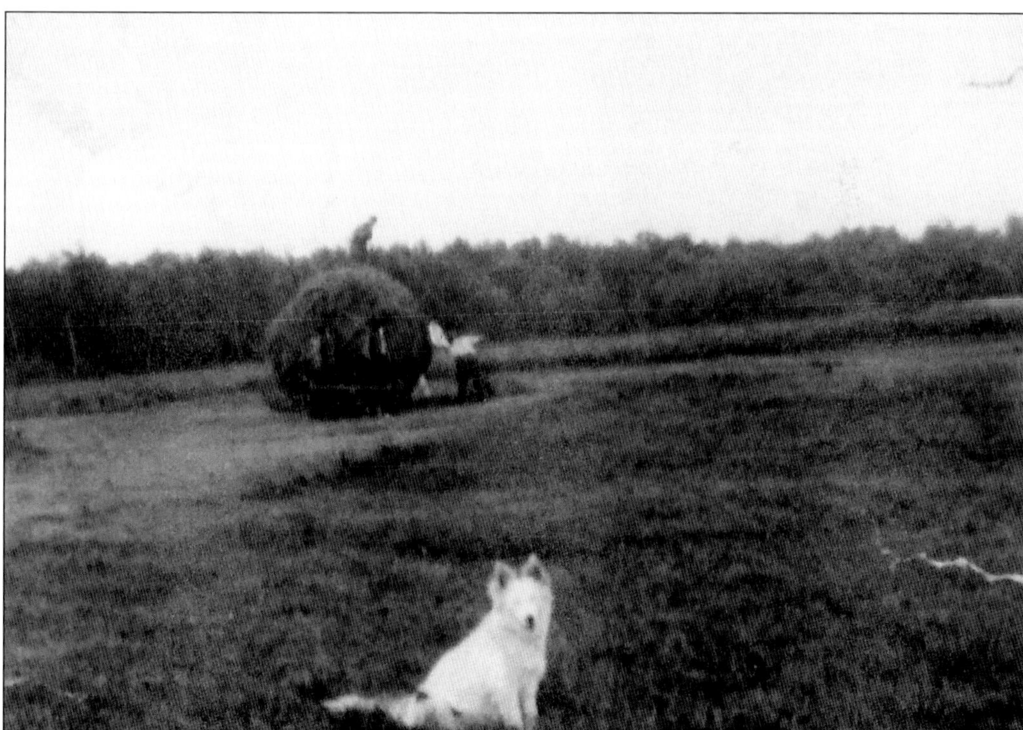

July and August of every year found the Hastys, like most farm families, getting in the hay.

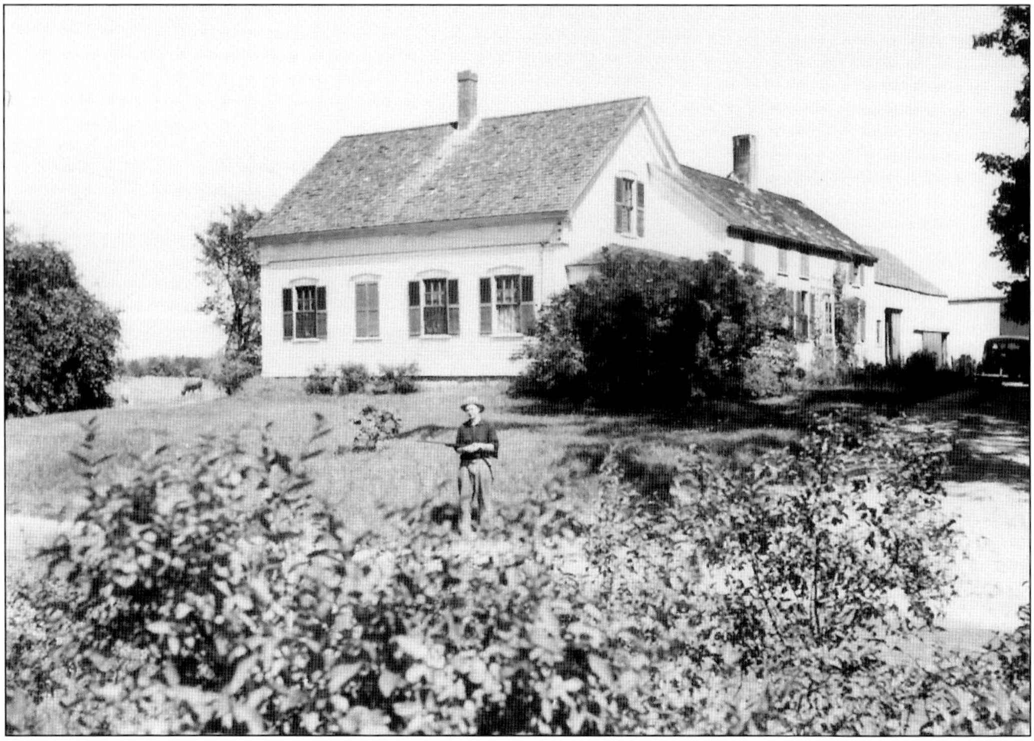

Some older farms were used for specialized crops. On the Meadow Road, Topsham, Rob and Samuel Strand and Velzora Bickell put in a nursery for landscapers on the latter's farm in the 1910s. Rob is shown here a few years later with the plantation of flowering bushes in the foreground.

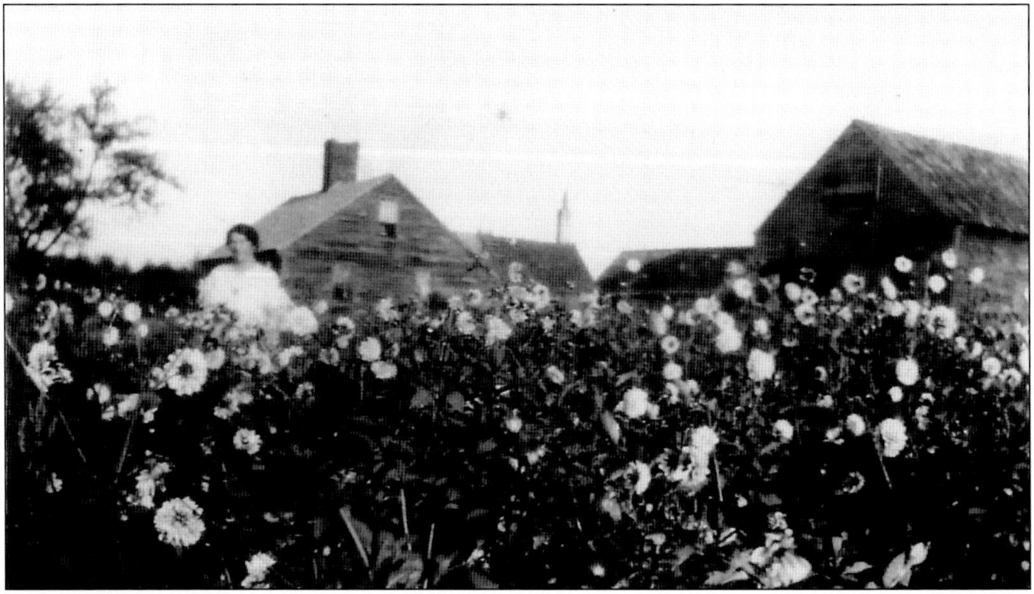

Farm wives might raise flowers for pleasure: Flora Moore is shown with her large bed of dahlias in Topsham.

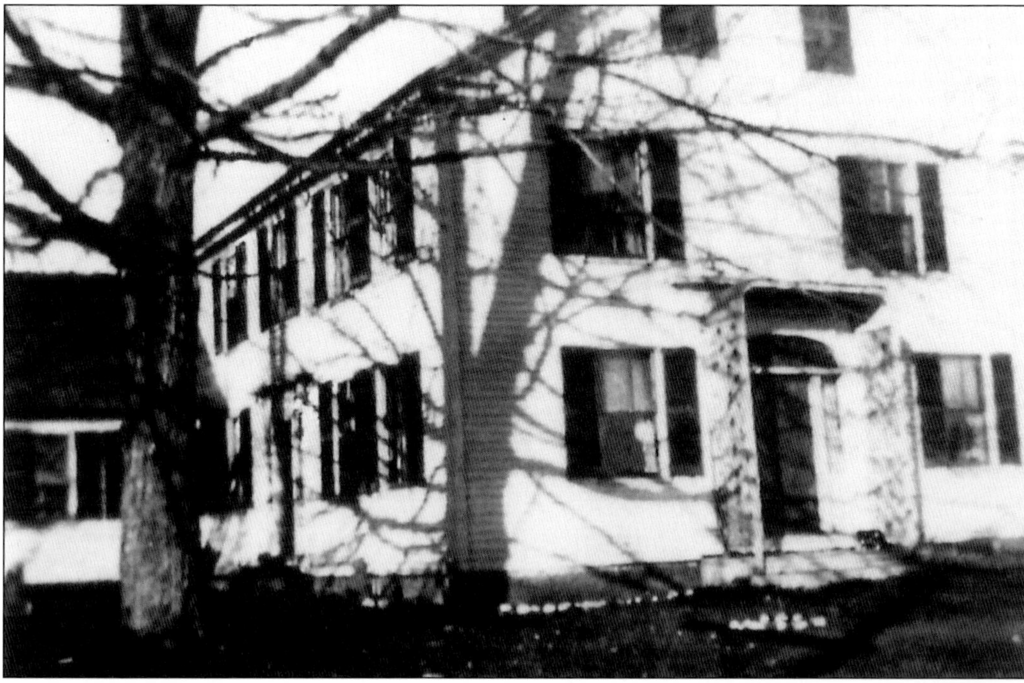

In the late 1920s Arthur Bisson bought another farm on the Meadow Road, including this large Federal-era house. Descendants recall that he made just a $5.00 down payment on a $5000.00 purchase price; yet the family worked hard enough to be able to buy more land the following decade.

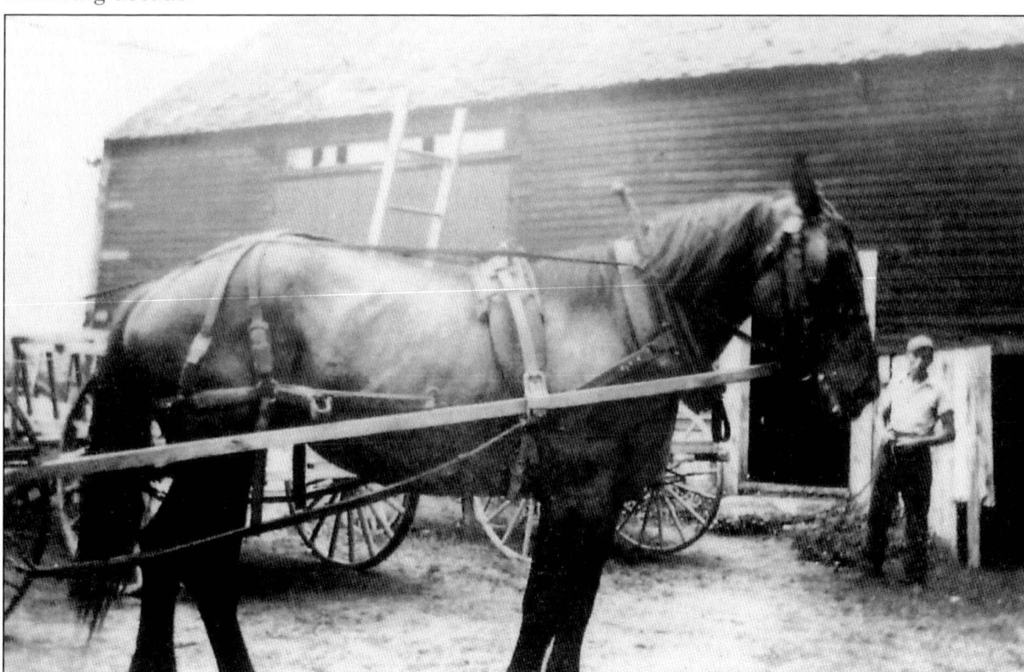

Horses provided early labor, this one looks to be hitched to a hay rake. In the background, by the old barn, stands Alderic Rossignol, a hired man.

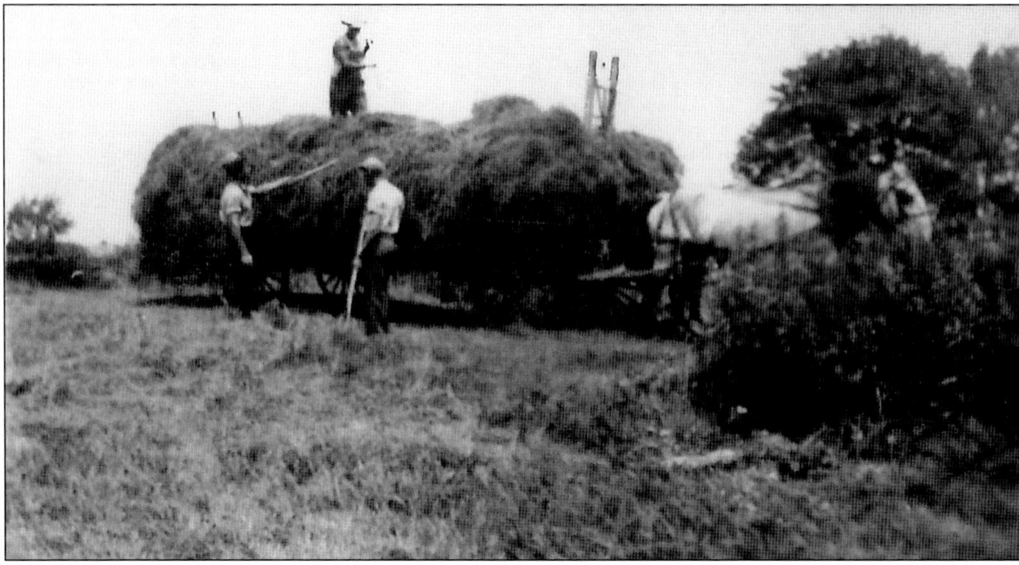

Getting in the hay required a crew: Paul Bisson builds the load, while Charles Perreault and Rossignol pitch him the hay.

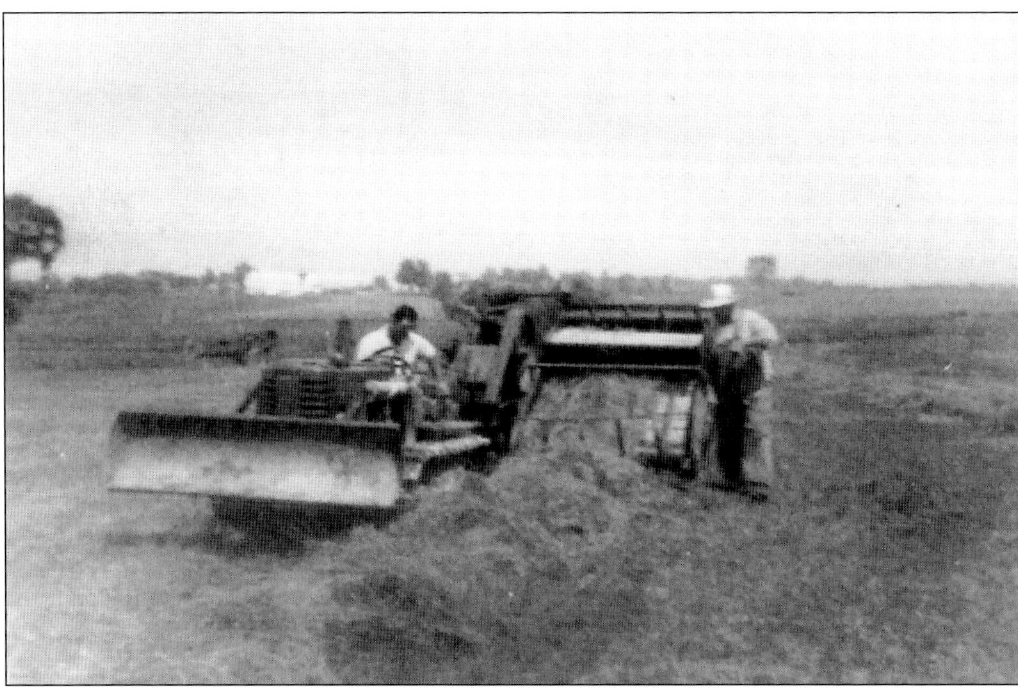

By the early 1940s, haying had become more mechanized. Paul Bisson drives the tractor, while his father, Arthur, oversees the hay being fed to the baler. The location is on the meadows of the Cathance River.

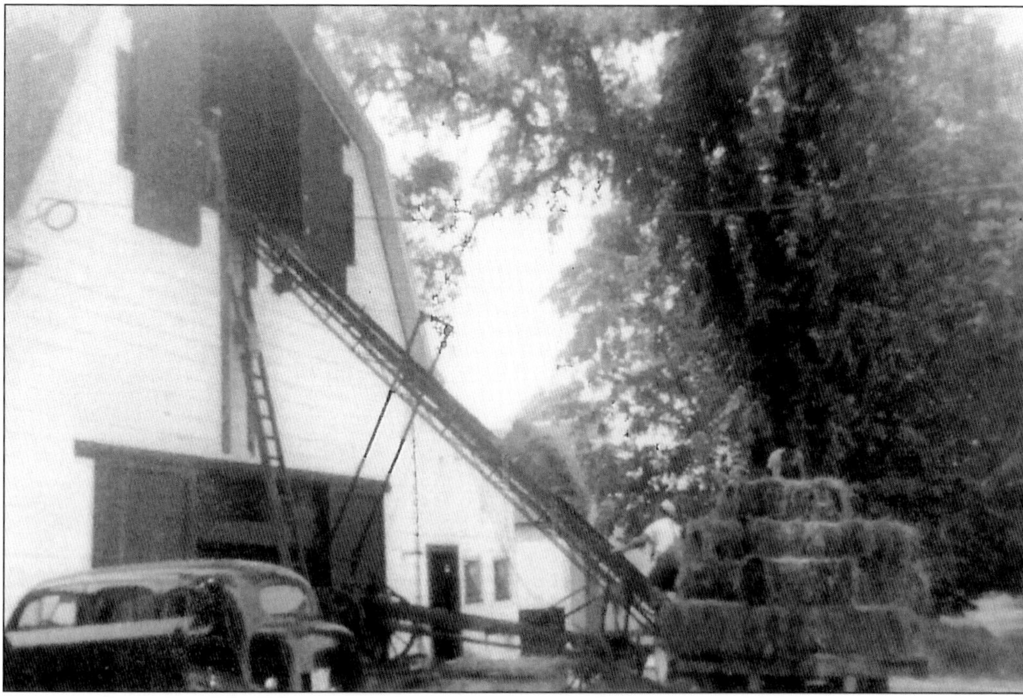

Mechanical means also lifted the bales of hay into the barn.

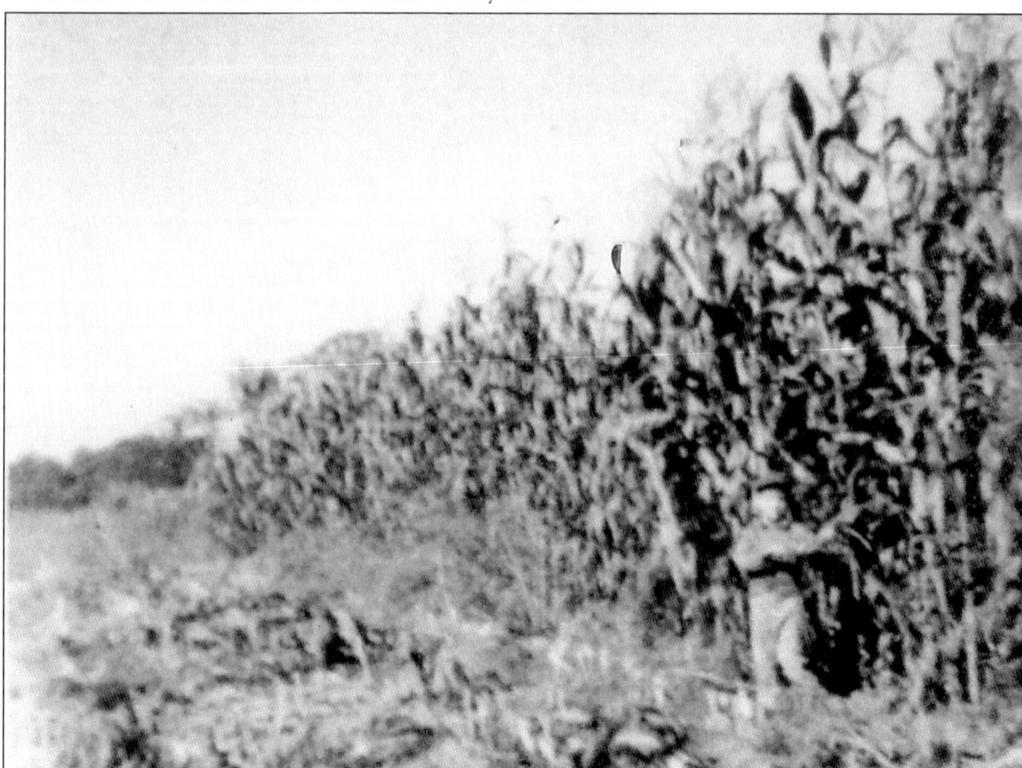

Corn was used for silage, its height measured by a younger Arthur Bisson in 1956.

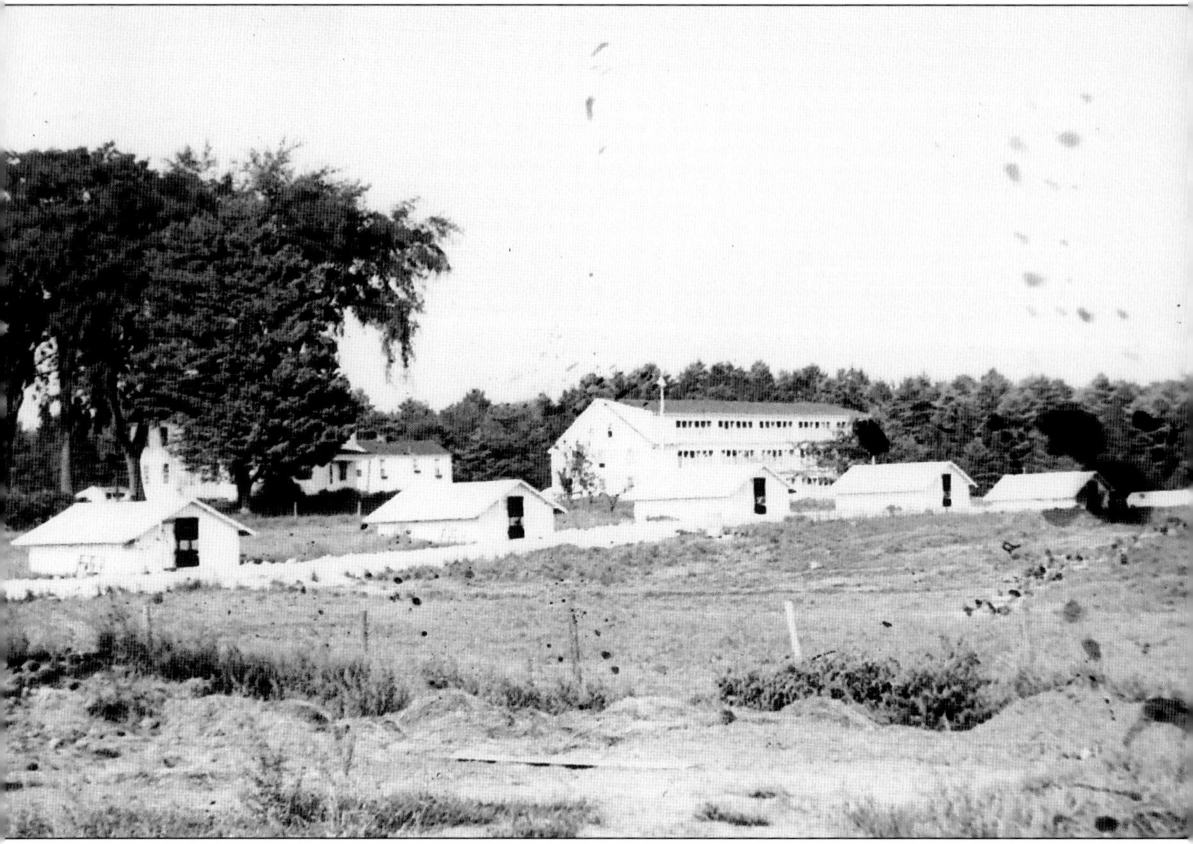

In 1938 George E. "Jim" and Jean Coleman purchased an old farm on the edge of Brunswick's Pennellville and developed it as a poultry breeding farm. By the mid-1940s, the barn had been enlarged to hold laying hens, and numerous small brooder houses had been built.

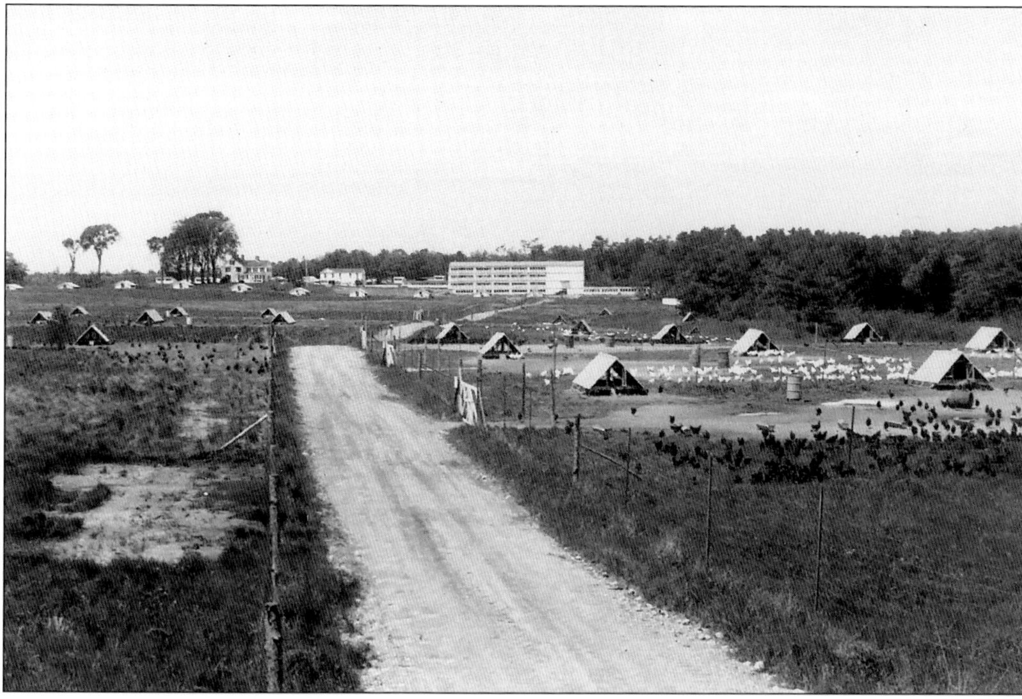

Shelters in a field housed young birds: the "Maine Red" was advertised as range-bred and sturdy.

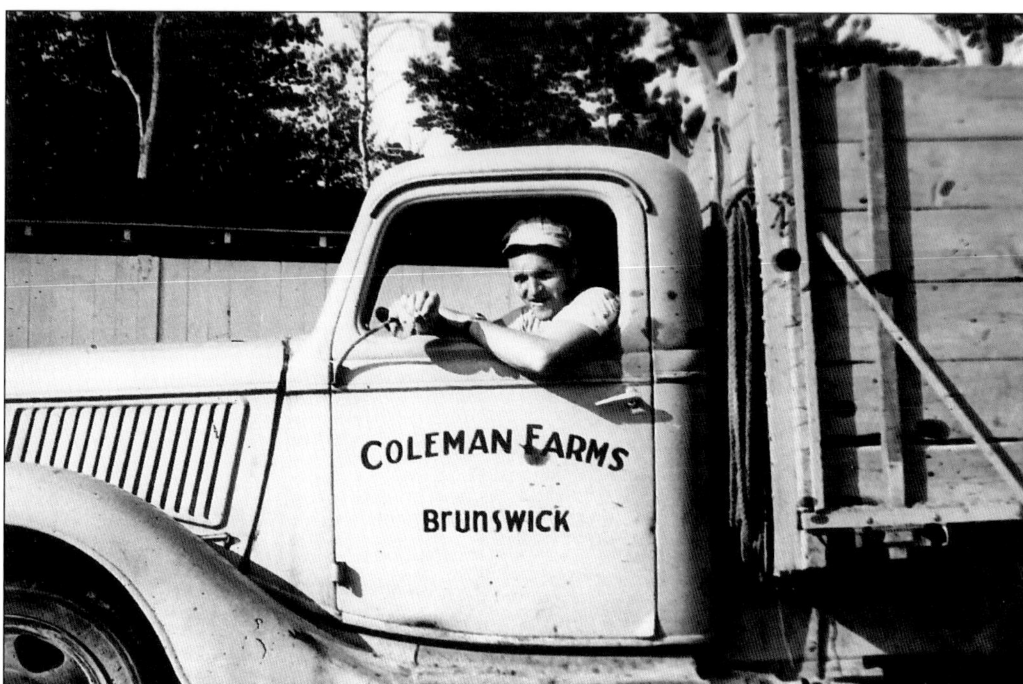

John Ring, farm manager, operates a company truck.

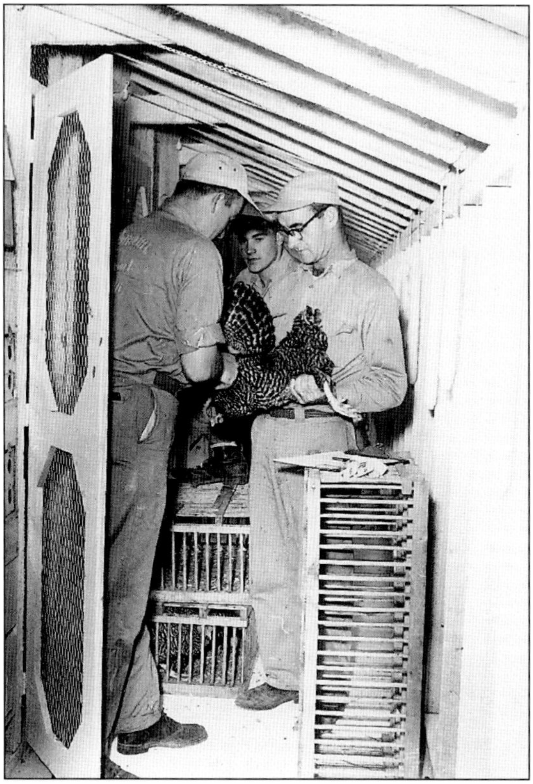

Lee Chipman and Ralph Eastman are banding breeding stock, while Elroy Bibber, Jr., looks on.

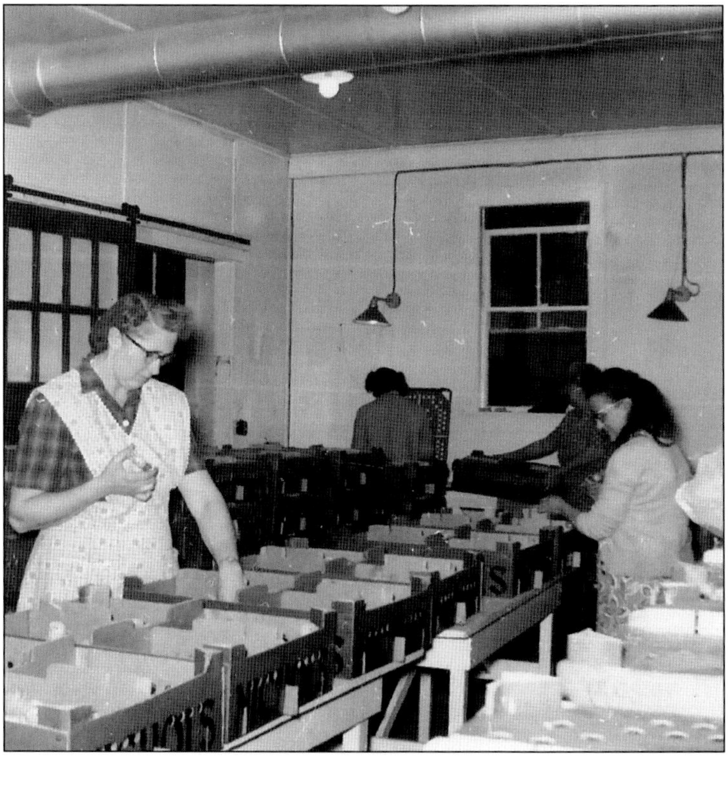

After a hatchery was set up on Middle Street, a program for vaccinating newly hatched chicks was instituted, run by part-time employees. On the job, left to right, are: Viola Bibber, Florence Rose, Thelma Martin, and Evelyn Wing.

Seven

Topsham Fair

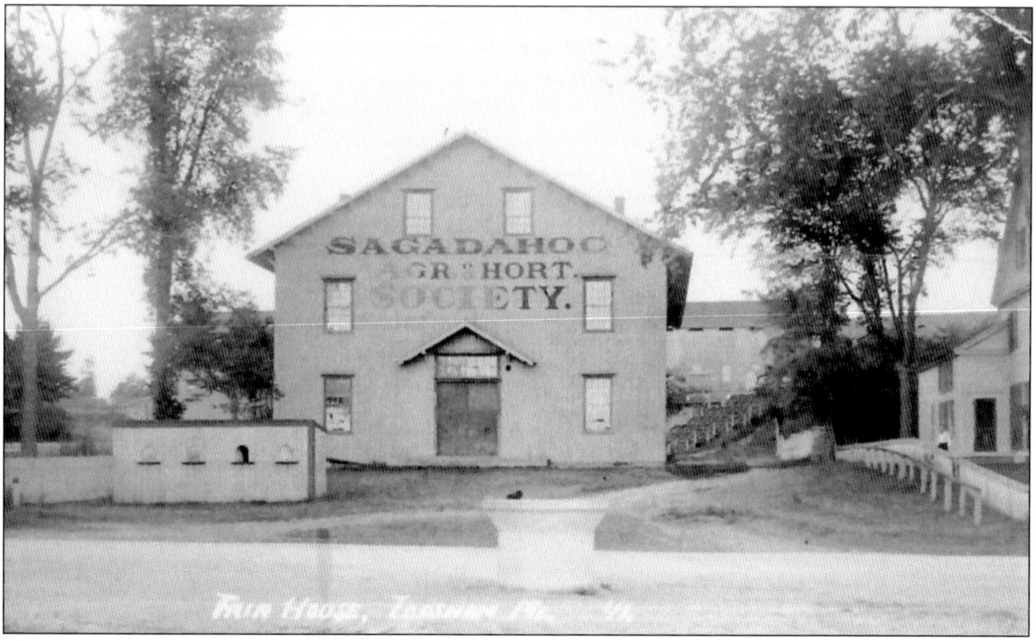

The Sagadahoc County Agricultural and Horticultural Society was formed in 1854. The following year they held a fair and shortly thereafter purchased land in Topsham for a fairgrounds. For many years, the main entrance on Elm Street led through this building, where booths held displays of fruits and vegetables entered for competition and different Granges exhibited members' produce or crafts. The grandstand can be seen up a rise on the right.

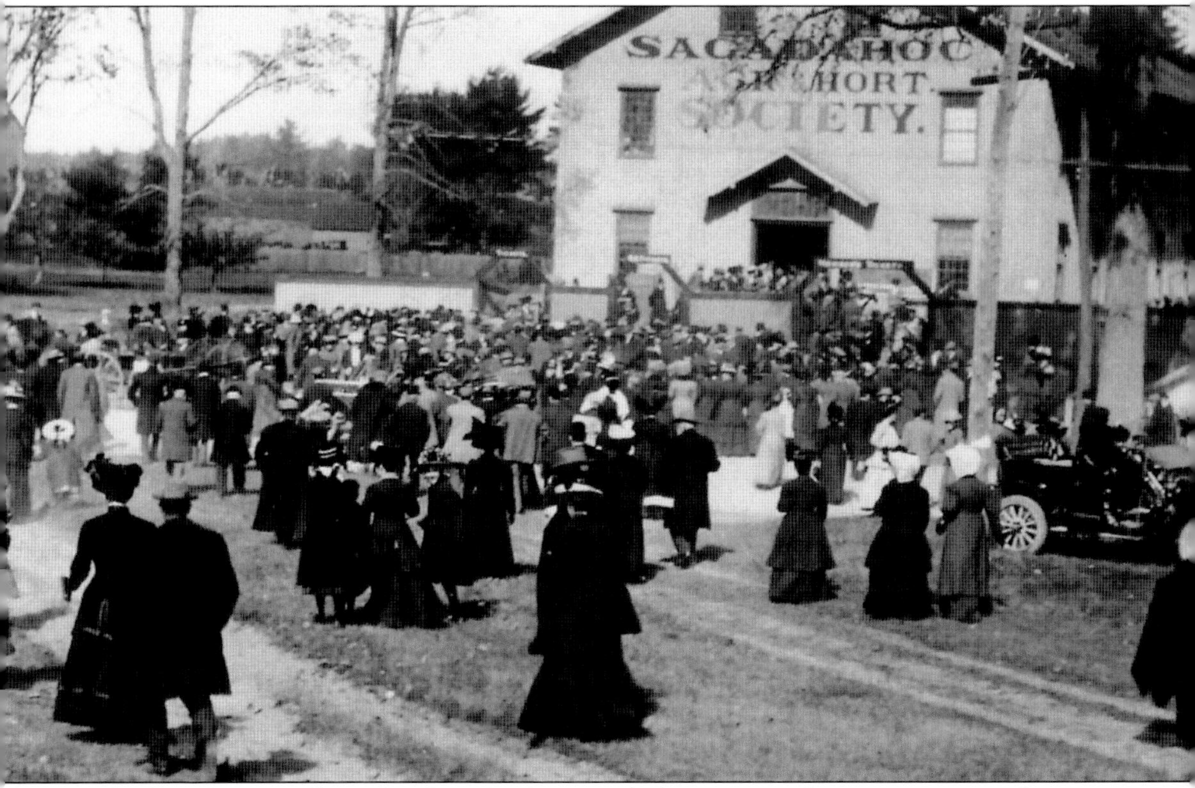

On Fair Day, usually in October, the fairgrounds drew visitors from many surrounding areas. Although nominally for Sagadahoc County, the fair also attracted visitors and competitors from Brunswick and other nearby Cumberland County towns. They arrived by private vehicle or on foot, some walking to the entrance from the train station across the street.

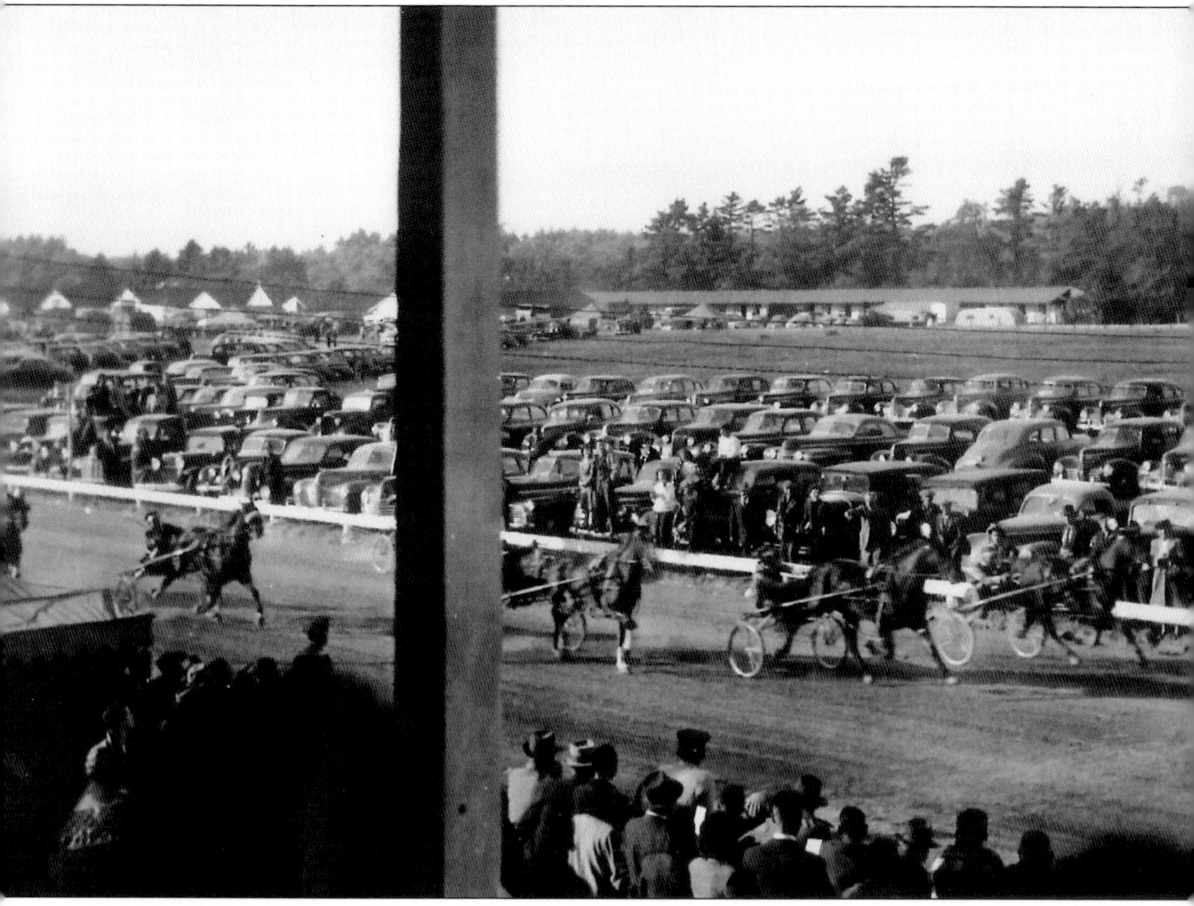

From the grandstand, one could see the harness races, the parking area within the track, and the barns and stables beyond.

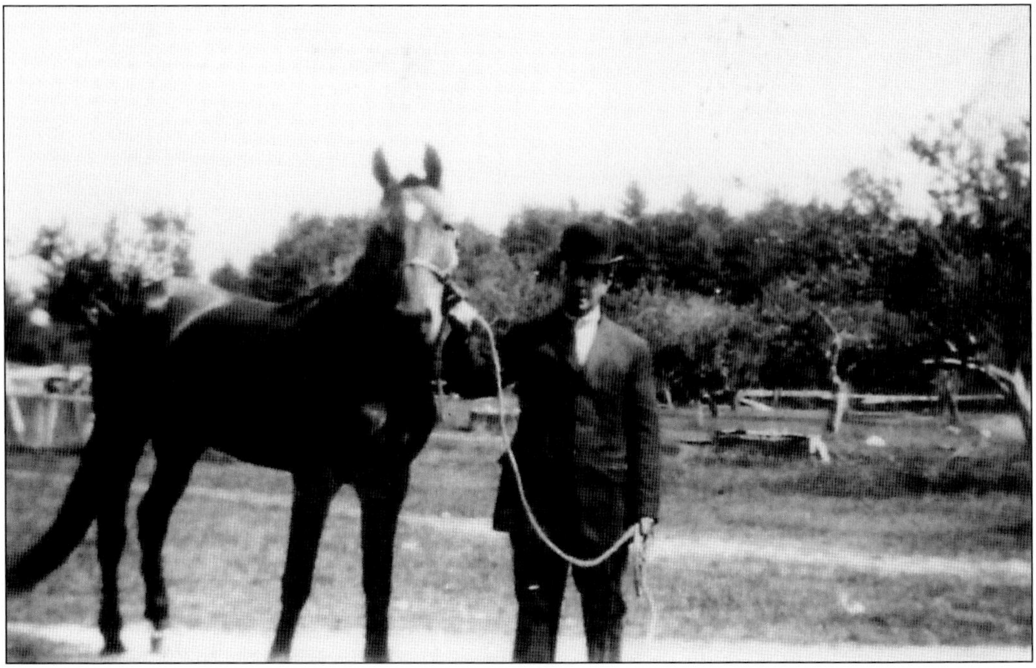

The harness races encouraged local men like Walter Foster to raise racehorses. This photo was taken in the 1910s: Foster died in the 1919 flu epidemic.

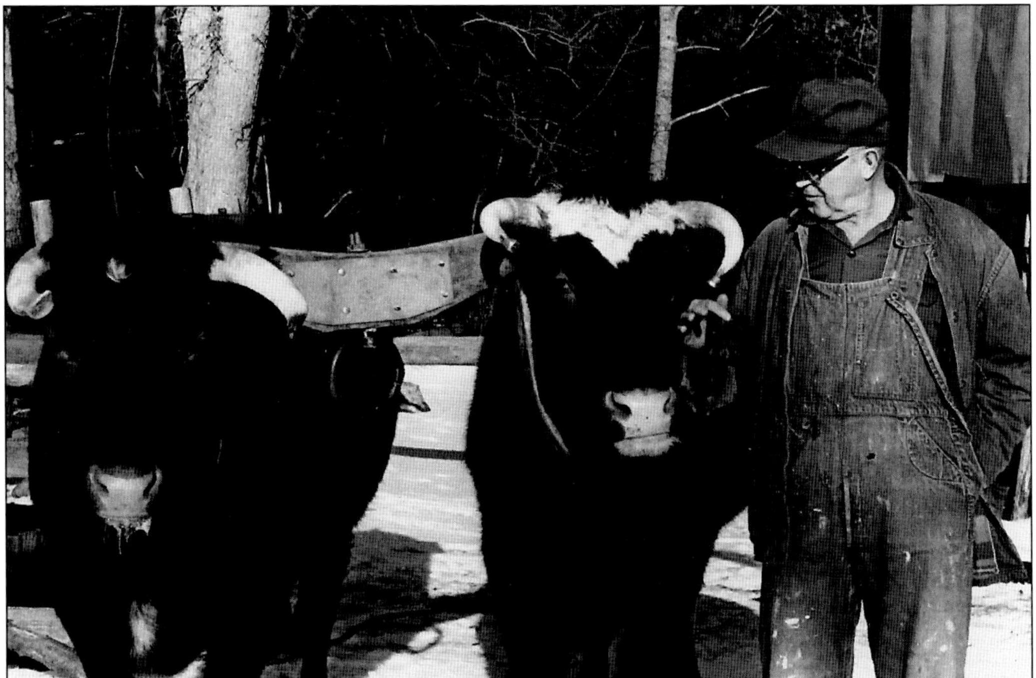

Oxen-pulling was a part of the first Topsham fair and remained popular. Holman Foster shows off his steers, Stumpy and Jerry, who, when entered in ten competitions, won ten prizes.

Eight

Transportation

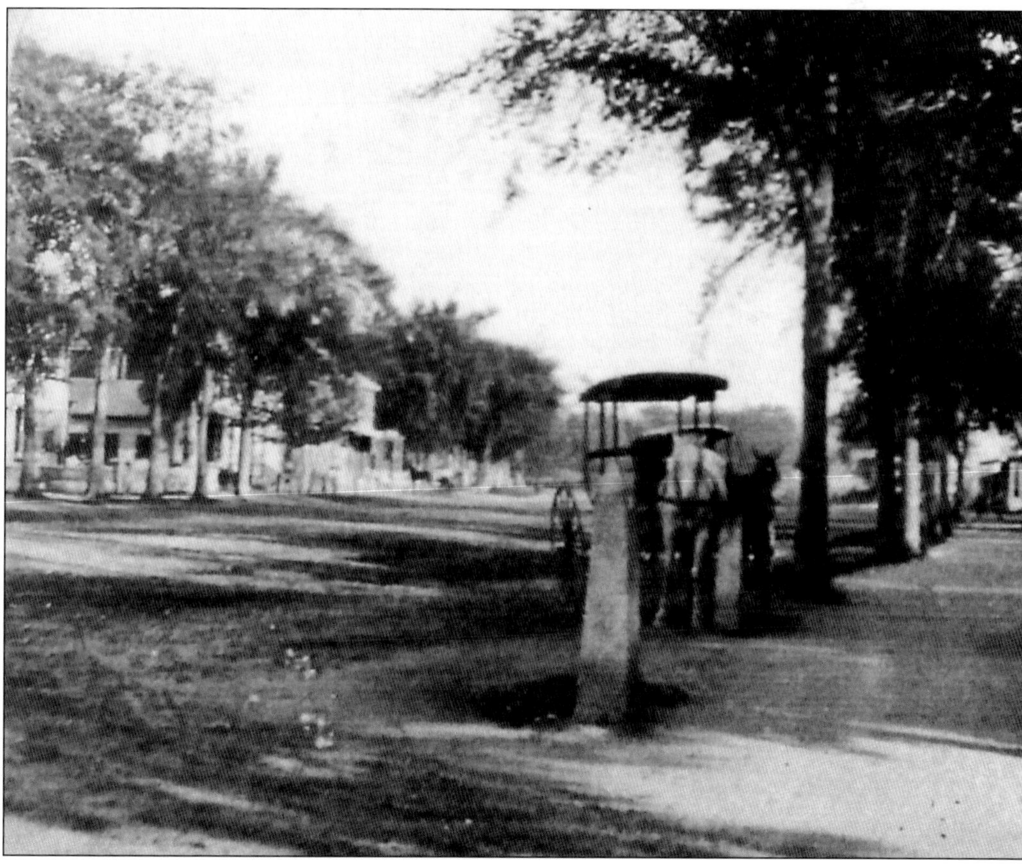

Horses and buggies were the main means of getting about before the early twentieth century. Dr. Lincoln's horse, tied in front of his house to one of the stone hitching posts which lined Maine Street, would have been a necessity in his work.

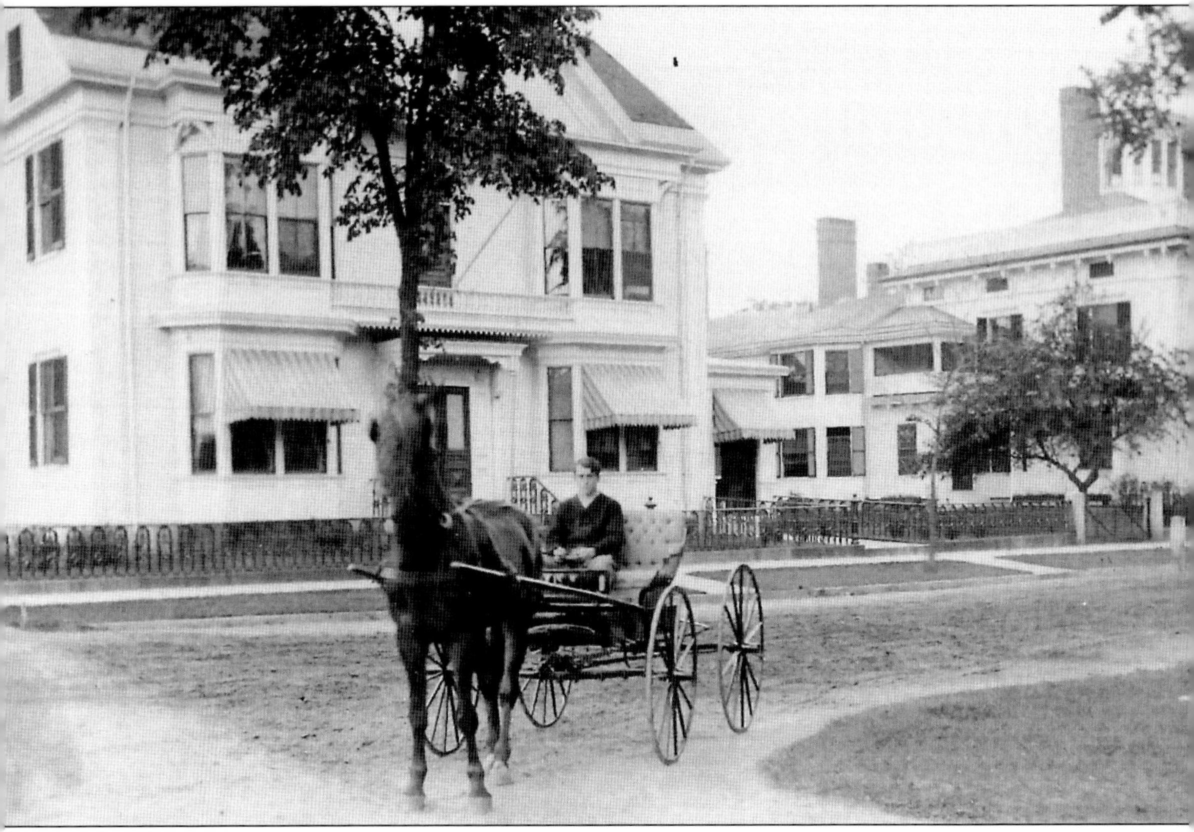

A young man in a carriage near Park Row around the turn of the century appears to be on a pleasure drive. Behind him are the houses of Captain Isaac L. Skolfield and Dr. Alfred Mitchell. The former was built early in the century and remodelled, while the latter was new in 1885-6.

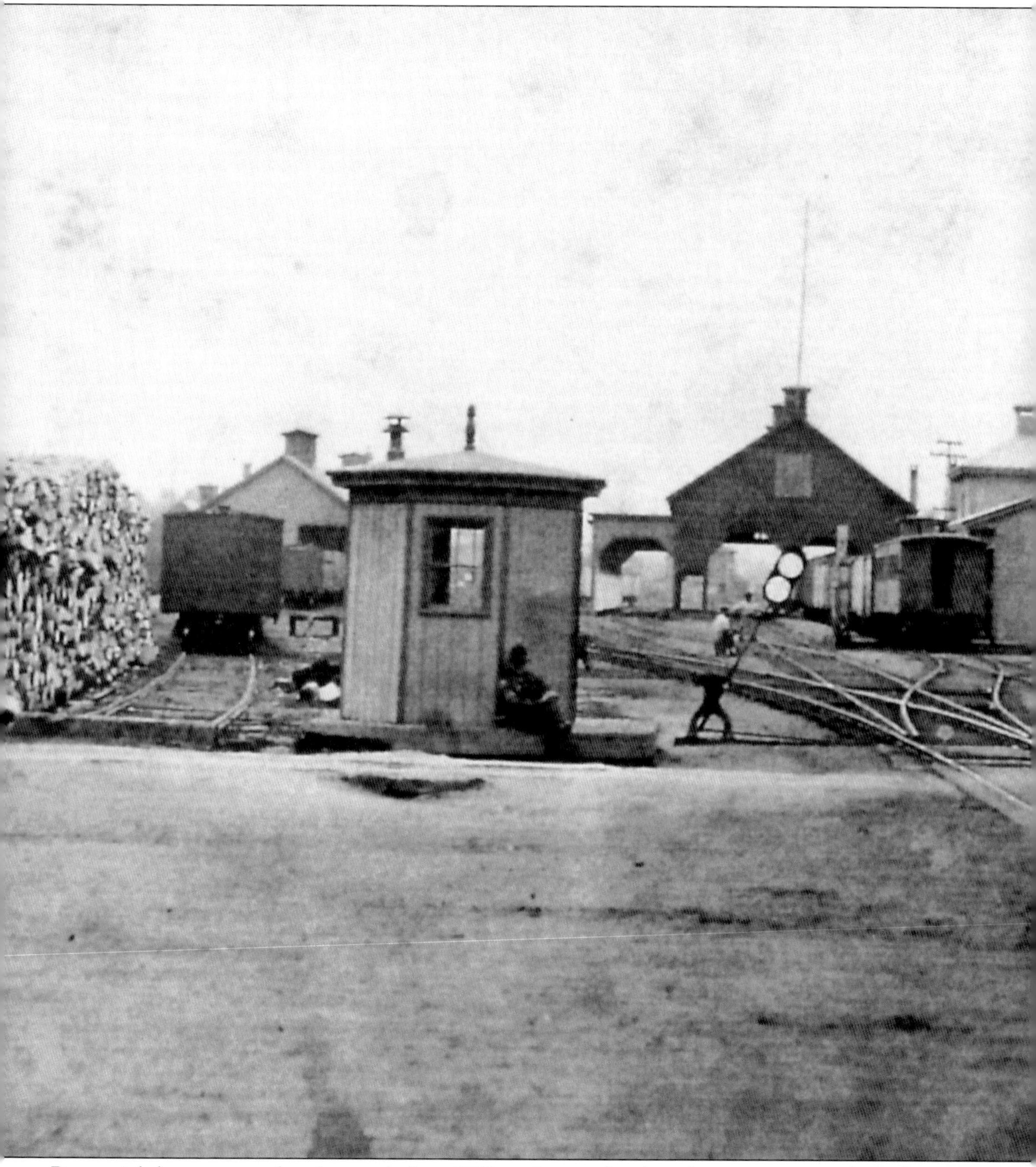

Brunswick became a railroad town before 1850 and soon developed connections with Bath to the east, Portland to the west, and Augusta to the north. Topsham's station was built by 1851. A fourth line, to Lewiston, was built in the 1860s. Another station was opened at Pejepscot after the mill and village were built; soon after a Brunswick depot called Harding Station and one west of the village at Oak Hill were built. The train shed of Brunswick's main depot of the 1870s overshadowed the freight and passenger spaces, although the latter was extensive enough to include a dining room. The signal man does not look very busy.

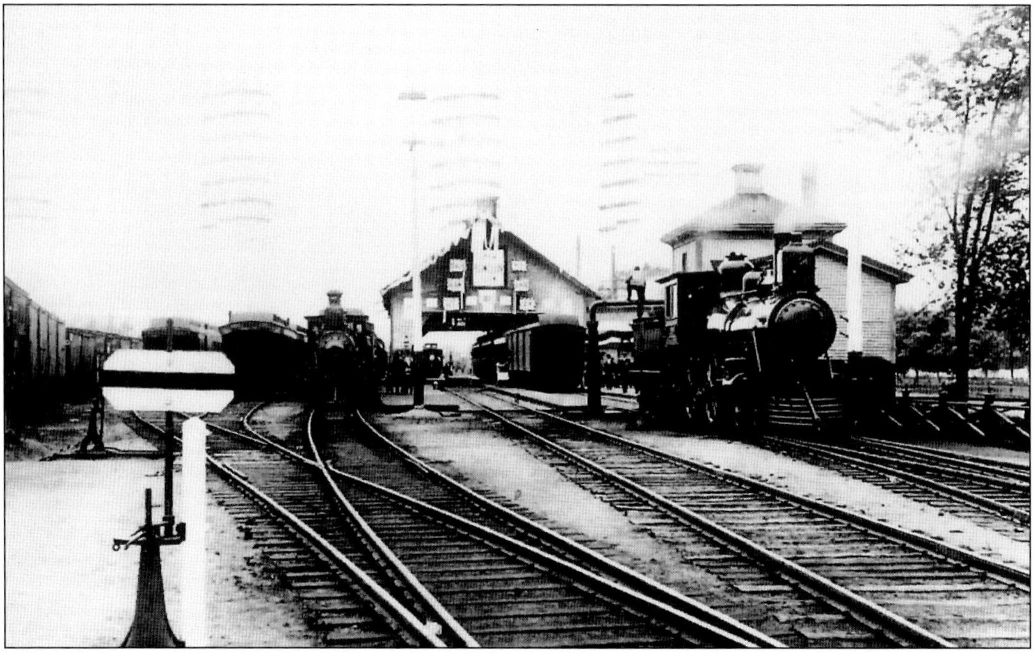

Two decades later, fewer tracks were covered, but more activity was apparent, including engines 14 and 21 in the yard at once. Note the neatly fenced grounds.

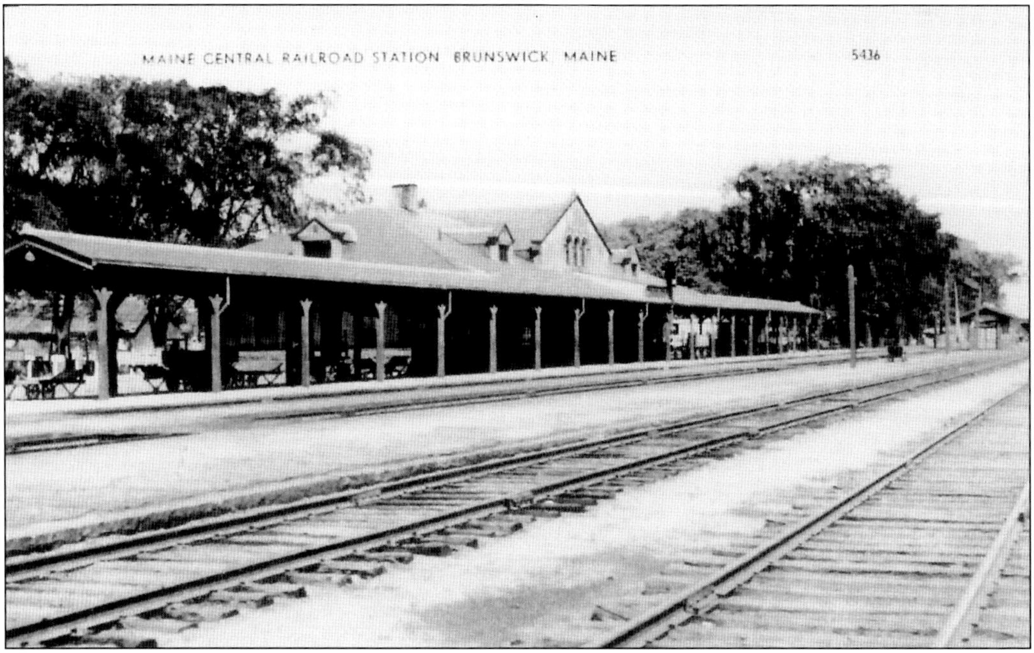

The station building built in 1899 remained in use until the end of passenger service.

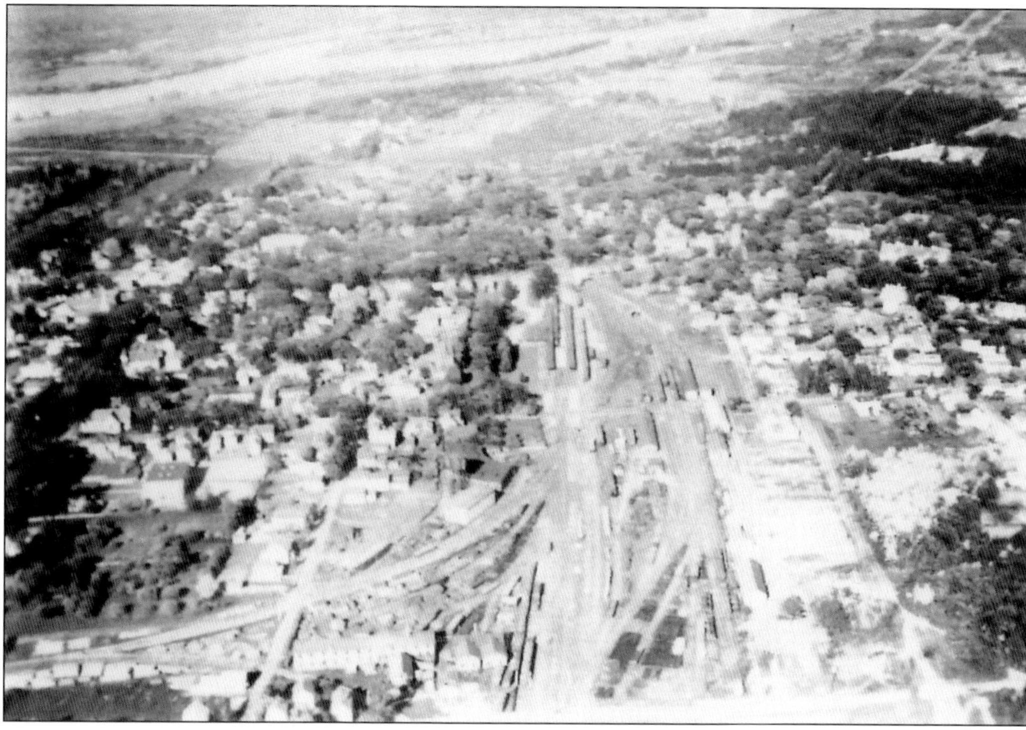

An air view in the summer of 1922 shows the railroad yards, looking east from above Spring Street. Tracks to Lewiston are in the foreground, and the Augusta route is apparent near the railway bridge in the upper left.

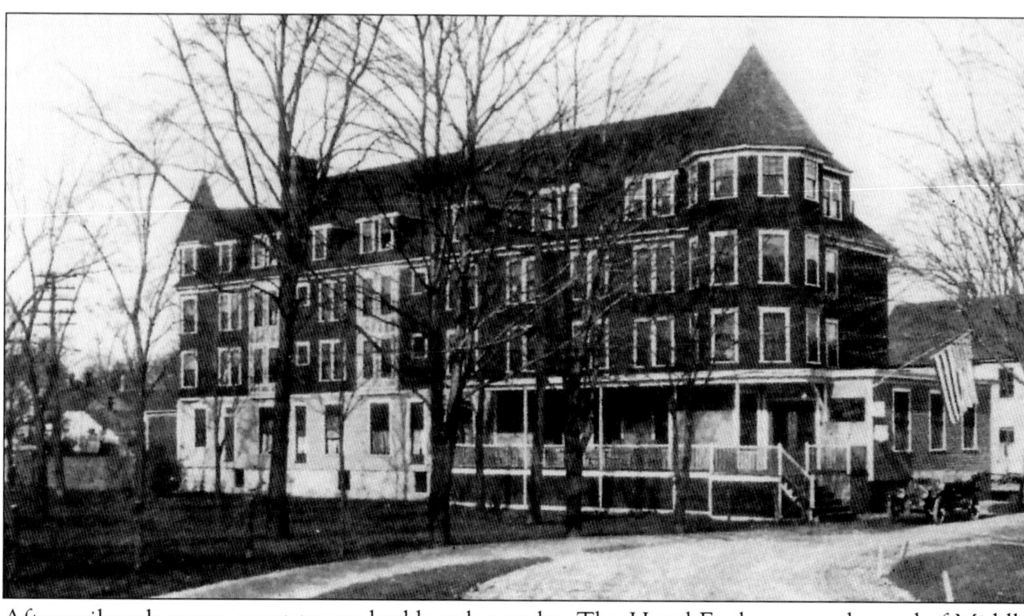

After railroads came, most towns had hotels nearby. The Hotel Eagle was at the end of Middle Street and almost adjacent to the train station.

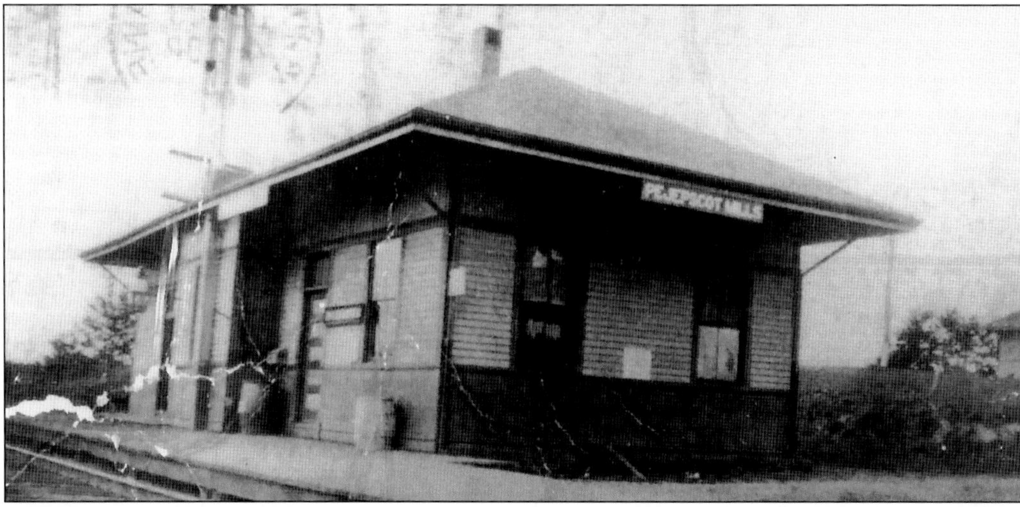

The Pejepscot Station served that village and had its own manager and telegraph operator.

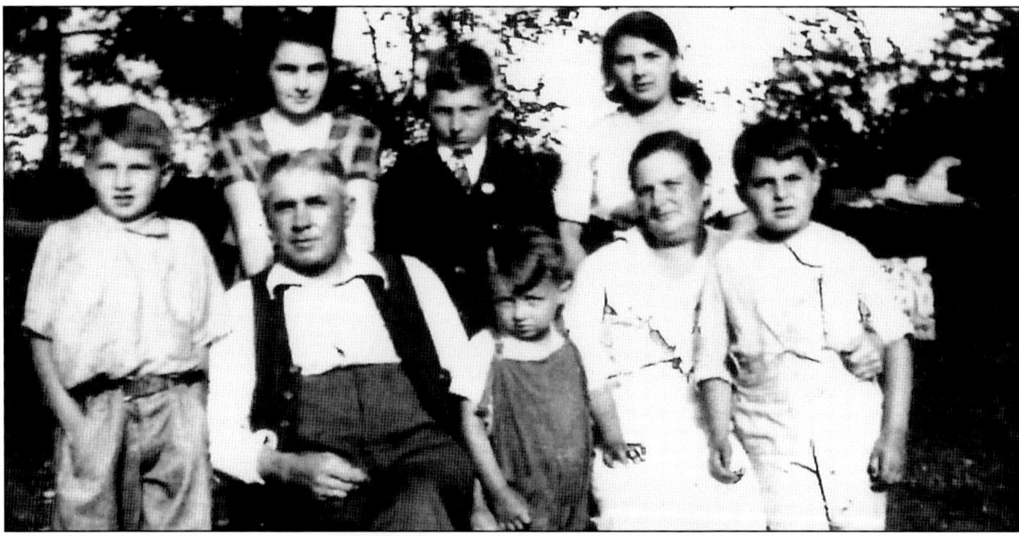

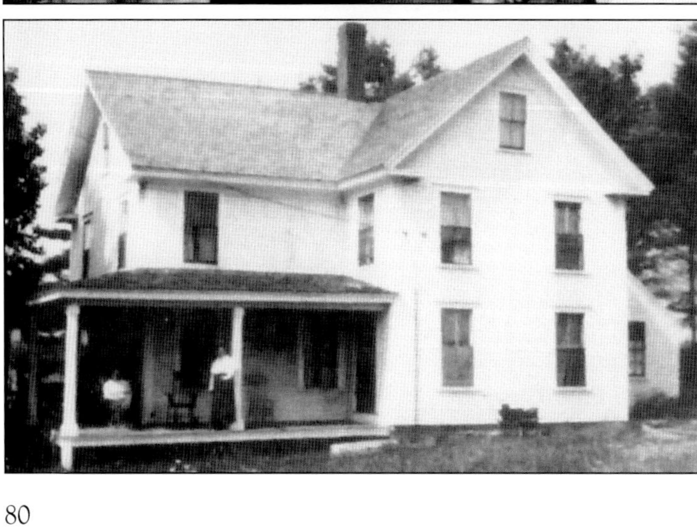

In the 1920s, the manager was Henry Vigeant, shown here with his wife, Jessie, and children Ralph, Richard, and Philip in the front row, with Helena, Arthur, and Ruth standing in rear.

The Vigeant house was one of the few in the area not part of the mill property.

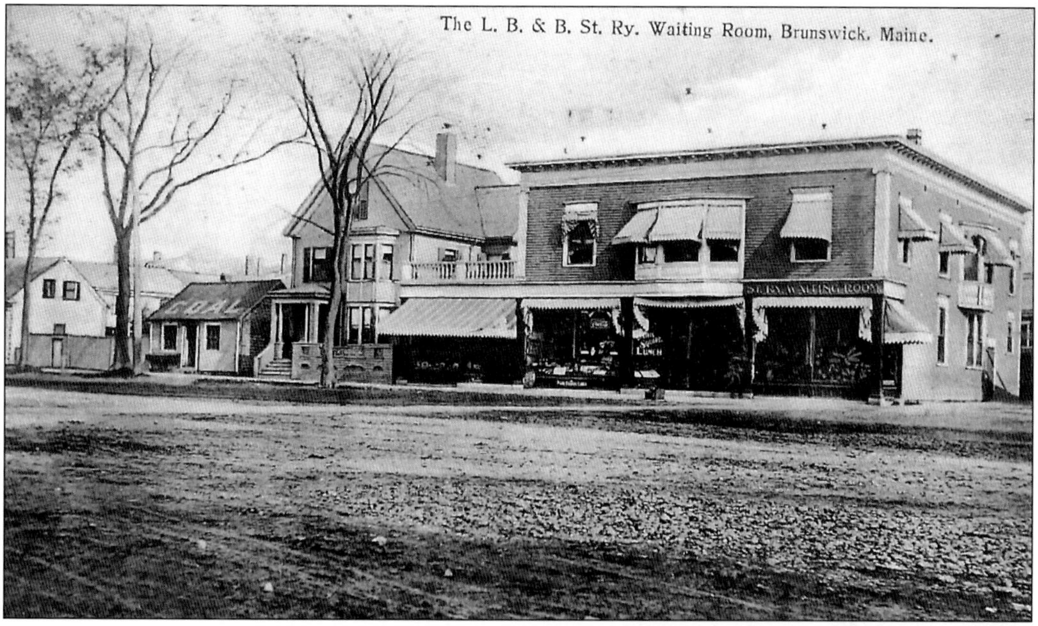

Electric cars, or trolleys, flourished for decades, with service to Lewiston beginning in 1896, to Bath in 1898, and a line to Portland via Freeport opening in 1902. A waiting room for the Lewiston, Brunswick, and Bath Street Railway was on Maine Street, a few doors north of the Mall.

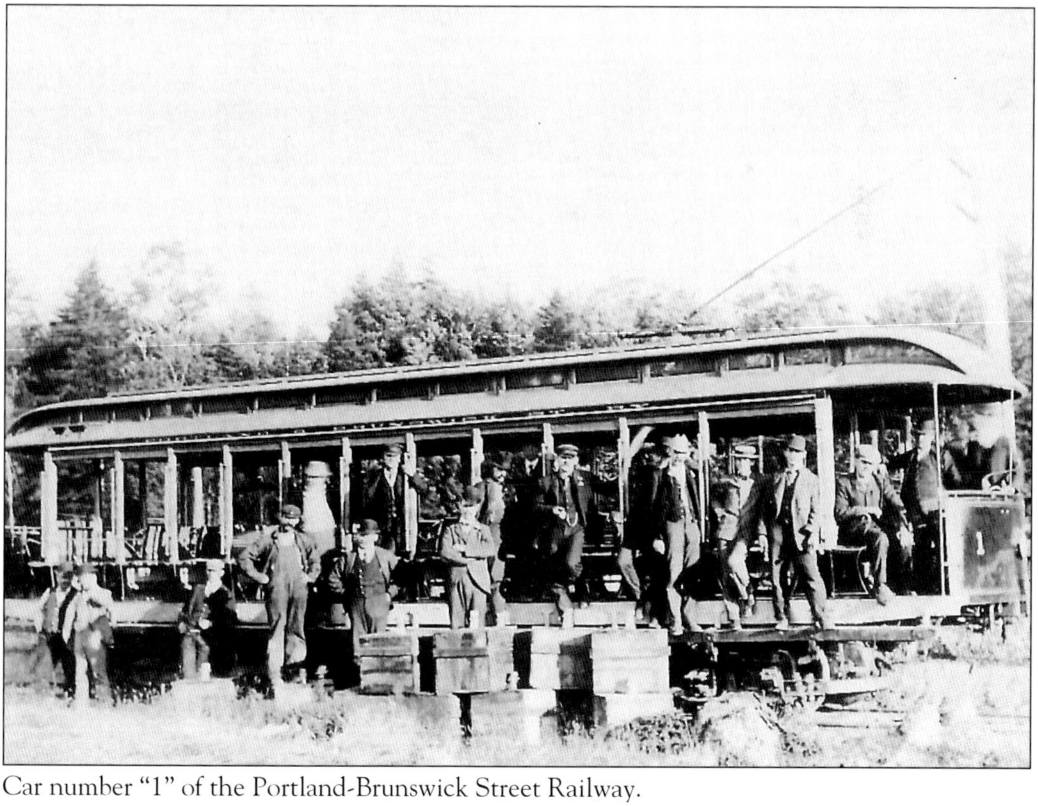

Car number "1" of the Portland-Brunswick Street Railway.

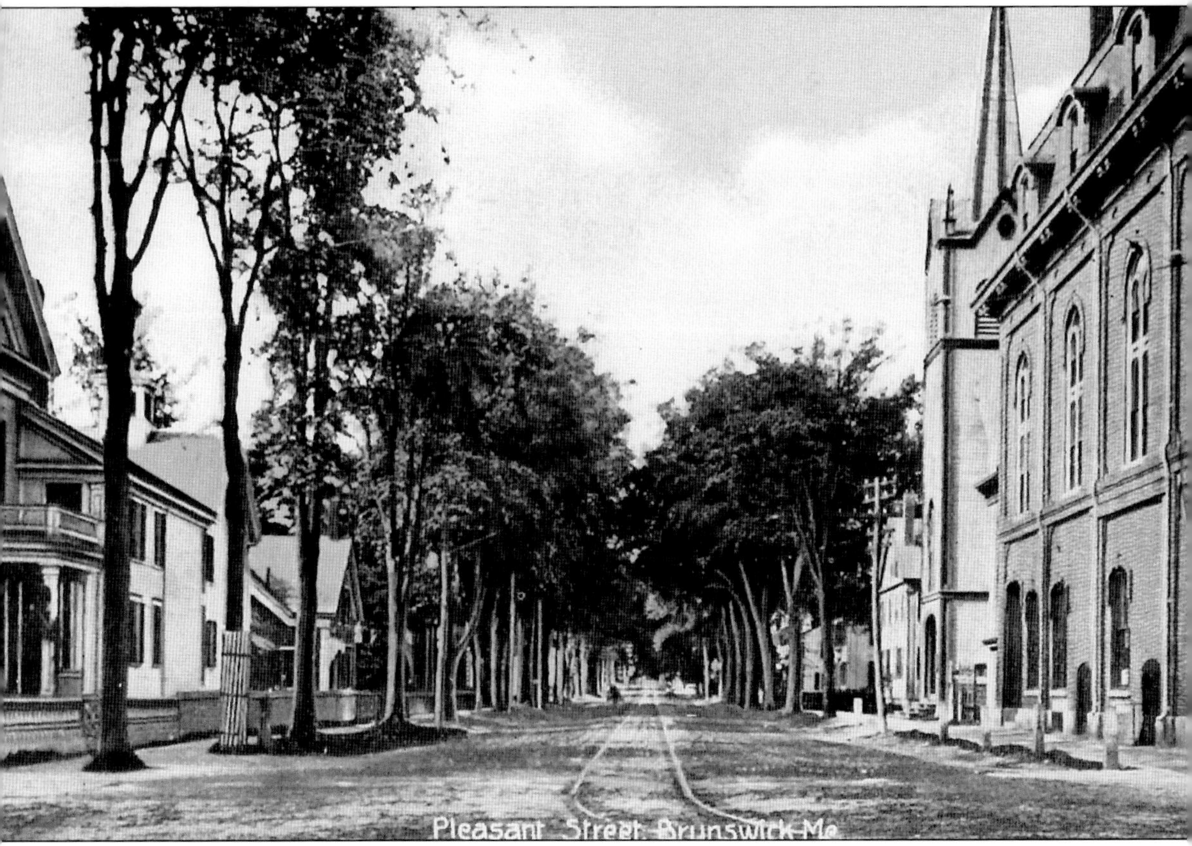

The car tracks from Portland ran along Pleasant Street, which was in 1910 mostly residential. The Methodist Church of 1866 stood just behind Chandler's College Bookstore, on the corner of Maine Street.

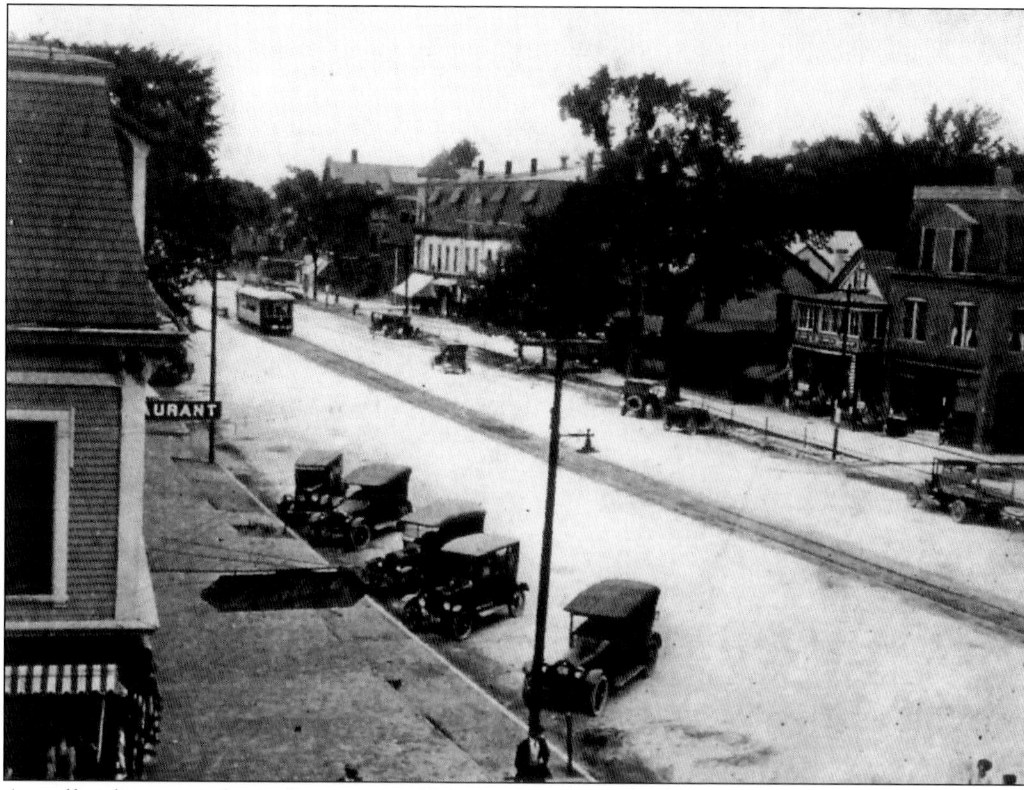

A trolley line ran along the center of Maine Street, with the autos and trucks which would eventually cause its demise using space on either side.

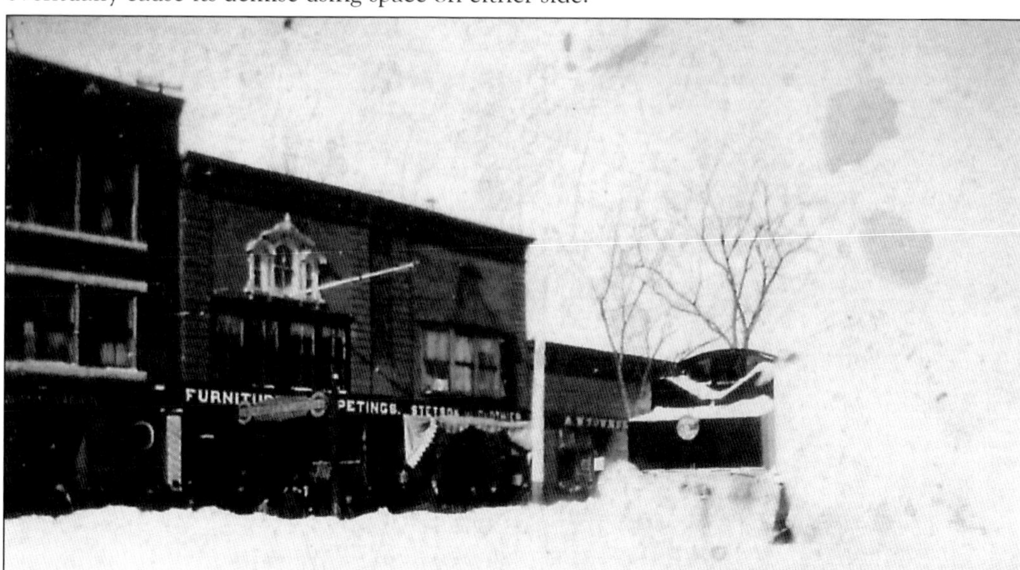

Whereas snow could be packed on the roads for use of sleighs, the trolley tracks had to be cleared. Here snow flies from an L.B. & B. rotary plow on Brunswick's Maine Street. Local power came from the Cabot Mill's plant, but the cars had to adapt to different voltages in the different towns served.

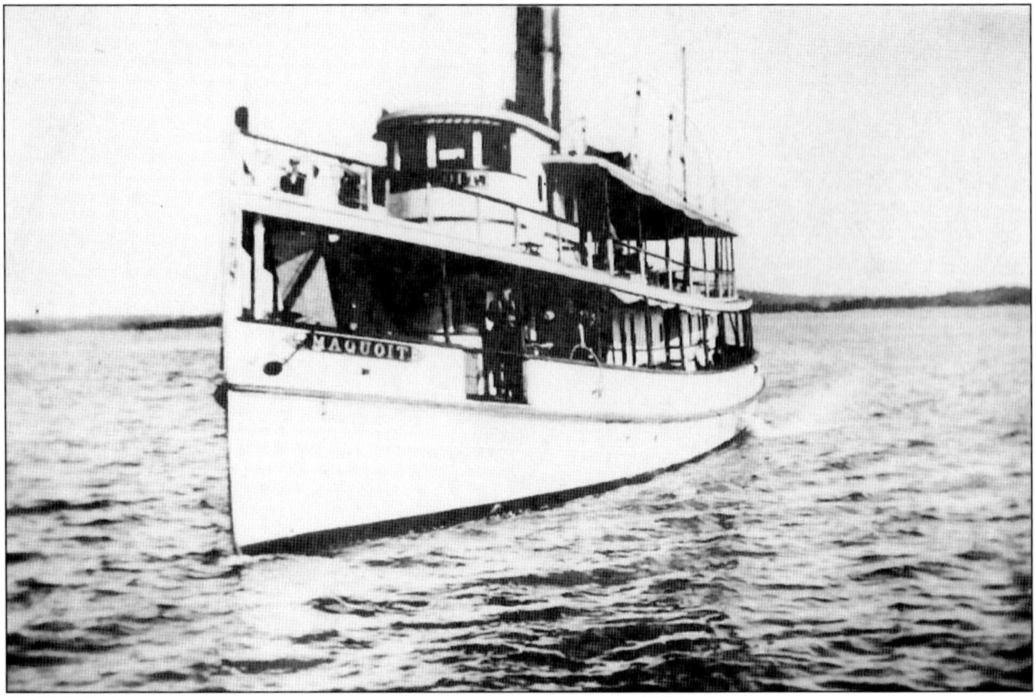

Train and trolley routes made most water passenger services unprofitable for Brunswick or Topsham, but a few steamboats, including the *Maquoit*, sporadically served Mere Point.

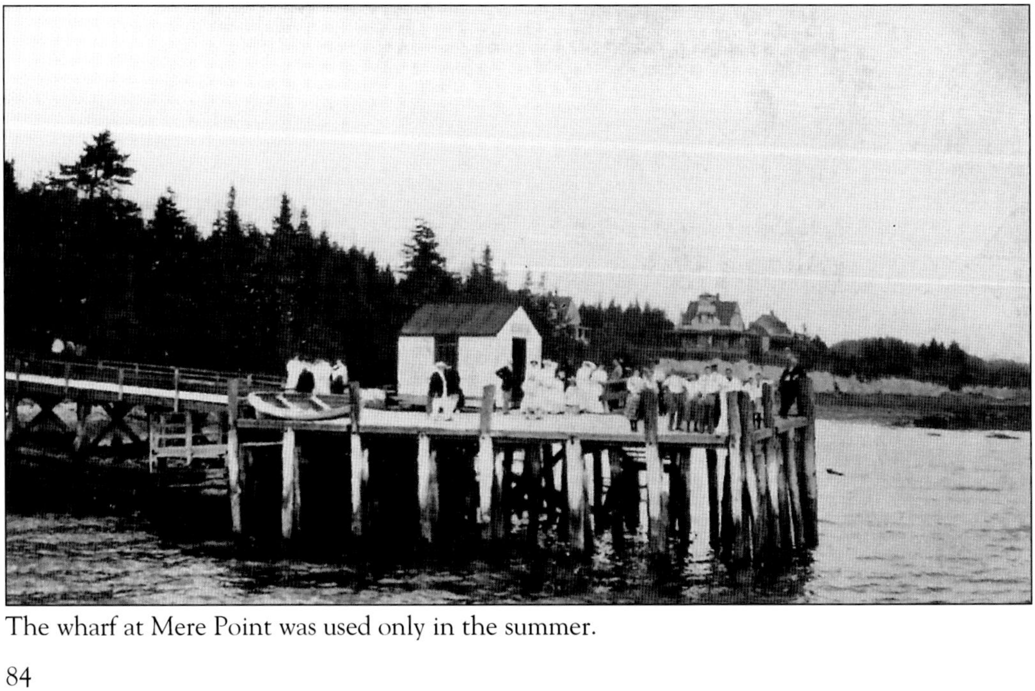

The wharf at Mere Point was used only in the summer.

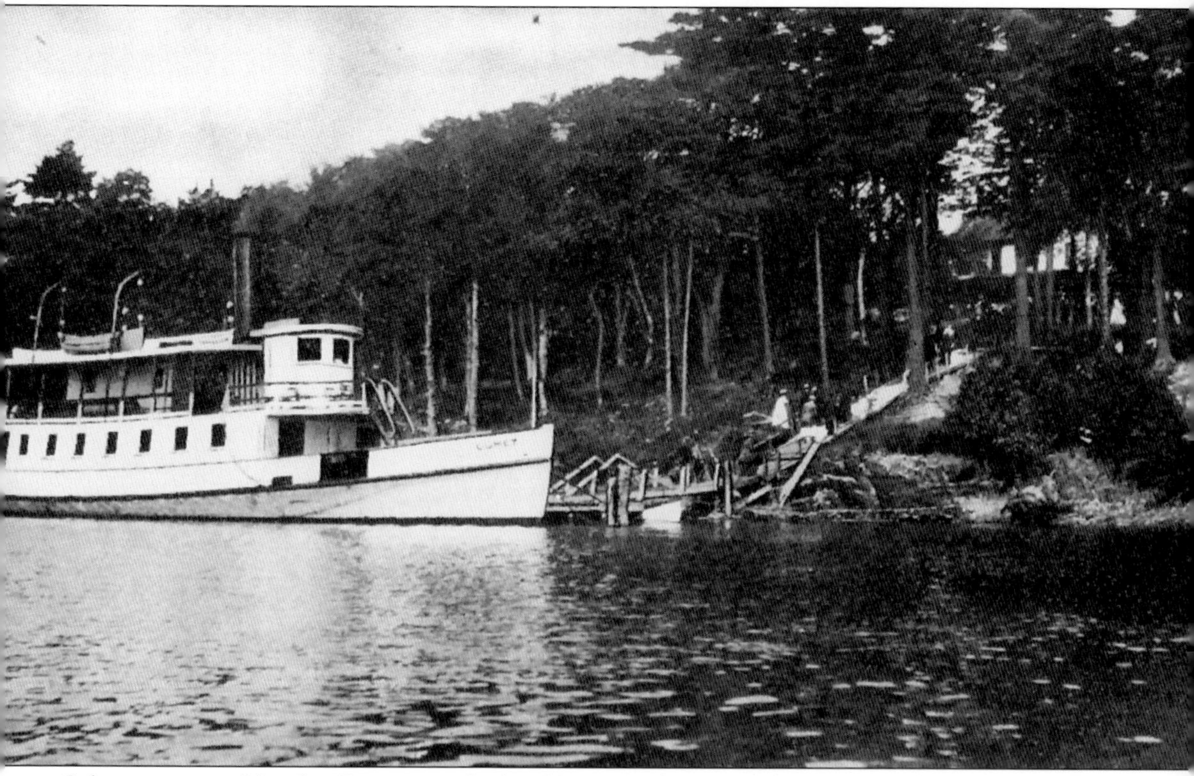

Other steamers, like the *Comet*, touched at New Meadows and the Gurnet, although in both cases the main wharves were across a bridge from Brunswick.

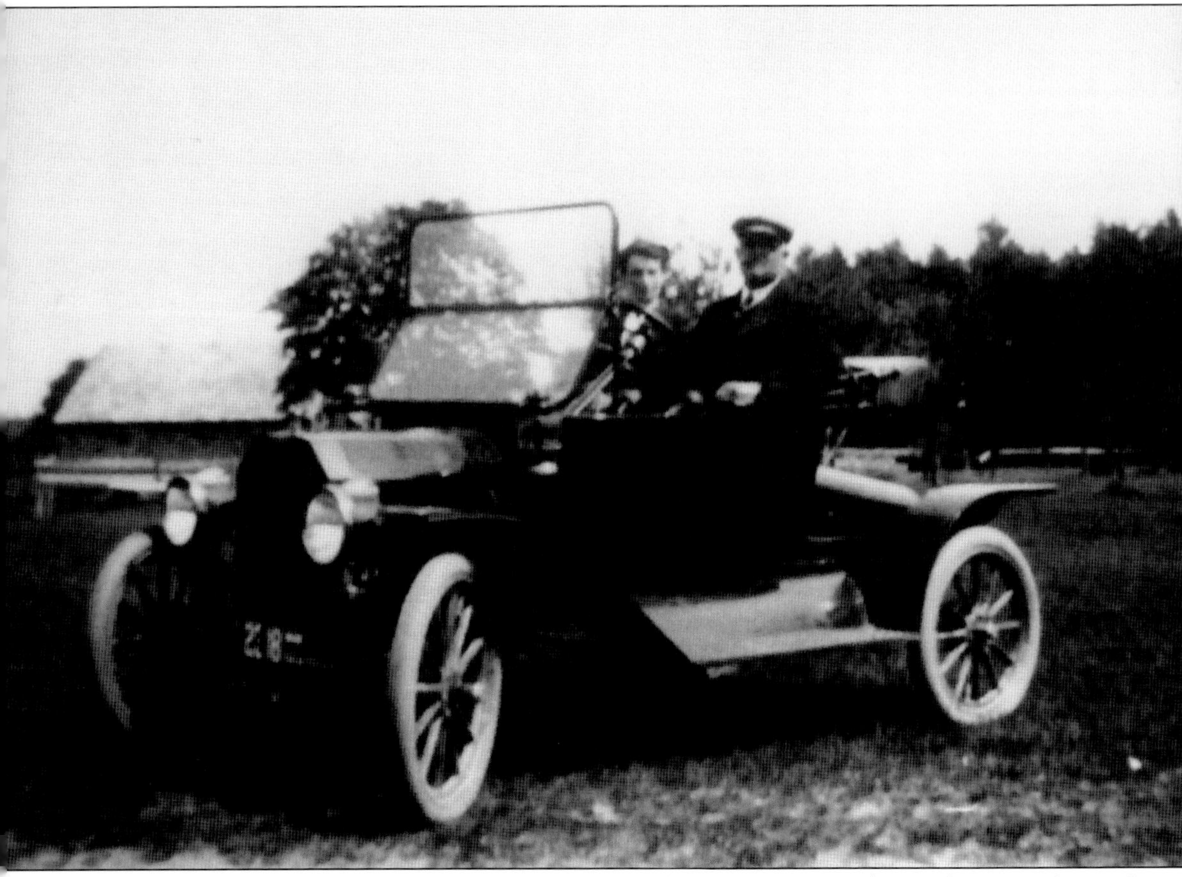

The first auto in town was bought about 1903, and the entire Brunswick-Topsham area boasted fewer than eighteen in 1906. Still, the new contraption caught on; and by the 1920s, the Sunday drive had become popular. Grace Foster and Mr. Stoddard are ready for a spin in his pre-war runabout.

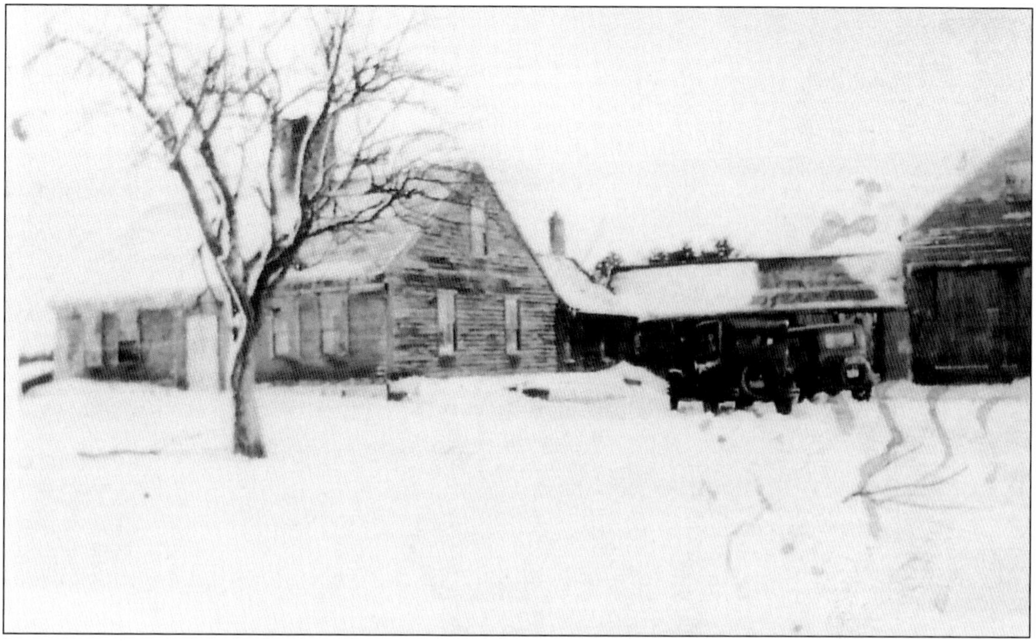

Cars soon became necessities, owned not just by the well-to-do but by the average worker and farmer. The Clarence Moore family, of Topsham's Middlesex Road, apparently sacrificed house paint in order to be on wheels about 1930.

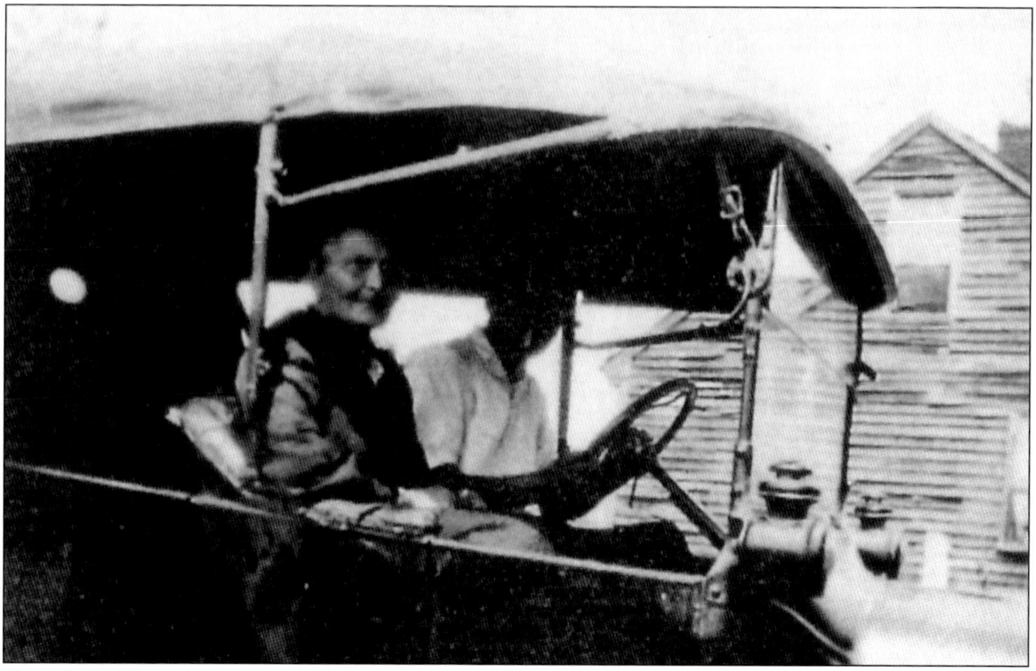

Flora Moore's mother, Sarah Cowan, adapted to motorcars at an advanced age.

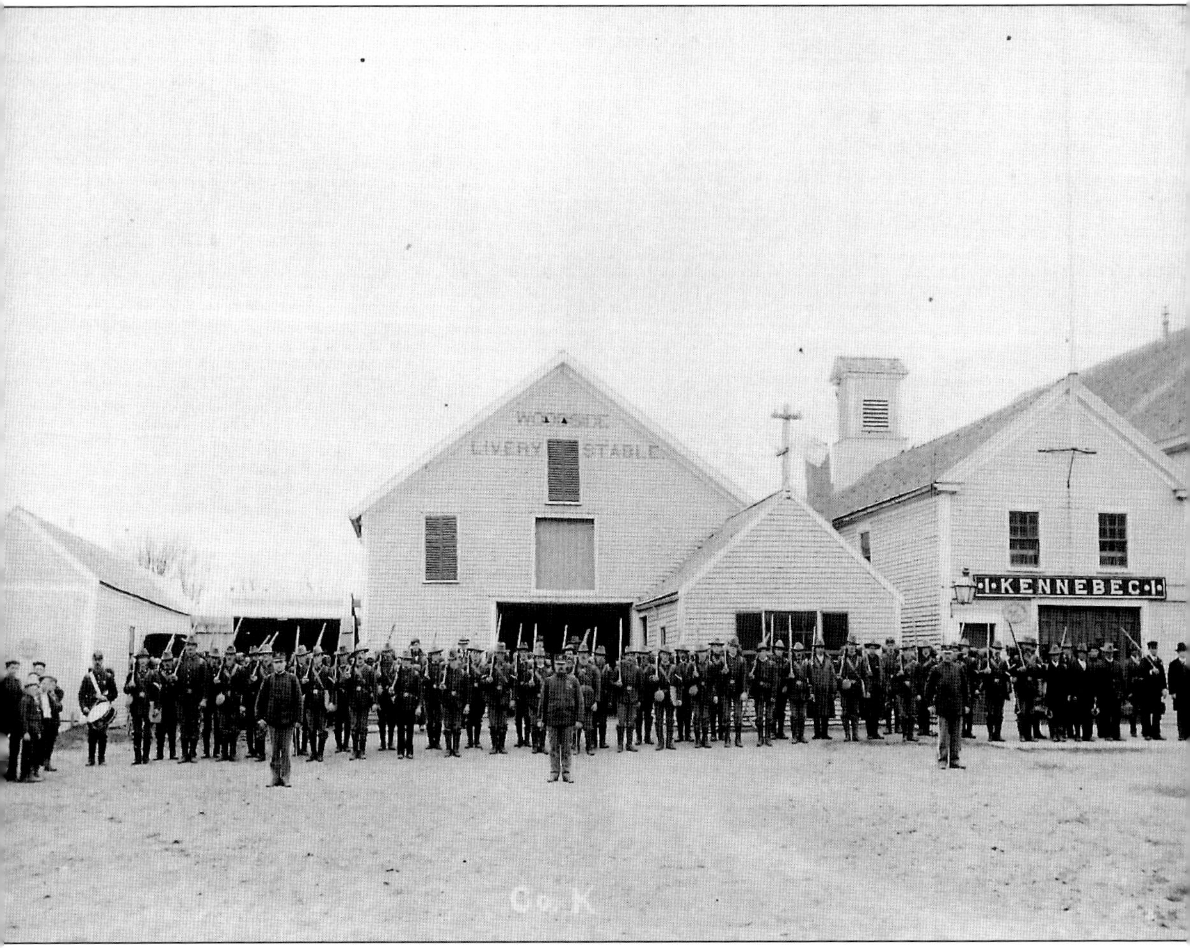

It took years for autos to fully take over. E.H. Woodside's livery stable, shown here behind a militia unit at about the turn of the century, remained in business into the World War I period. It was located behind the old post office and later the town hall. Next to it, the "Kennebec No. 1" engine, added to the town's fire-fighting capabilities in 1875, had its own house, with a hose tower at the rear.

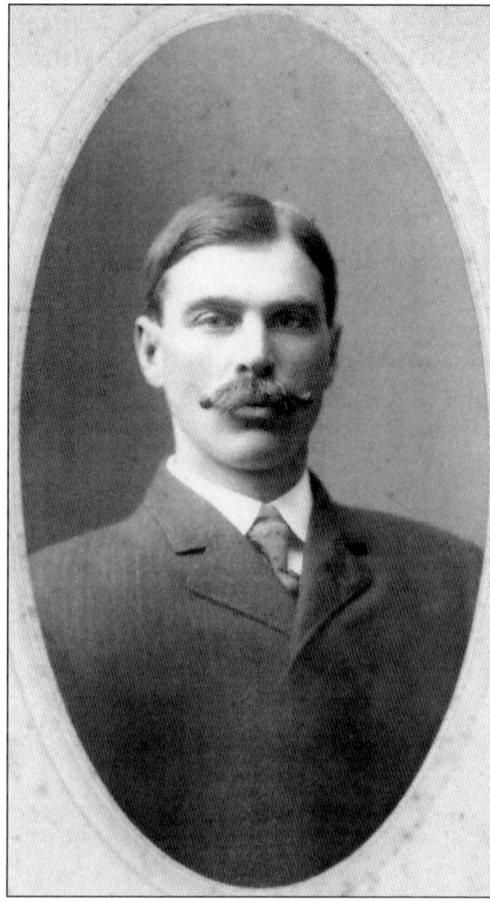

Among the pioneers in the auto business was Theodore S. Allen, who became an agent for Ford Motors while operating an auto and bicycle repair shop on Dunlap Street in 1910, then ran a modern dealership in a specially-built structure (with a ramp from the door to the second-floor showroom) from 1913 to 1917. He closed that concern to open a repair shop next to his widowed mother's home in Pejepscot.

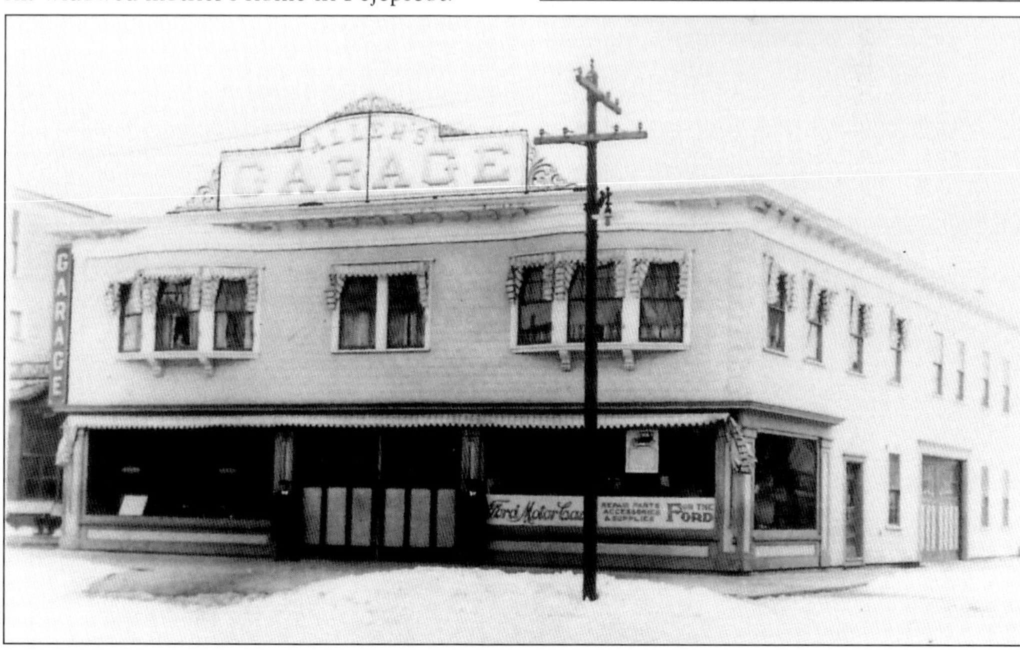

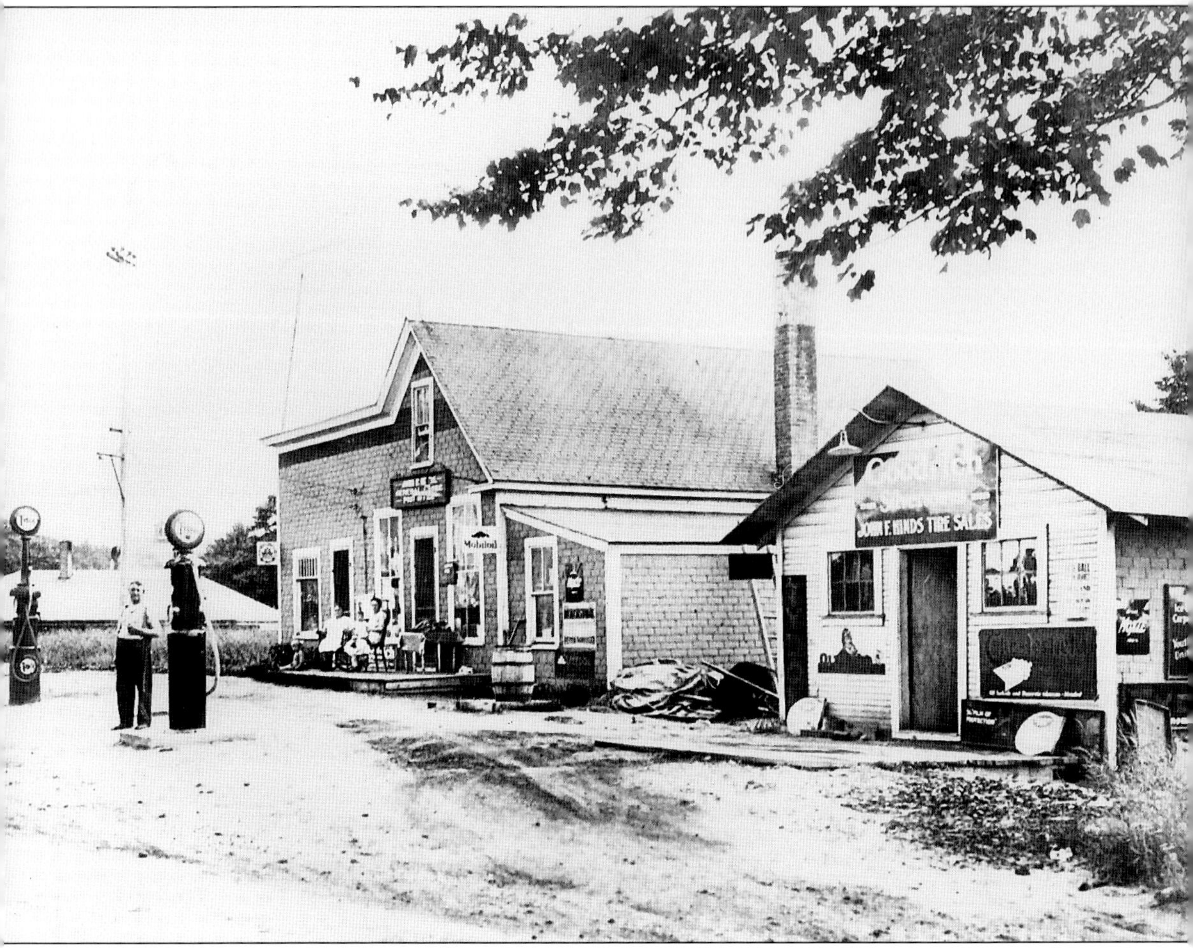

The auto era also ushered in the gas station. John Hines stands by the pumps in front of his Pejepscot grocery store in about 1929. On the entry platform are his wife, Nellie, and daughter-in-law, Mary Hinds. Mary holds her daughter Marilyn in her lap, while Walter, Jr., sits on the platform.

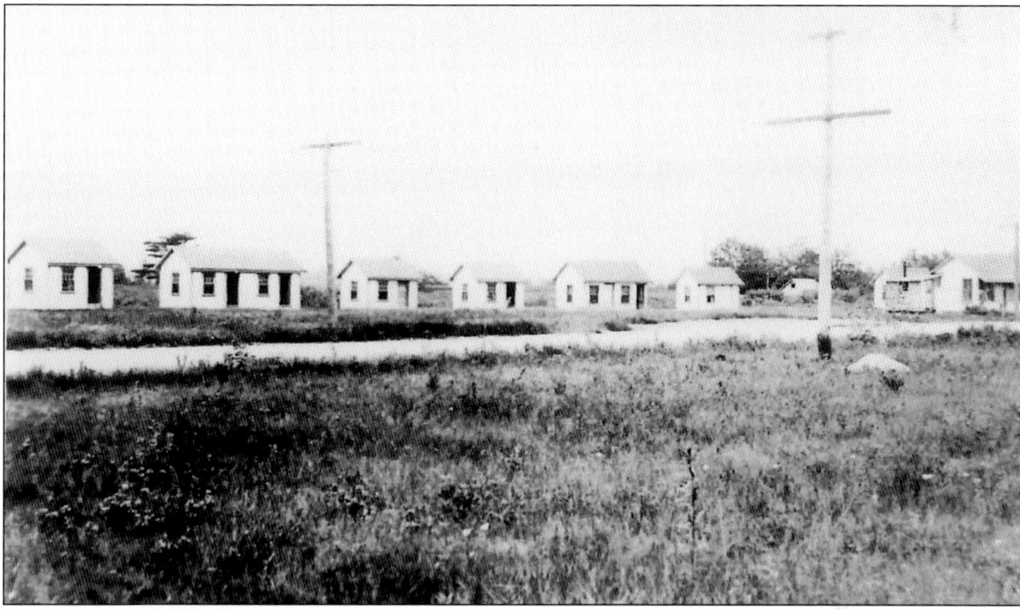

Another contribution of the era was the tourist camp. These cabins were on the road between Brunswick and Bath.

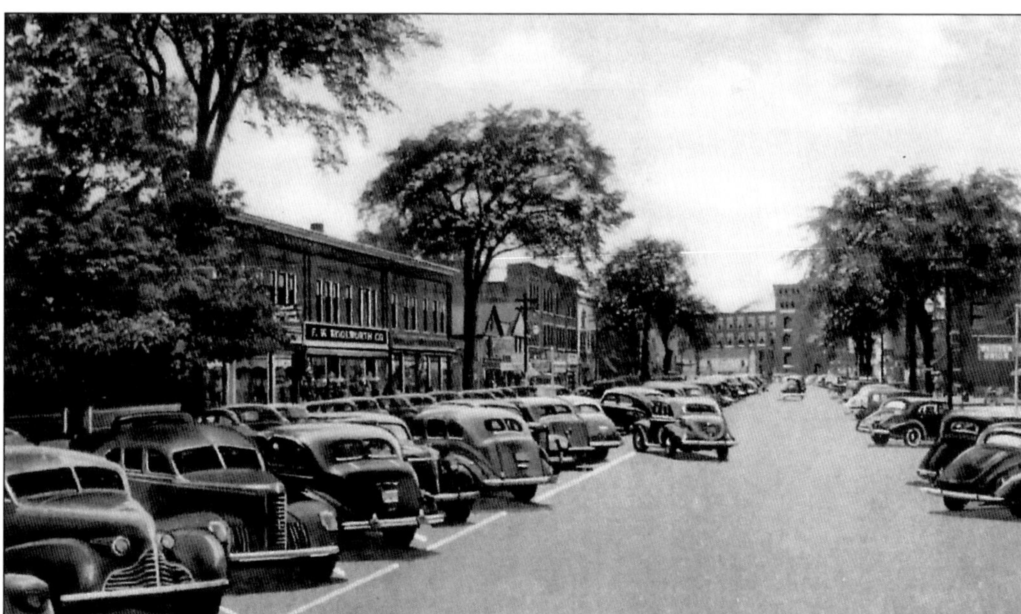

In many towns, parking became a major problem, but Brunswick's wide Maine Street could accommodate three rows of cars parked at angles in the late 1930s, when cars were shorter and two travel lanes sufficed.

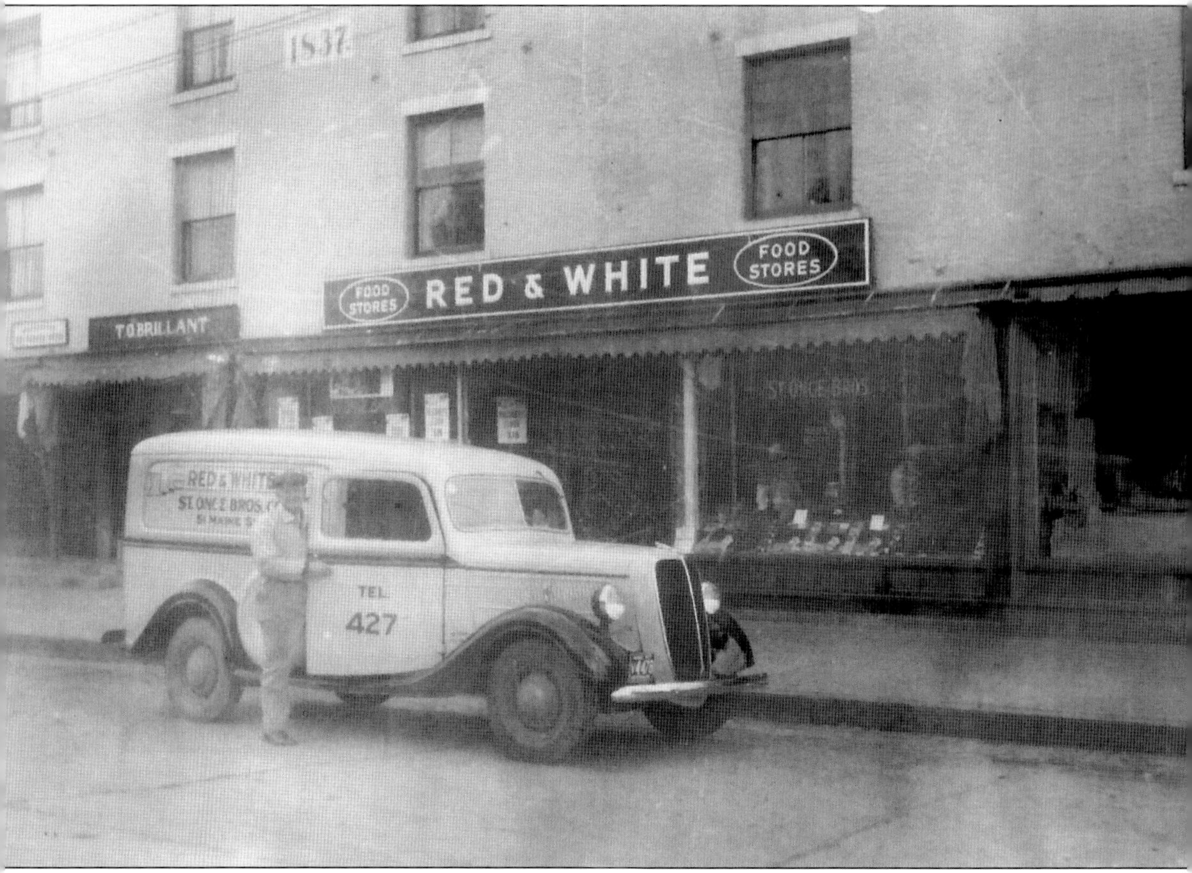

The internal combustion engine also changed delivery methods. The firm had employed a horse and wagon earlier, but St. Onge Brothers were among those changing to trucks, probably before this 1930s example.

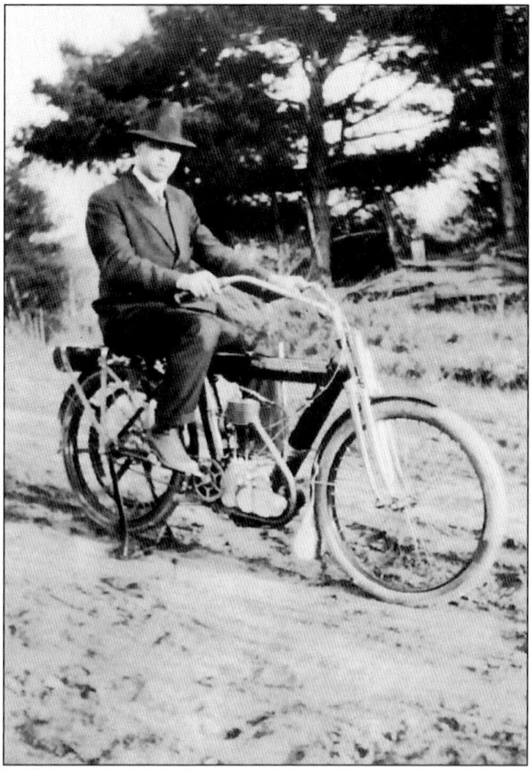

Percy Hyde, of Foreside Road, Topsham, used a 1910 Pierce-Arrow motorcycle to court Blanche Watson in East Brunswick. They wed in 1911.

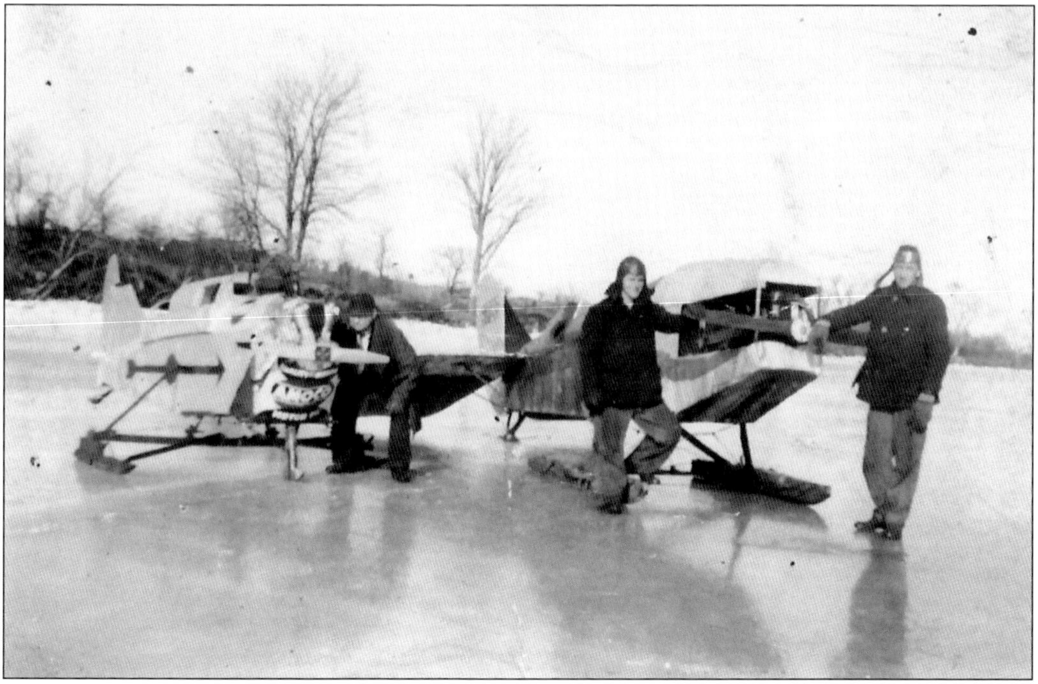

Percy Hyde, Jr., looked to other transportation. As teenagers, he (on right) and Arthur Williams (center) built ice boats resembling wingless airplanes on which to speed up and down the river near Hyde's home. "Frankie Fixit" Leblanc examines a motor.

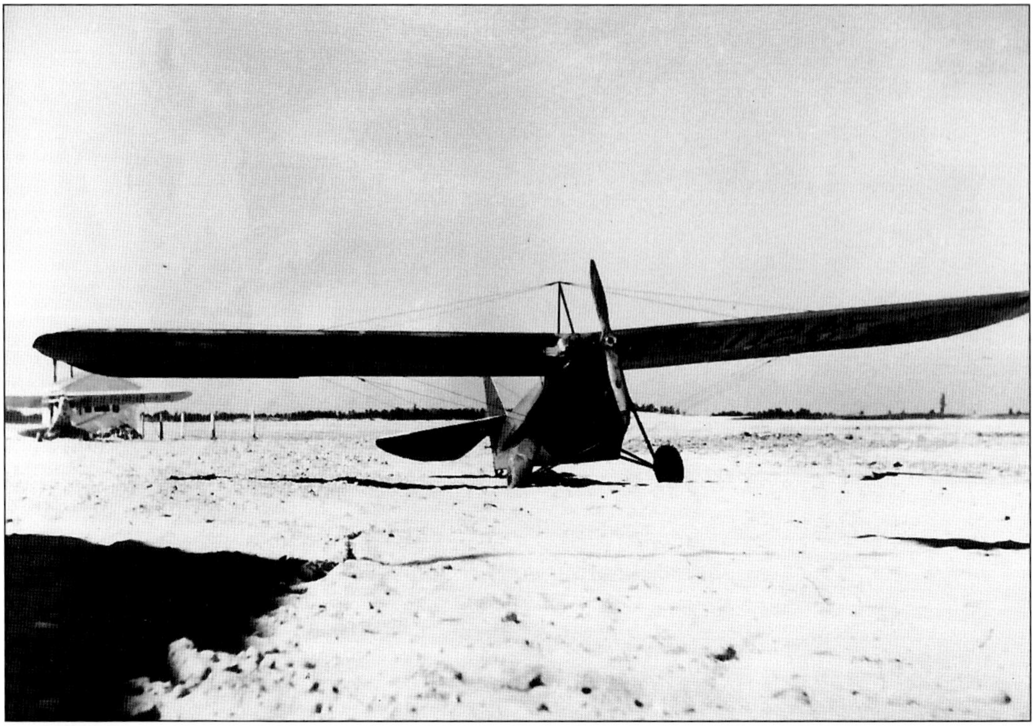

By 1939 Hyde and Williams had saved to purchase a 1931 Aronica airplane, here standing on the sandy strip which was Brunswick's airport before the U.S. Navy established a base there.

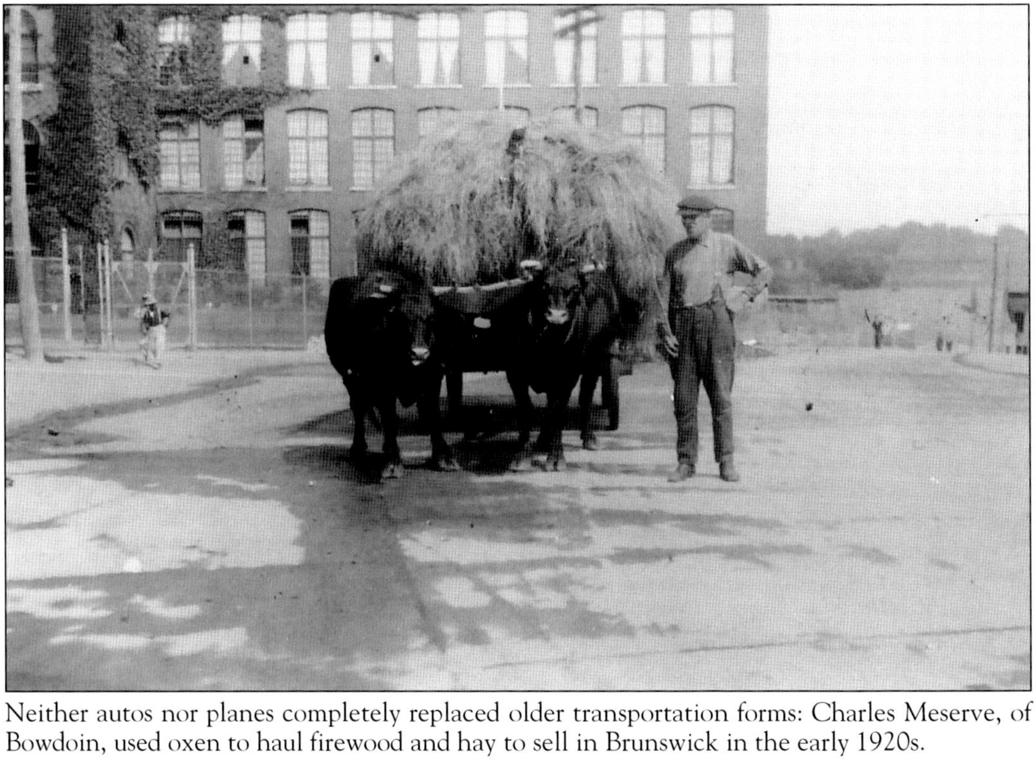

Neither autos nor planes completely replaced older transportation forms: Charles Meserve, of Bowdoin, used oxen to haul firewood and hay to sell in Brunswick in the early 1920s.

Nine

Wartime

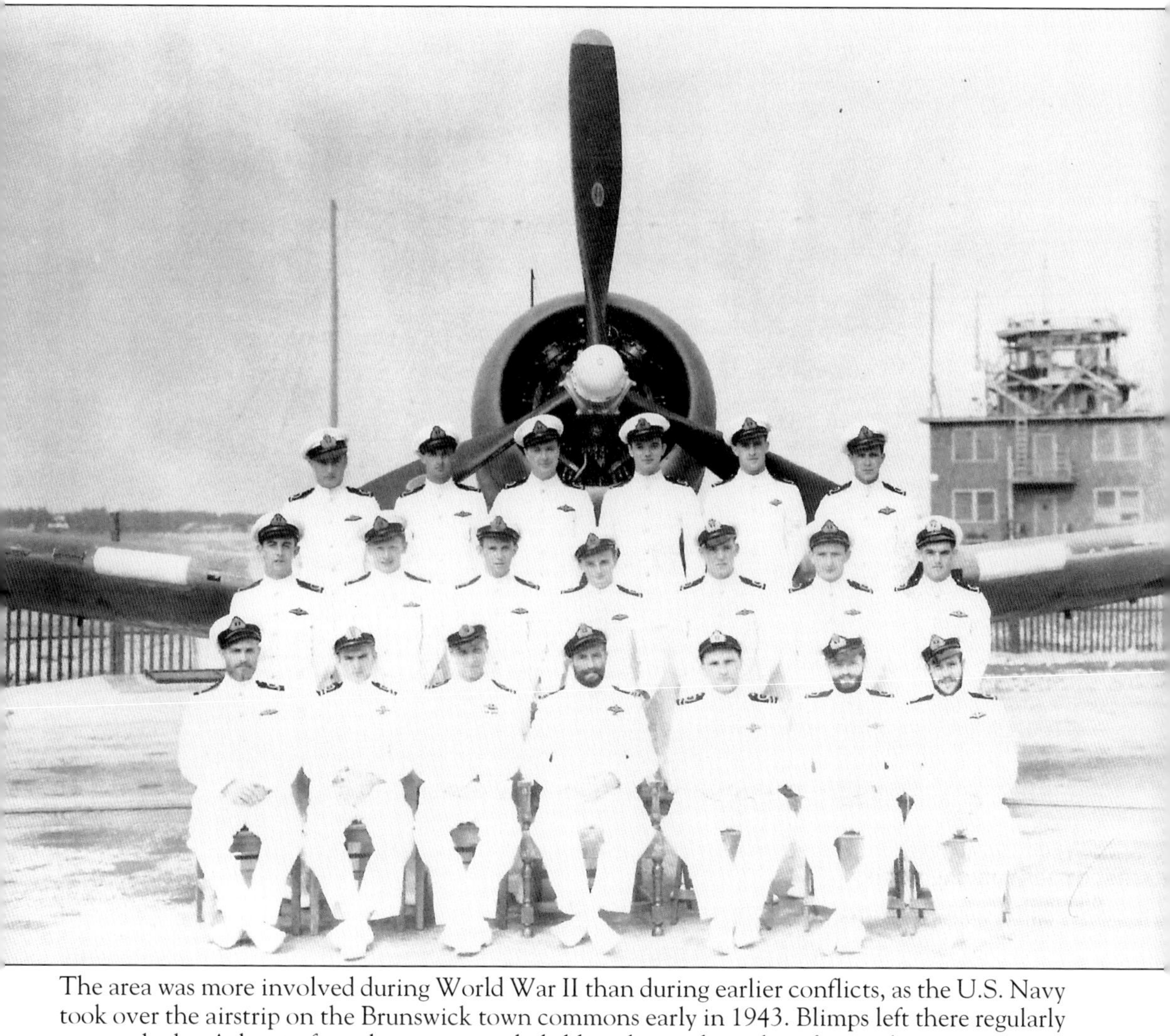

The area was more involved during World War II than during earlier conflicts, as the U.S. Navy took over the airstrip on the Brunswick town commons early in 1943. Blimps left there regularly to search the Atlantic for submarines, and children learned to identify warplanes. Moreover, when the new base received squadrons from the British Navy for training, men in "different" uniforms appeared on the streets of town. Here young British officers pose on the base before a Corsair fighter, easily recognized by its bent wings.

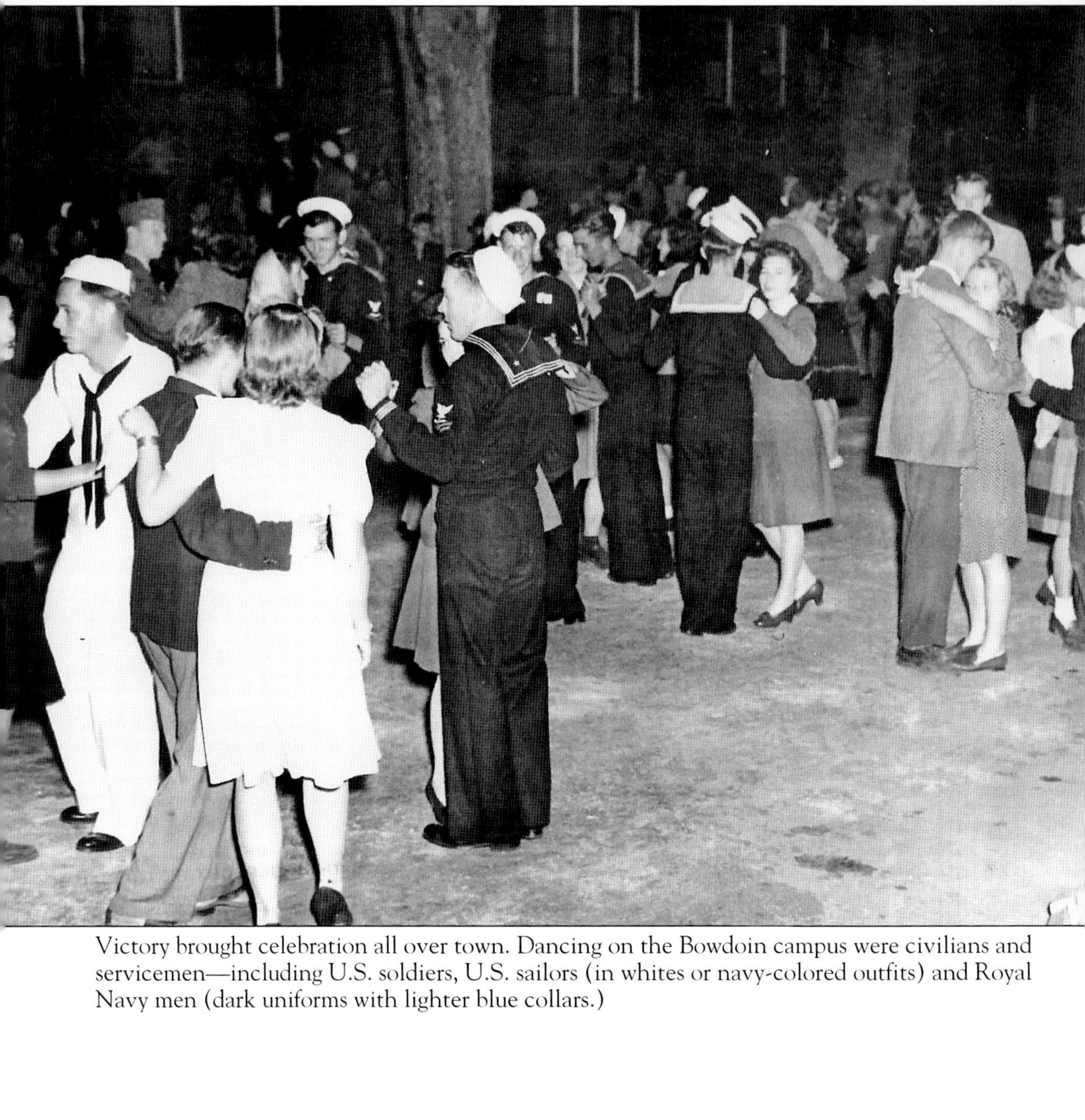

Victory brought celebration all over town. Dancing on the Bowdoin campus were civilians and servicemen—including U.S. soldiers, U.S. sailors (in whites or navy-colored outfits) and Royal Navy men (dark uniforms with lighter blue collars.)

Ten

Getting Away From It All

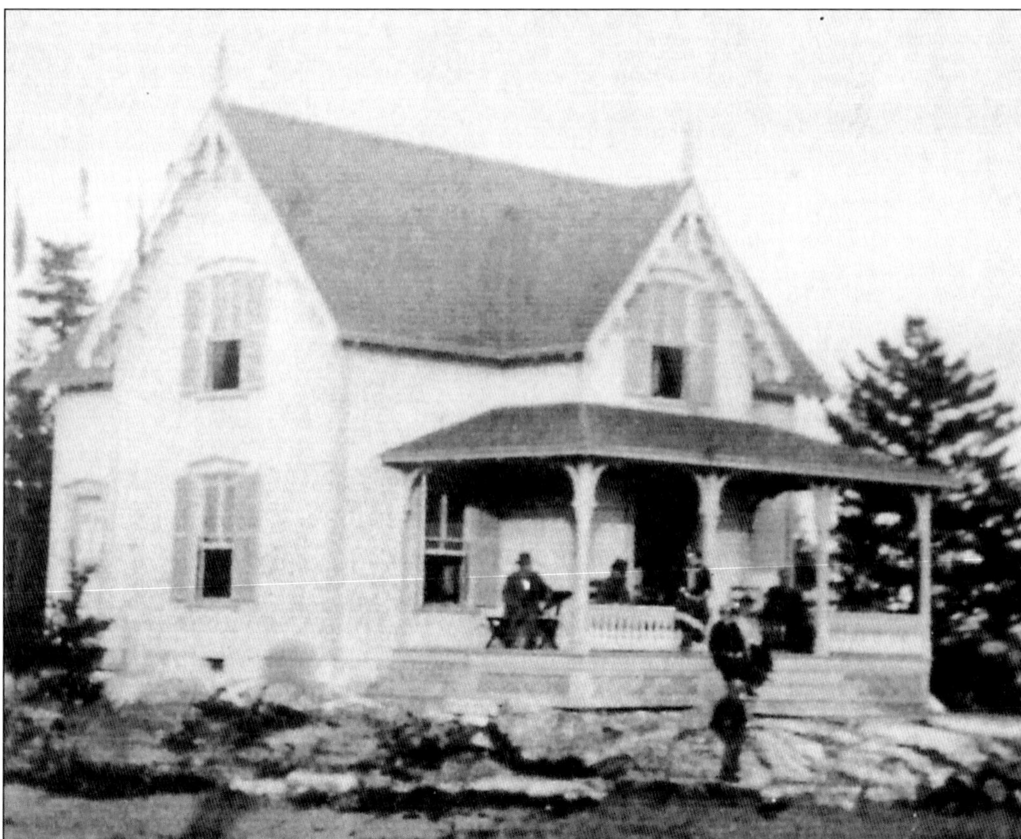

Many areas around Casco Bay became summer resorts in the late nineteenth century, but Brunswick's only real development of the sort began when the end of Mere Point was surveyed for cottage lots in 1877. Lots at "Sea Point" were offered at $100 each. By 1888, the enclave included a bowling alley and a restaurant, and was described by the *Brunswick Telegraph* editor as "next to Bar Harbor as a summer resort," although he mourned the presence of "only four Democrats" there. "Summit Cottage" is shown here in the 1870s.

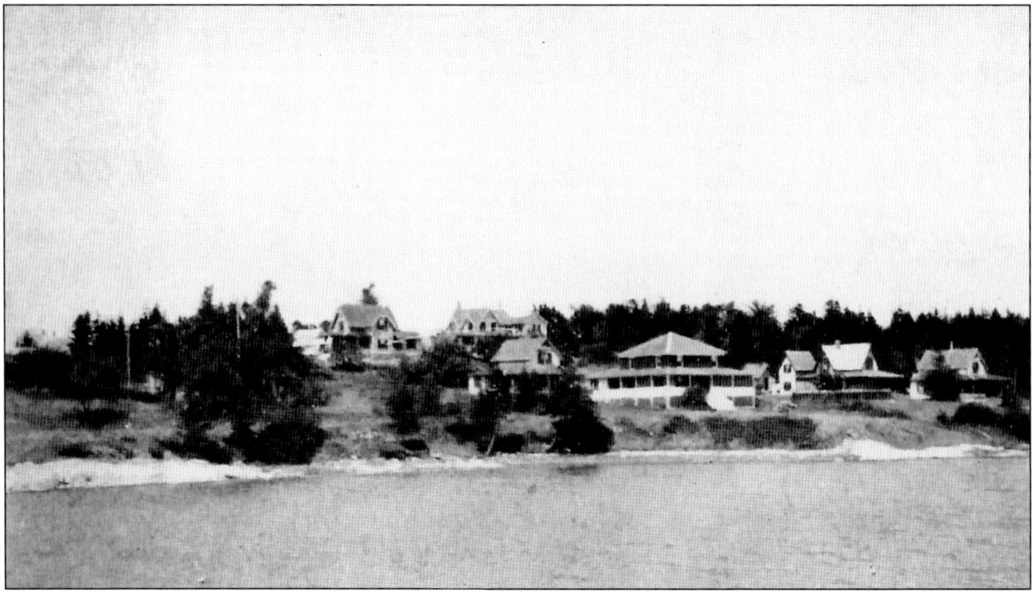

Some of Mere Point's cottages were photographed from the water at the turn of the century.

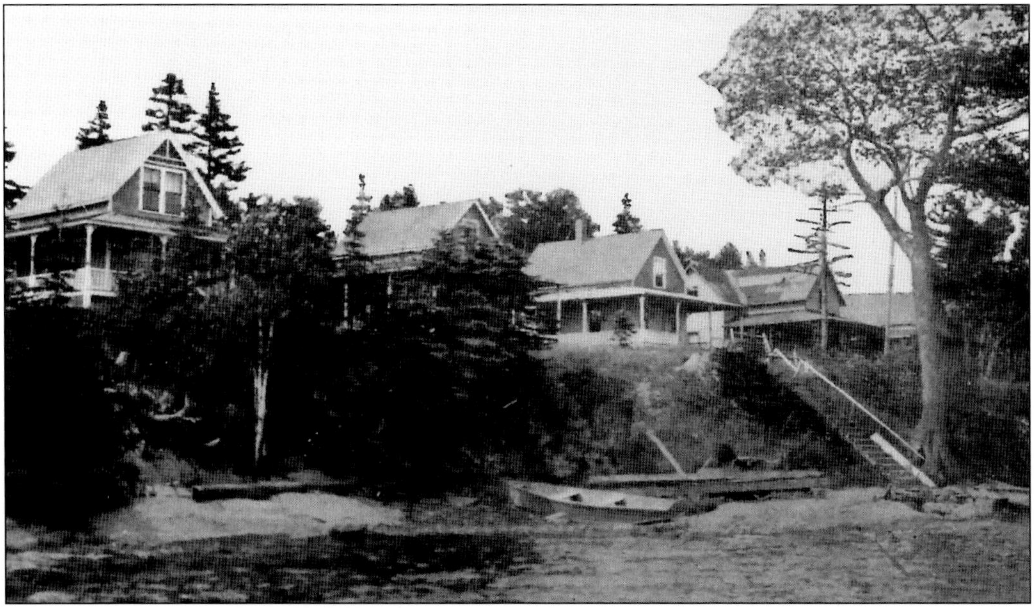

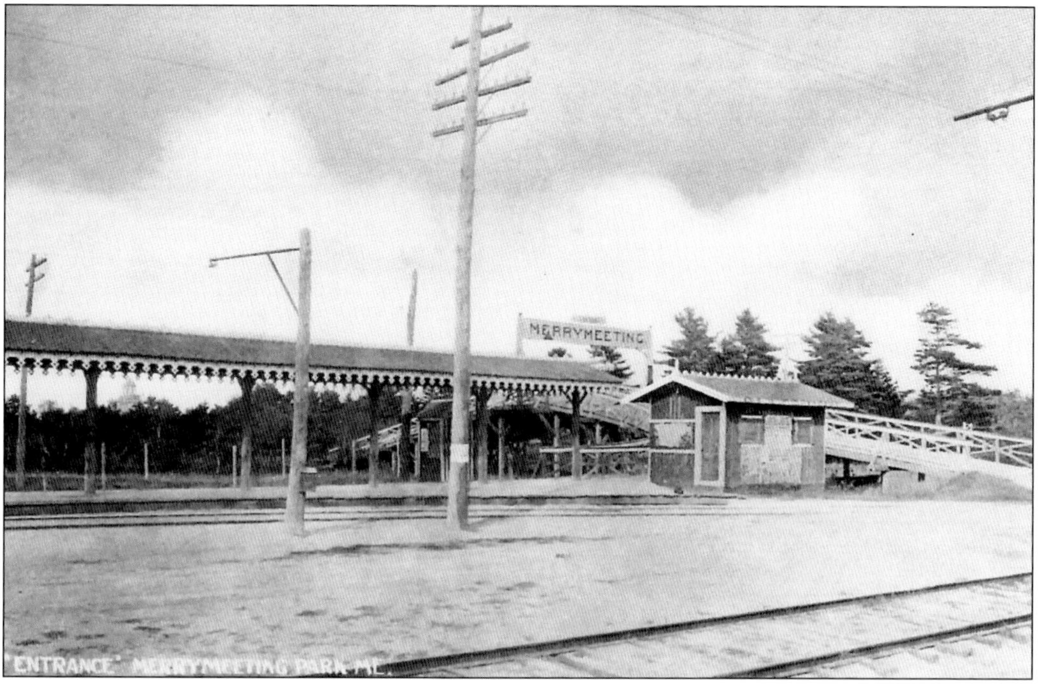

In order to encourage day trips, trolley interests in 1898 constructed Merrymeeting Park, located two miles east of Brunswick village between the river and the trolley route to Bath. Entrance was by way of an arched bridge over the adjacent train tracks.

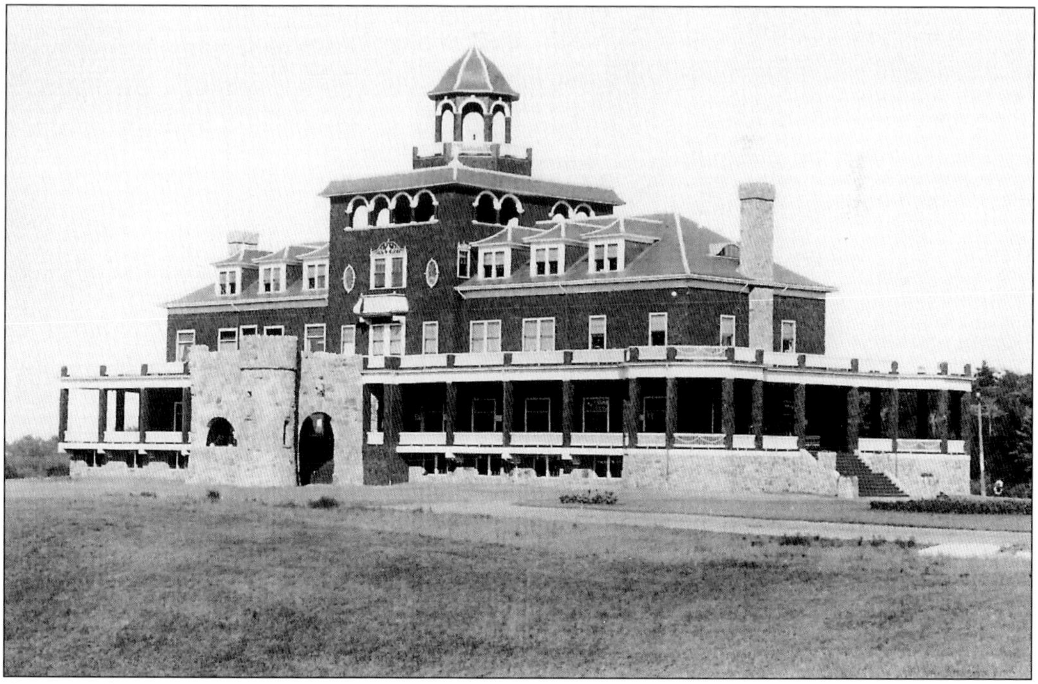

Once in the park, the visitor found many attractions, including a small zoo. The casino stood on an elevation with views of the river. Its restaurant offered "Regular Table d'Hote" dinners for 75 cents, shore dinners for 50 cents.

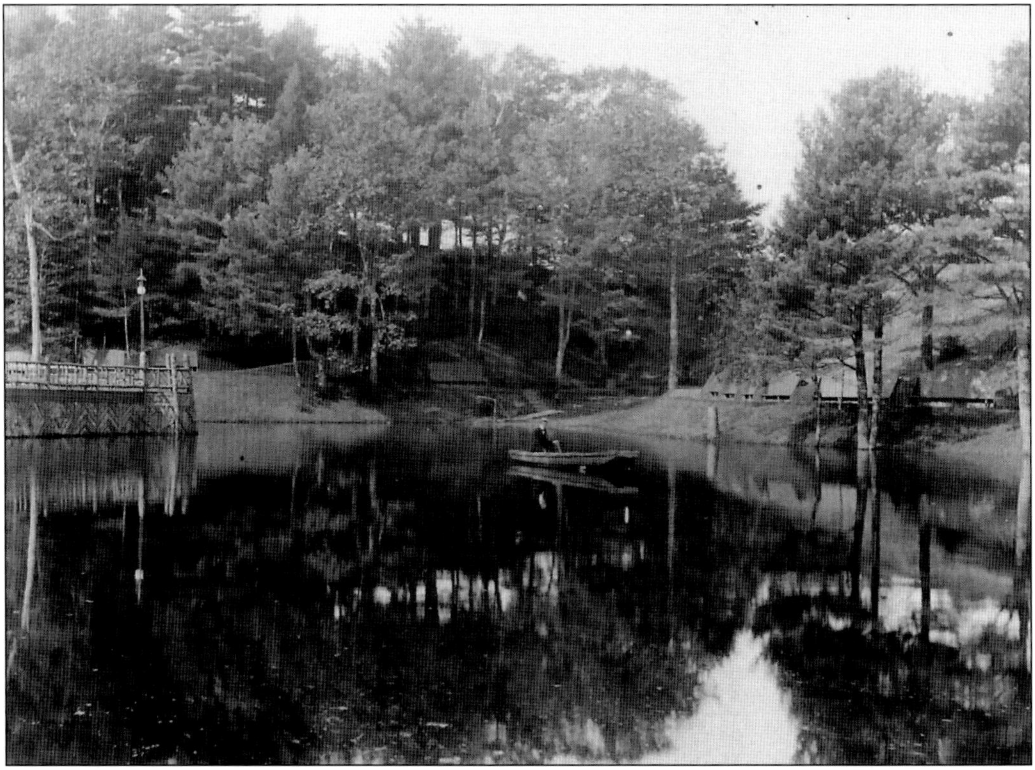

Paths for strolling were laid out around a series of man-made ponds. The boat shown here would have been unusual, as no boathouse was included on a visitors' map: ducks and swans were more common occupants of the waters.

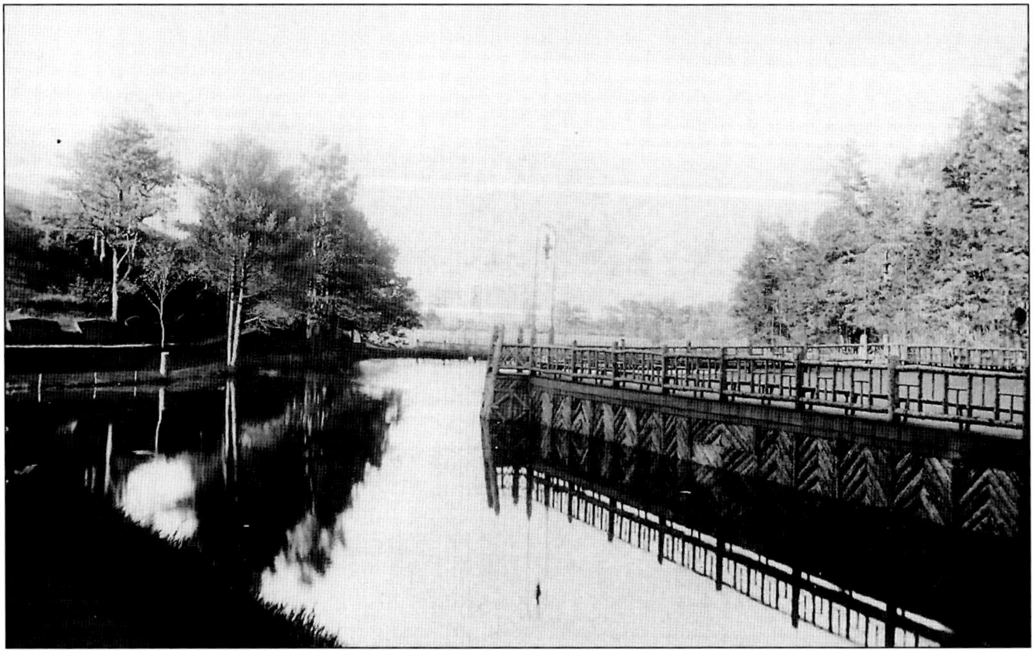

Protruding into a pond was an out-of-doors dance floor, lighted by arc lights in the evenings.

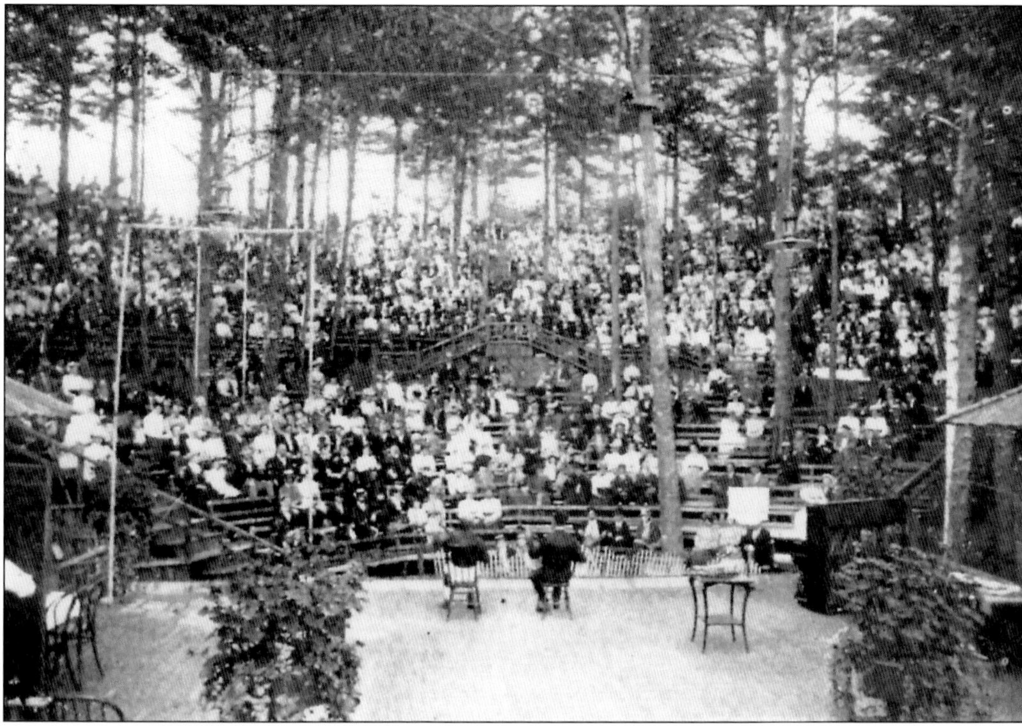

The open-air theater offered performances of music and vaudeville acts—even religious lectures. However, profits were not enough to keep the park going. It closed in 1906, too early to have felt any impact from autos, of which there were still perhaps no more than a dozen in the region. Trolleys ran until the 1930s.

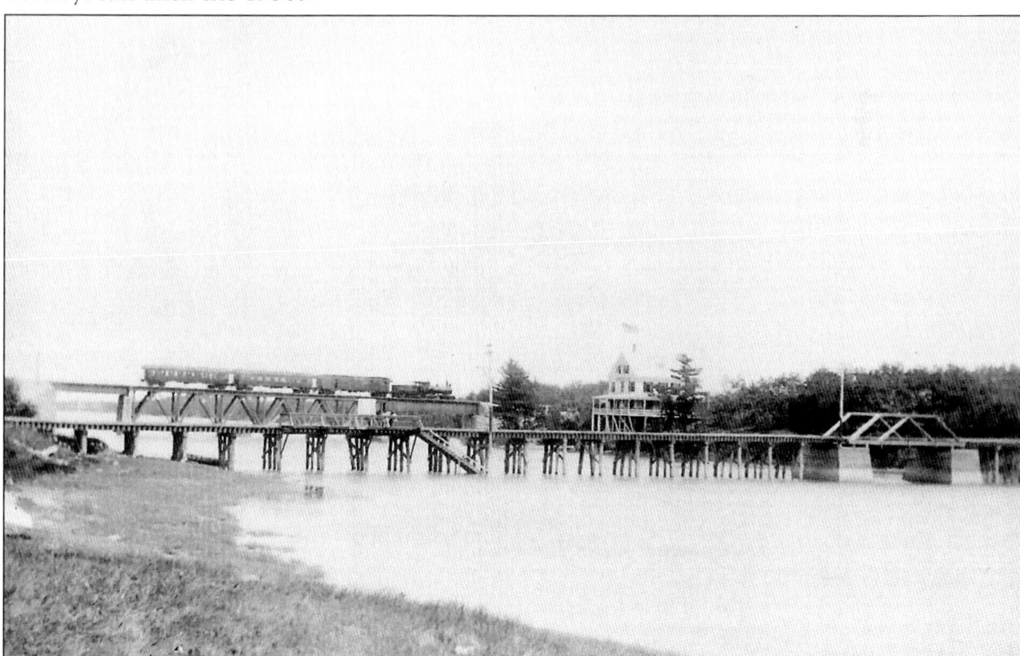

Near the bridges across the New Meadows River, an inn on the Bath side attracted guests.

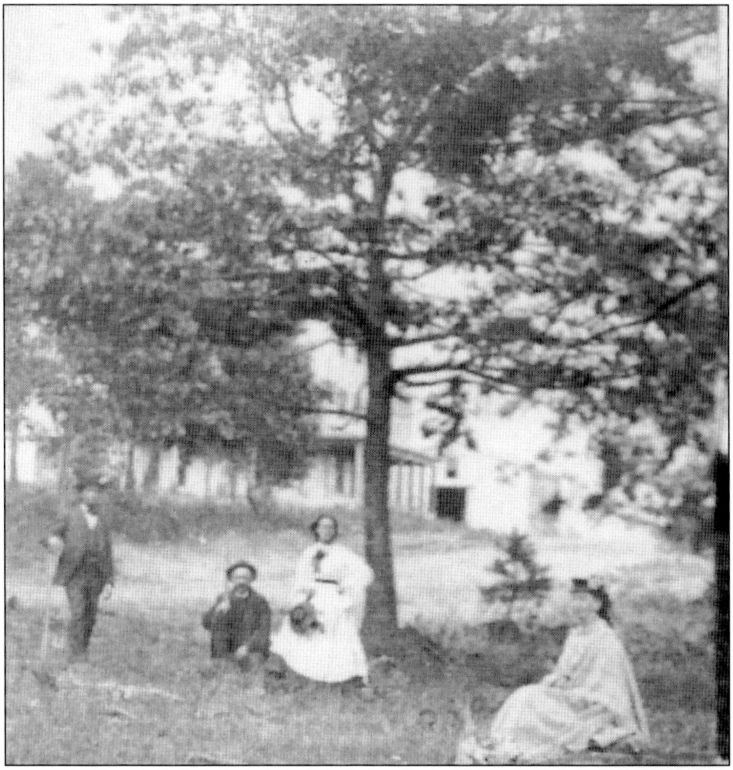

Other visitors spent summer weeks as boarders at the Hardings' Riverside House on the Brunswick side.

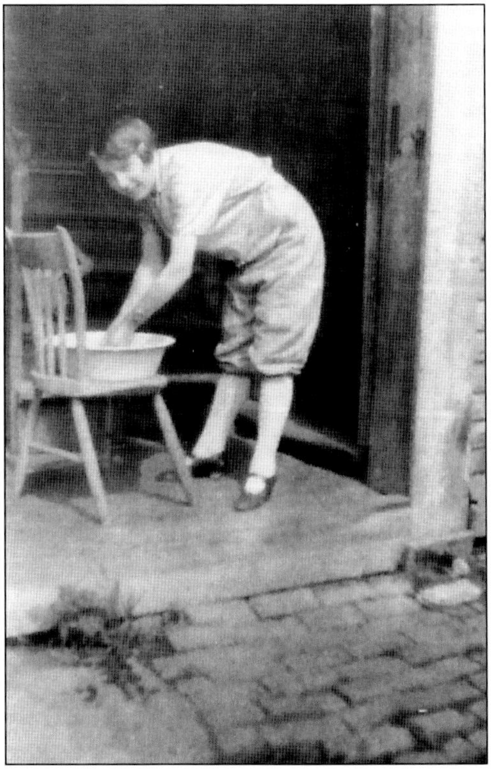

Taking in boarders was a common way for a farm wife to make extra money, as city dwellers enjoyed "roughing it." This knickers-clad young lady staying at the Tripp Farm on Topsham's Pleasant Point was obviously amused by having to wash up in the shed.

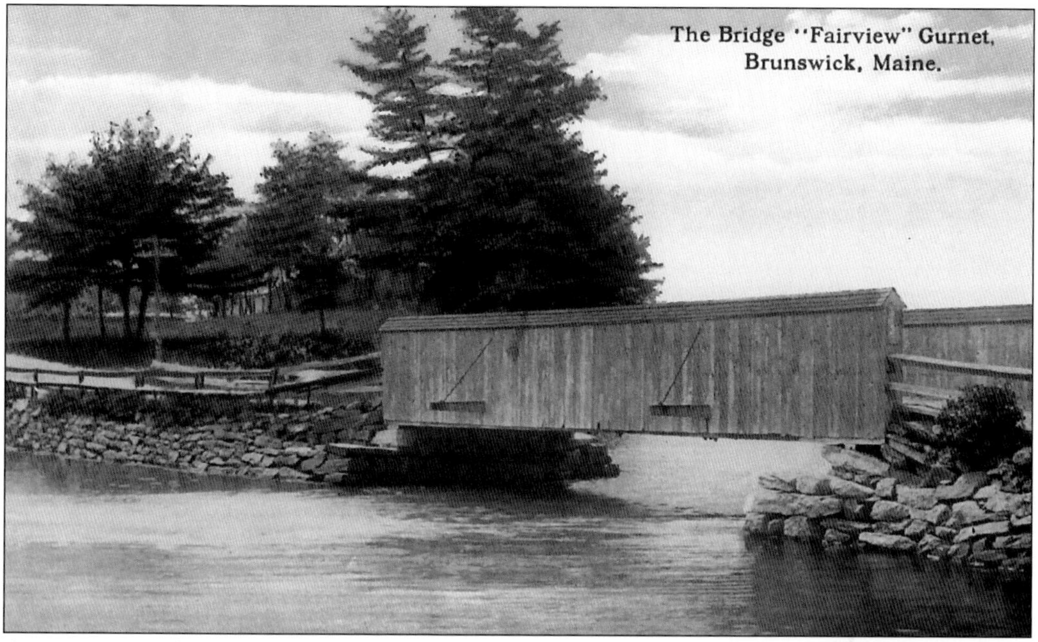

Attractions at the Gurnet were shared with Harpswell's Great Island, reached across a short bridge. The boards on the high sides of the early span would have protected wooden trusses.

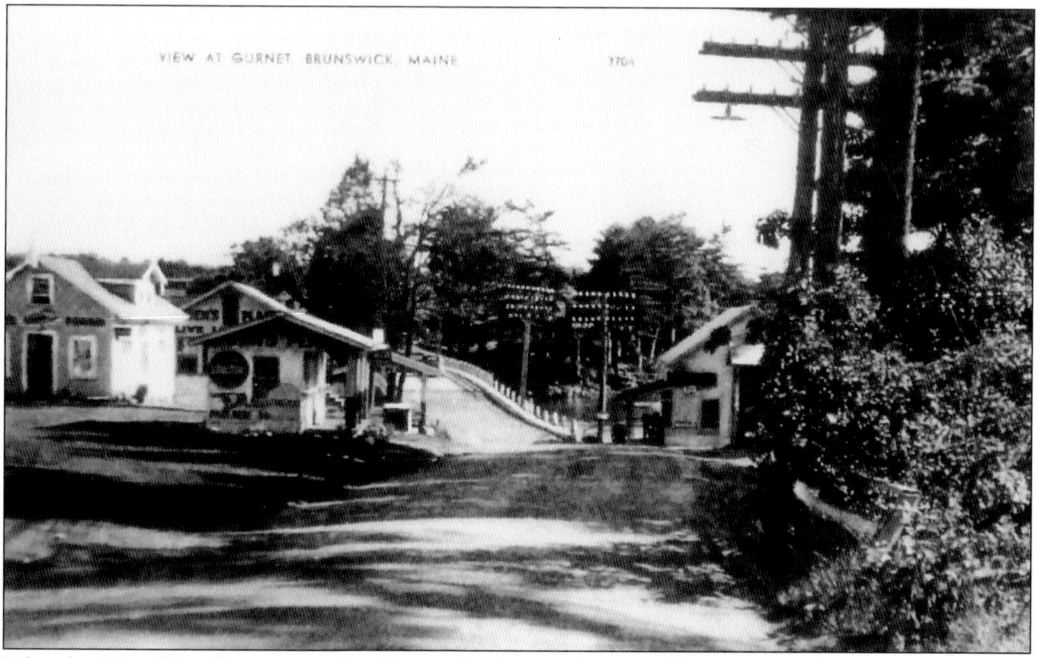

Like the New Meadows area, the Gurnet had sporadic steamboat service; but it became more popular in the early twentieth century after auto travel became common enough that town dwellers could drop in at restaurants and dance pavilions there. The bridge was widened after a demand by the state in 1915.

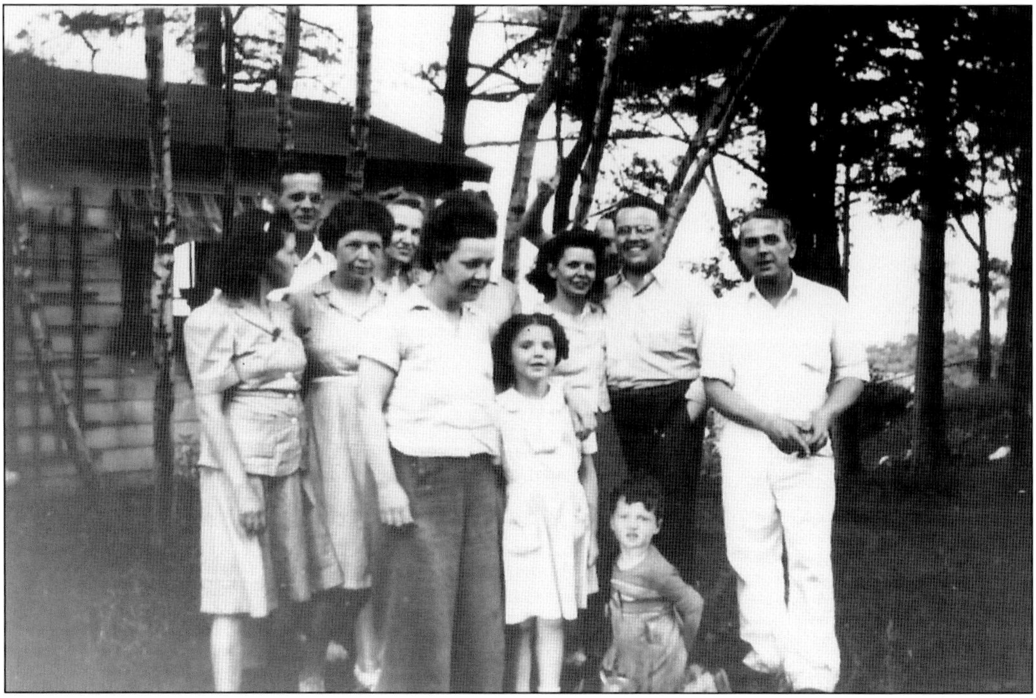

Automobiles also enabled laborers to commute to summer "camps" on rivers, lakes, and ocean. Here on a 1940s family outing at Pleasant Point, are: (front) Gladys Black, Anne Morin, and Paul Bouchard; (next row) Edith Morin, Laura Blanchard, Margaret Kelly, Lionel Gaudreau, and Michael Morin; (rear) Gerald and Gervais Blanchard.

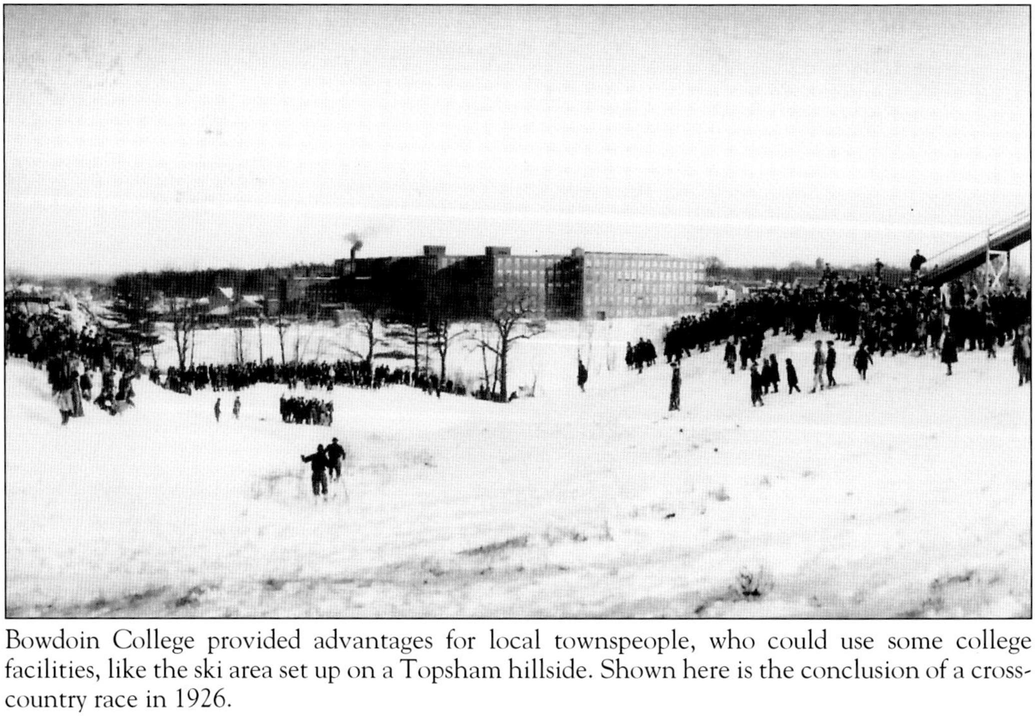

Bowdoin College provided advantages for local townspeople, who could use some college facilities, like the ski area set up on a Topsham hillside. Shown here is the conclusion of a cross-country race in 1926.

Eleven

Parades

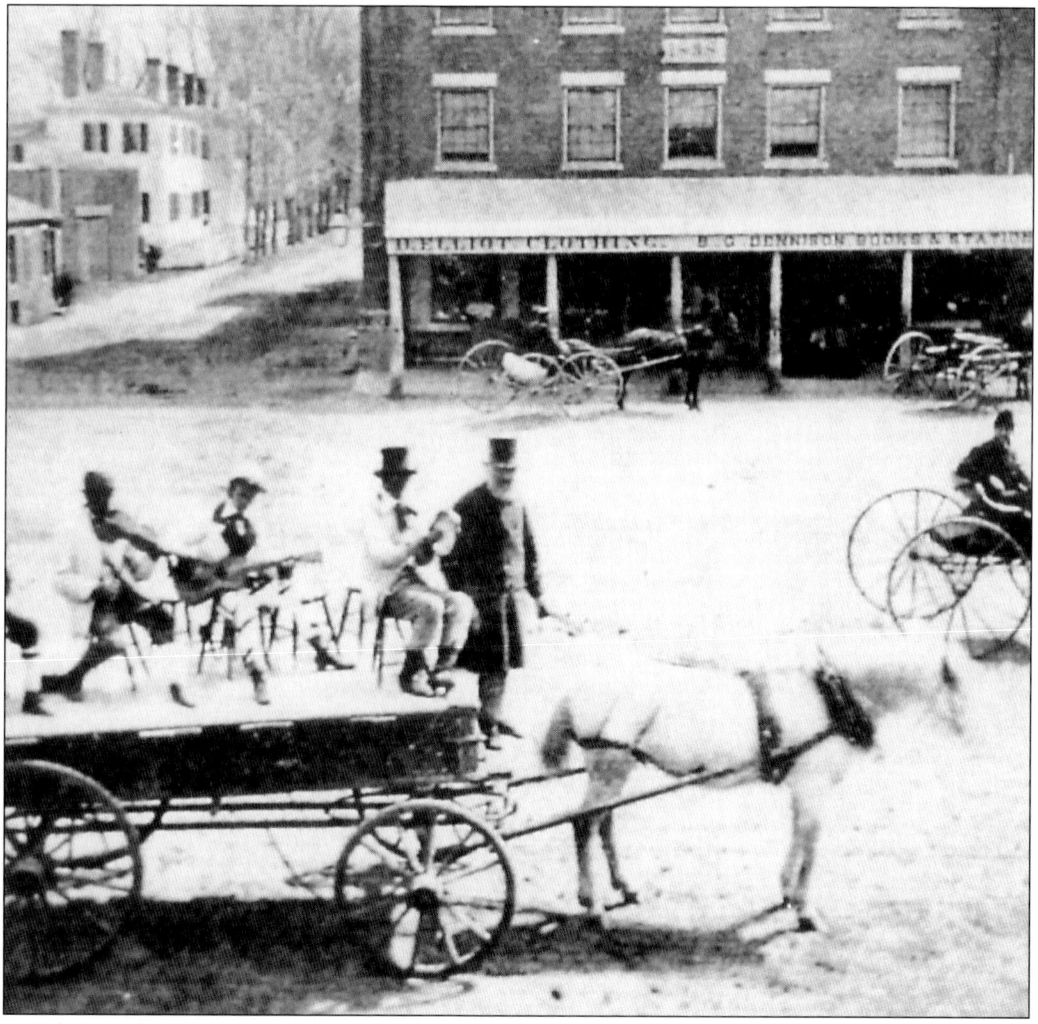

Parades or demonstrations regularly utilized Maine Street. The load of musicians here was not named, the stereoptic card publisher preferring to identify the old Dunlap Block in the background, which was altered in 1872 and again in 1880.

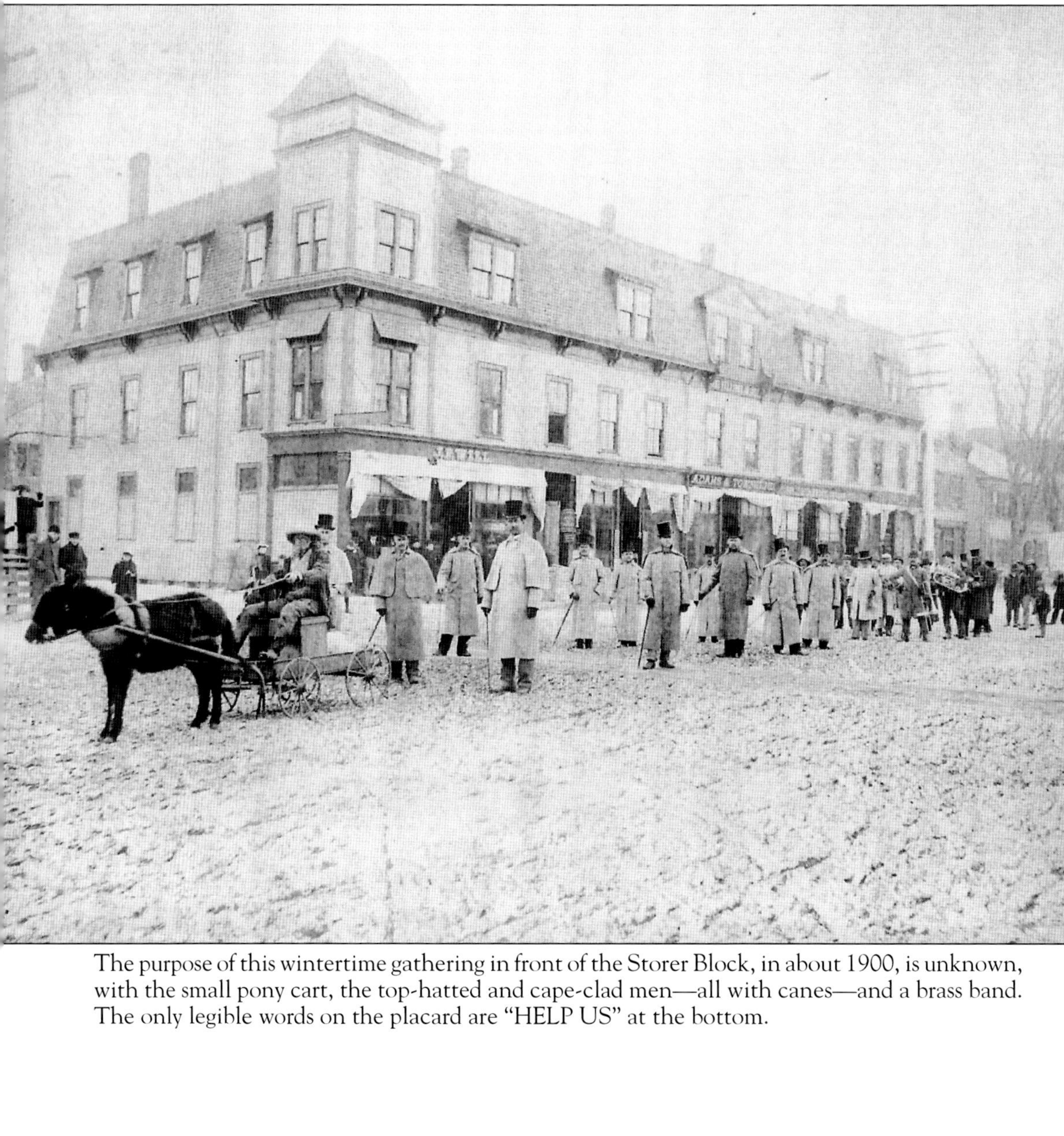

The purpose of this wintertime gathering in front of the Storer Block, in about 1900, is unknown, with the small pony cart, the top-hatted and cape-clad men—all with canes—and a brass band. The only legible words on the placard are "HELP US" at the bottom.

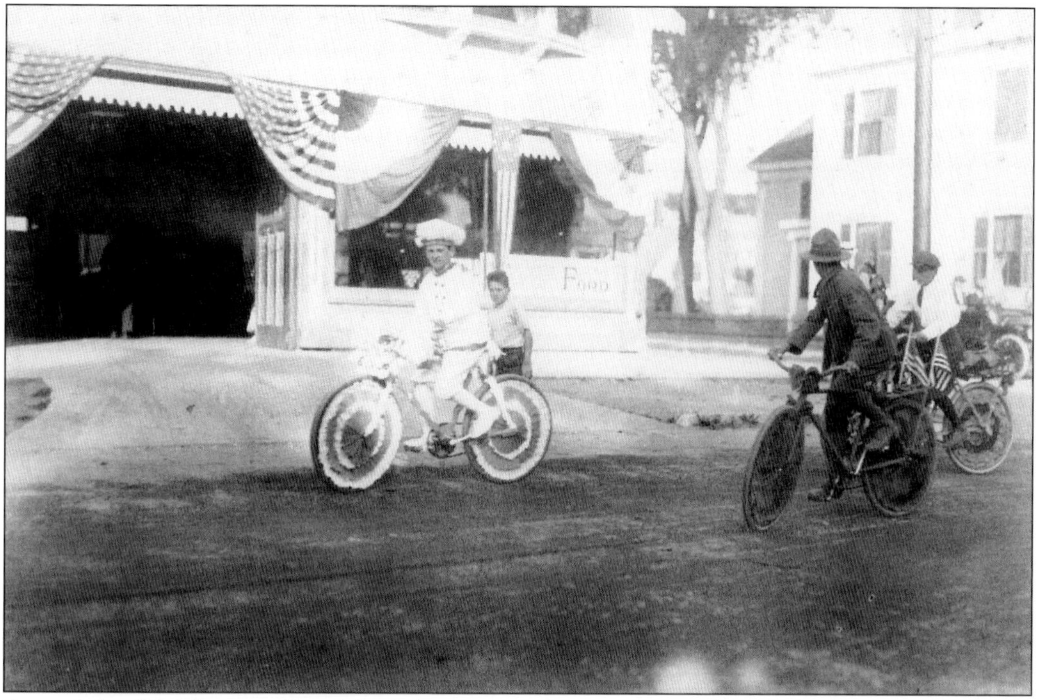

Part of the "Celebration Parade" of August 1916, at Maine and School Streets. This parade combined many types of transport.

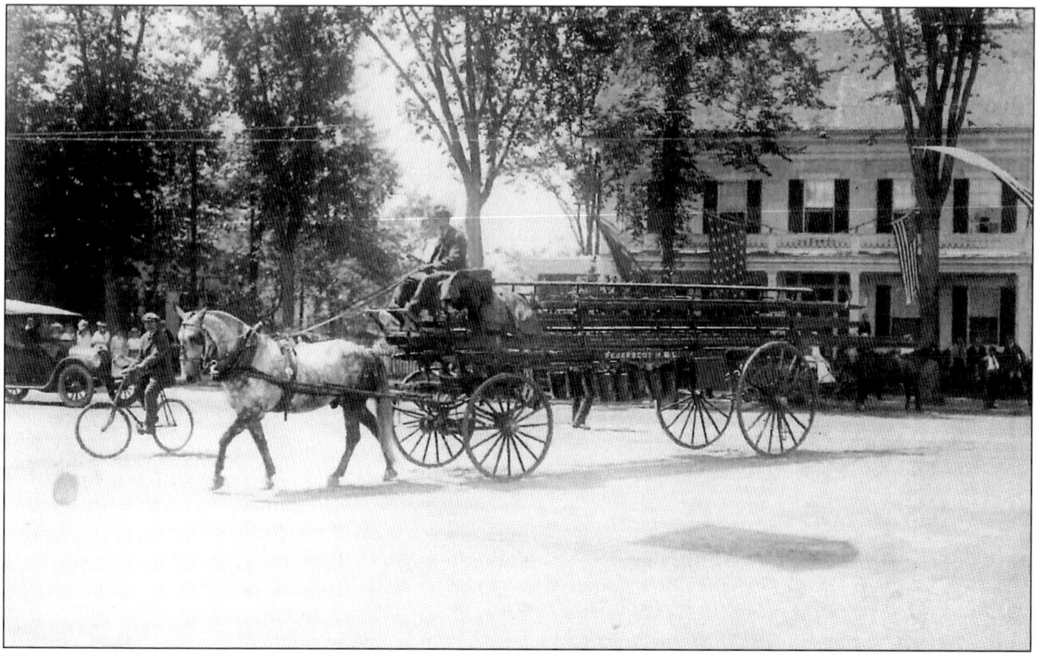

The Pejepscot Hook and Ladder, drawn by a proud horse, together with a bicycle and an auto.

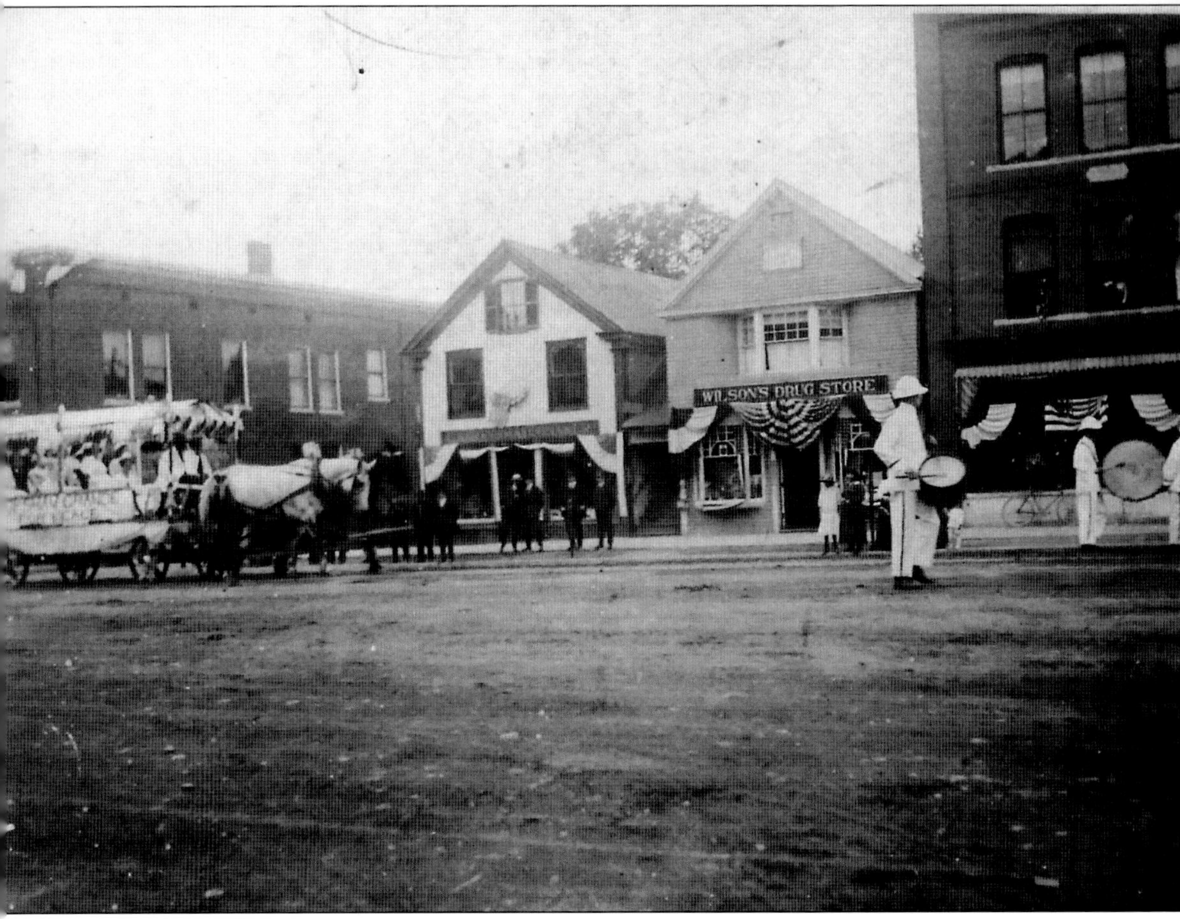

This horse-drawn float with the timely message "Topsham Grange for Peace" was awarded a first prize.

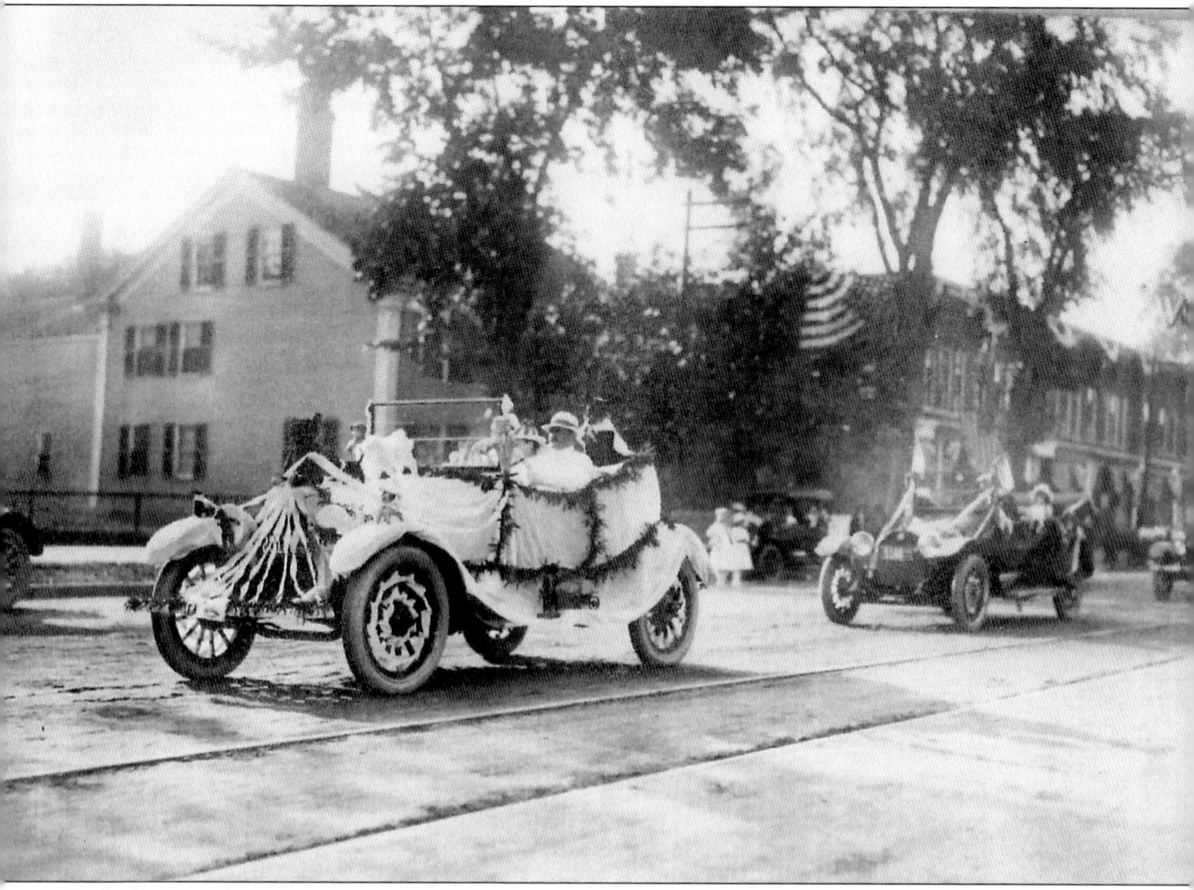

Well-decorated autos in front of the Forsaith House, later the last private home on lower Maine Street, and the Lincoln Block, erected in 1893 on the lot where Dr. Isaac Lincoln's home once stood.

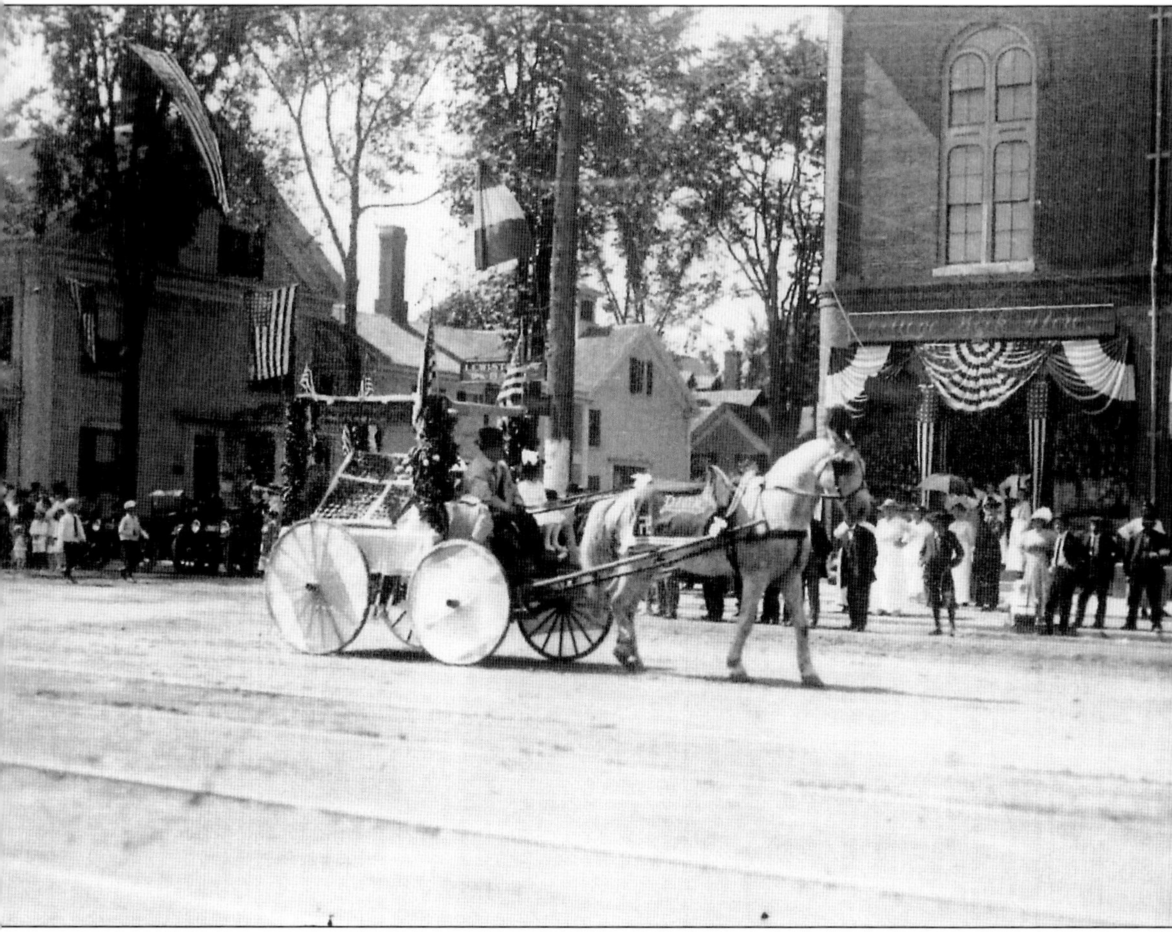

Kennebec Fruit Co., opened in Brunswick by Frank and Joseph Fiori in 1899, won first prize in the "trades" category. "Dick" was the horse.

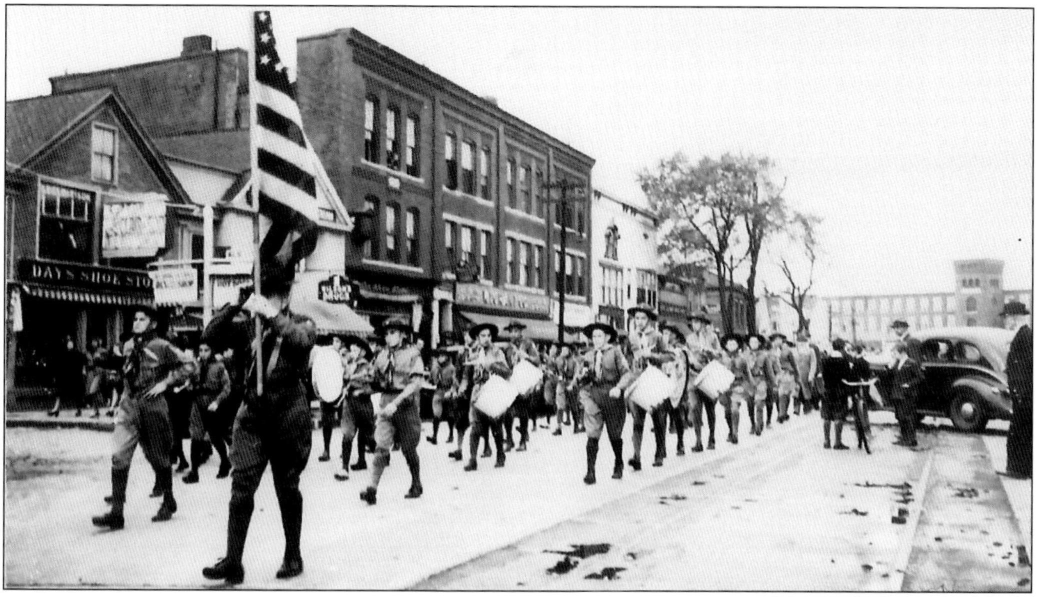

A Memorial Day parade of the 1930s marching south on Maine Street.

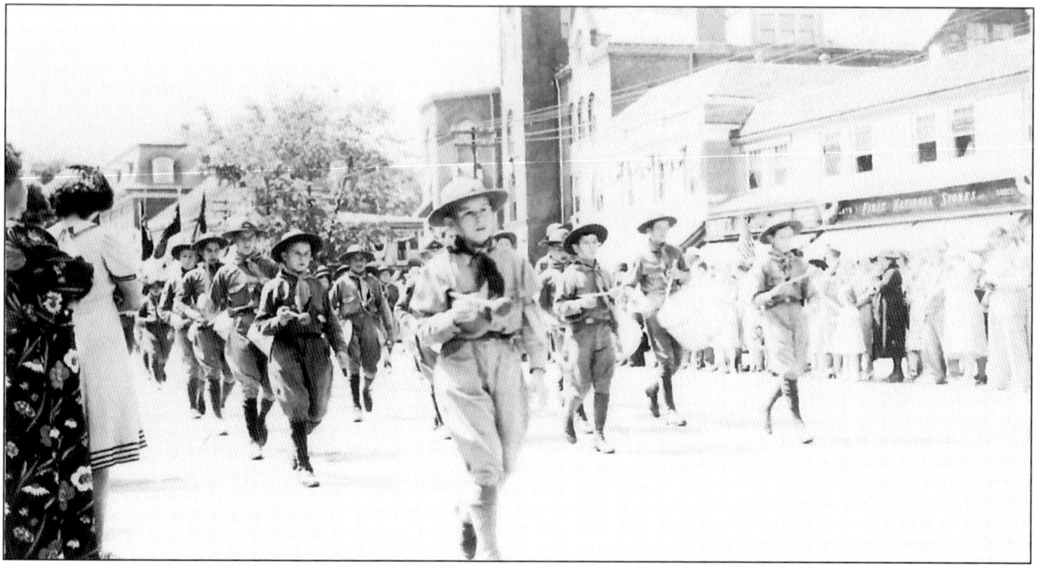

Boy Scouts were commended in the newspaper for their helpfulness at the time of Brunswick's 1939 bicentenary. Troops camped on the college campus and also joined the parade on July 3.

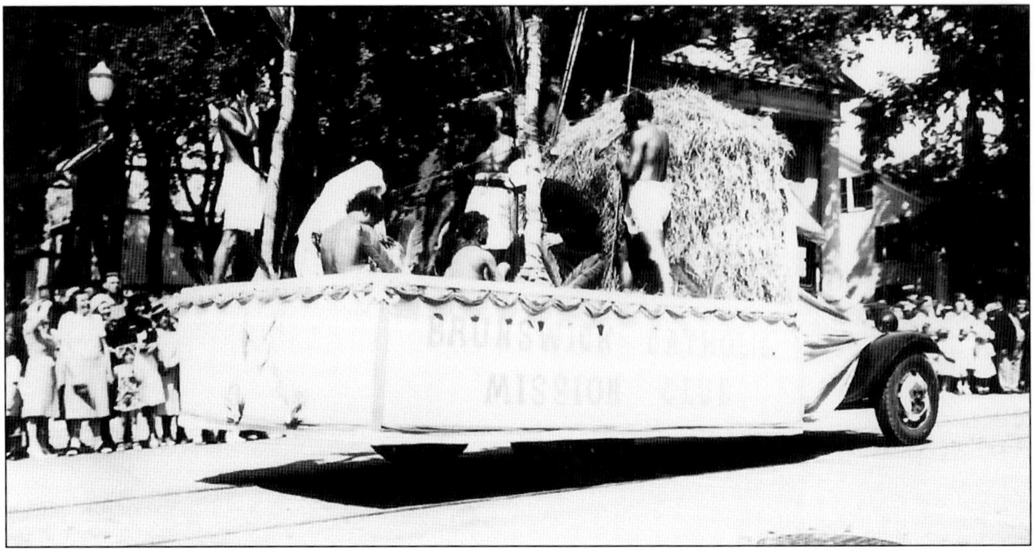

The parade showed that area interests were far-flung, insofar as the Catholic Mission Society's float represented missionary work in the Solomon Islands, where, a news report noted, "several" local missionaries were laboring.

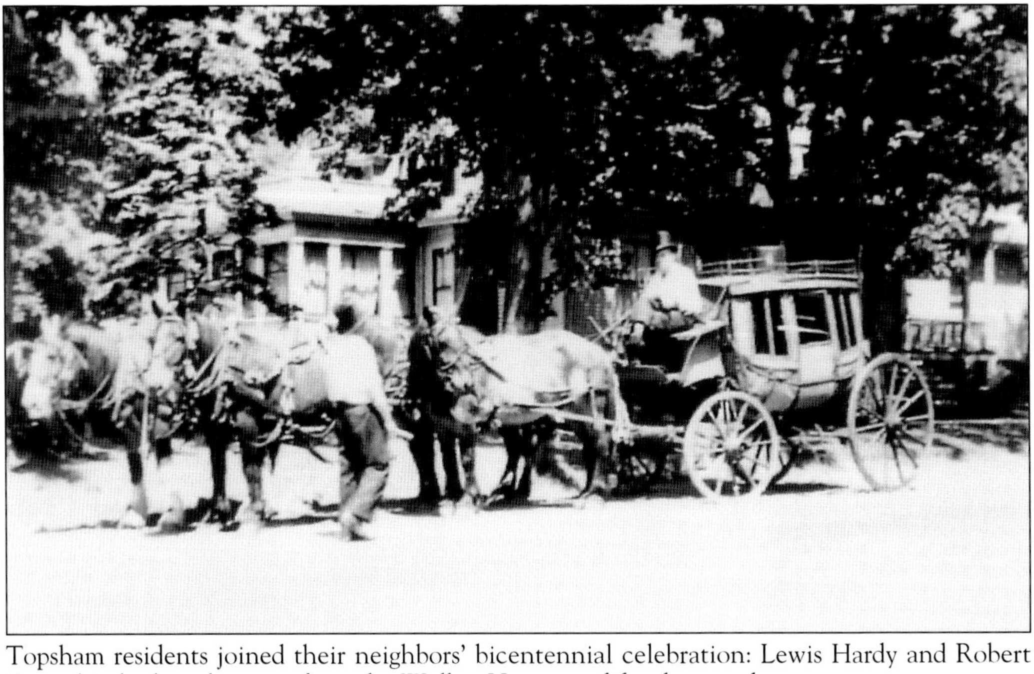

Topsham residents joined their neighbors' bicentennial celebration: Lewis Hardy and Robert Foster hitched up the stage from the Walker Homestead for the parade.

Twelve

Churches

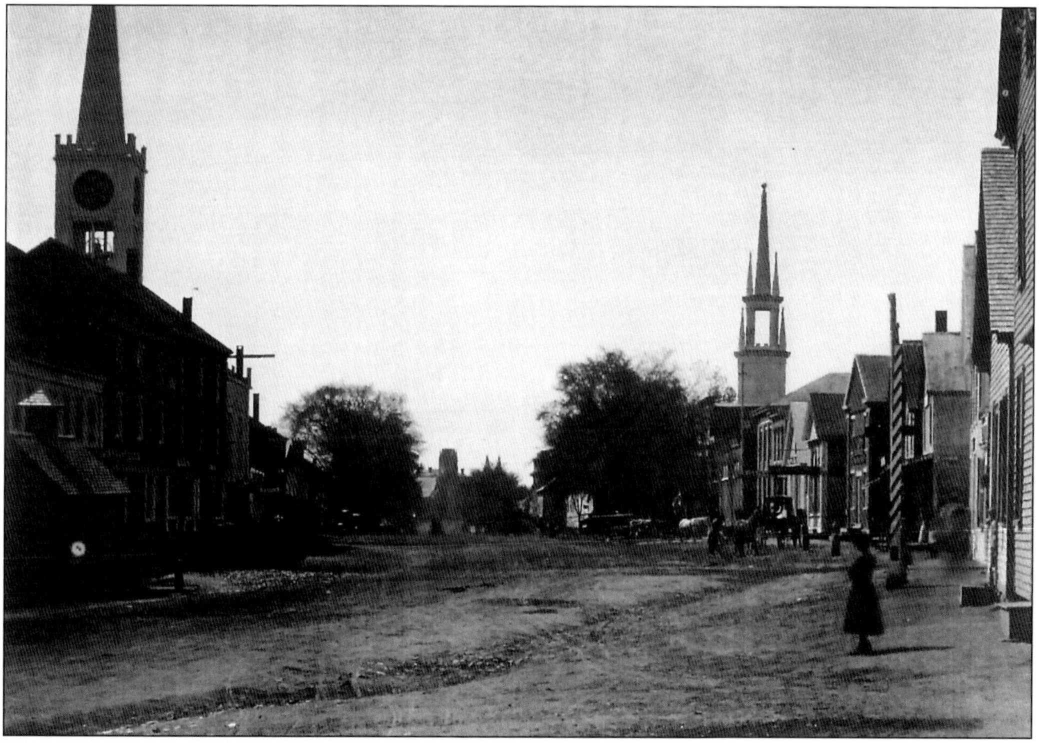

The skyline as seen from near the mill around 1870 was punctuated by spires of four churches. In the background are the First Parish Church, which lost its spire in 1866, and the twin spires of the college chapel. The steeple at the left, with a clock, was on a church built at the corner of Mason and Maine Streets by Universalists; it was later then used by Unitarians, but at the time of this photo it was serving members of both groups, joined as the Mason Street Religious Society. (Employing the street level for shops no doubt helped pay building costs.) To the right is the Maine Street Baptist Church, located between Lincoln and Gilman Streets. By 1890 the two latter churches would be given up, although the Mason Street building, shorn of its steeple, remained in use for decades. The lower level of shops remains.

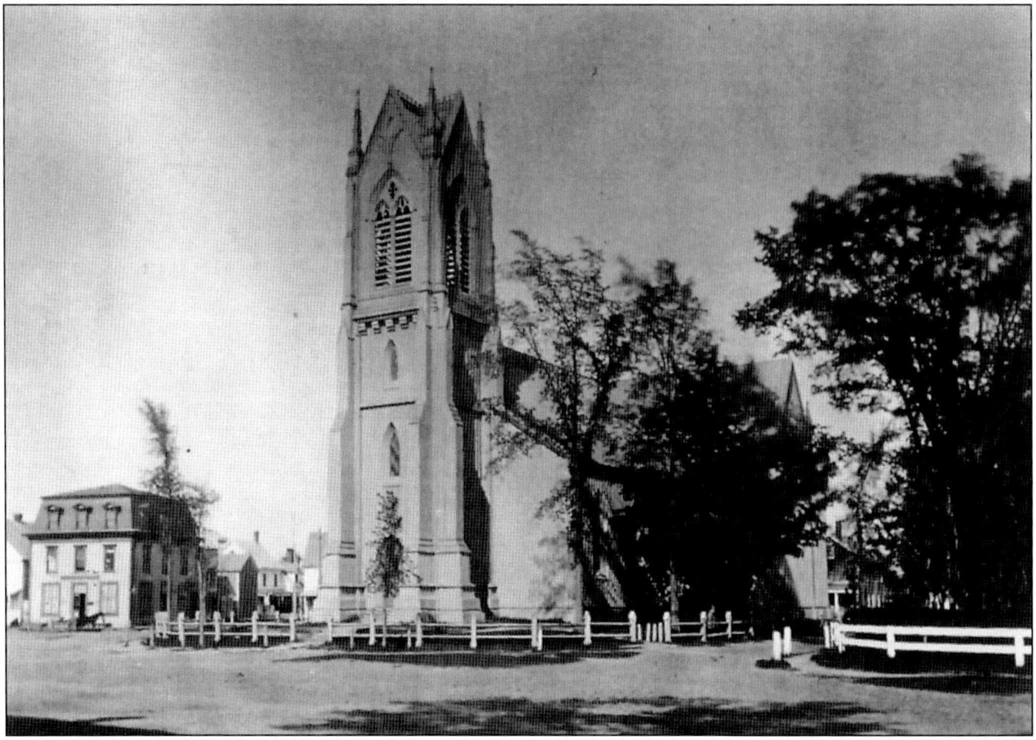

The First Parish Church, designed in 1845 by English architect Richard Upjohn, featured vertical boarding and pointed arches in the Gothic style, and was unusual for a Congregational Church of the era.

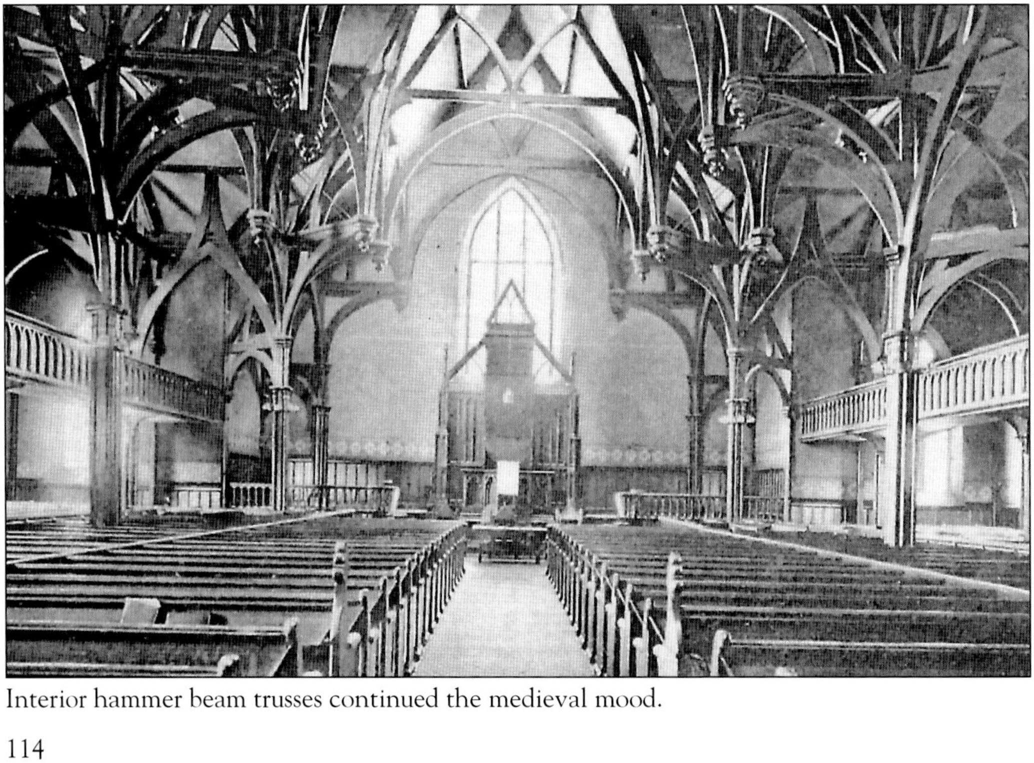

Interior hammer beam trusses continued the medieval mood.

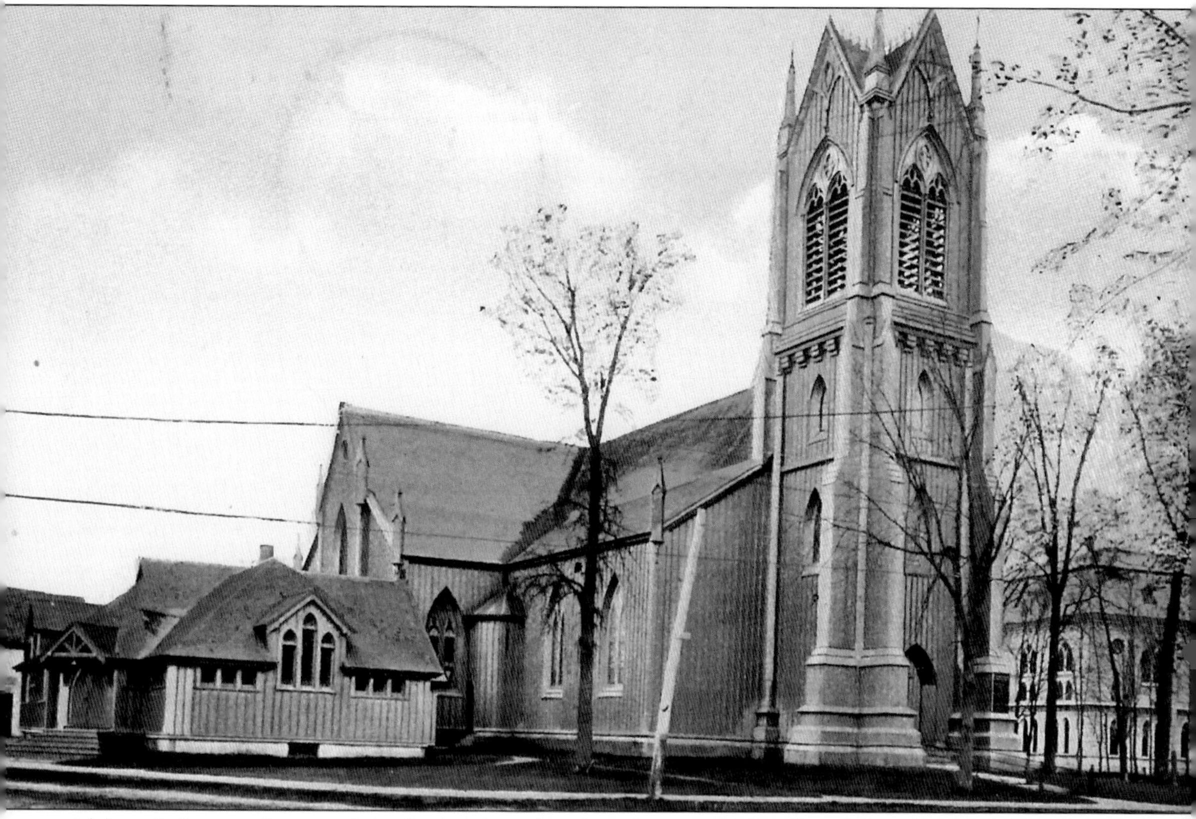

Although lower, the parish hall added to the church in 1892 displayed details which blended well with the earlier building.

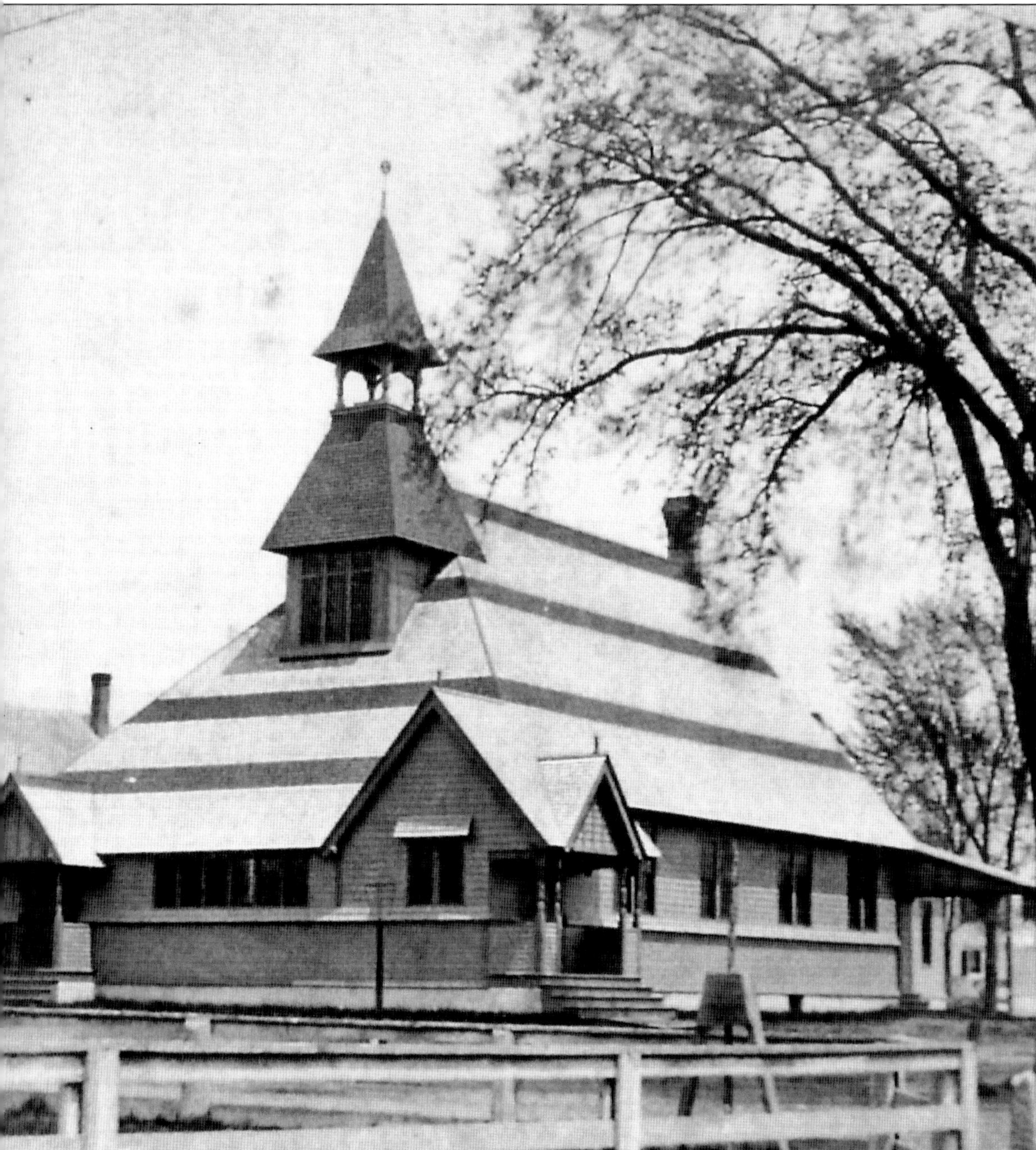

In 1875, a group of Unitarians purchased land on Federal Street and hired a Boston architect, Nathanial Bradlee, to design this church. However, their numbers were insufficient to maintain the congregation, and the structure, called Wheeler Hall after a local Unitarian preacher of the 1850s, had a varied career, providing classrooms for the nearby high school in the 1920s and a location for ballroom dance classes later. It again became a church in the late 1940s when purchased by a Church of Christ congregation.

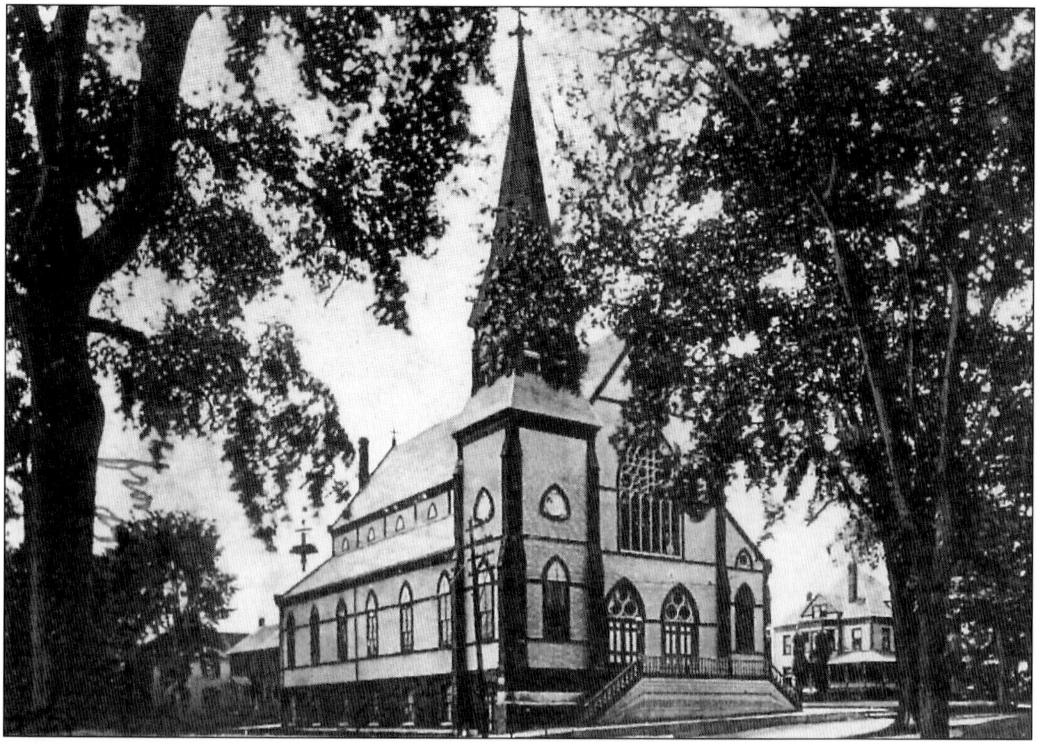

Other denominations changed church buildings. After Methodists left a Federal Street structure (built by Baptists) in favor of one on Pleasant Street, the former building served Brunswick's growing numbers of Roman Catholics. At first most were of Irish descent, but by 1877 the preponderance of French-Canadians enabled them to realize their desire for a French-speaking priest. Fifteen years later, they gave up the earlier building and moved into the large new St. John's Church on the corner of Pleasant and Union Streets, shown here. The rectory, designed by Brunswick architect Samuel Dunning in 1888, stood on the right.

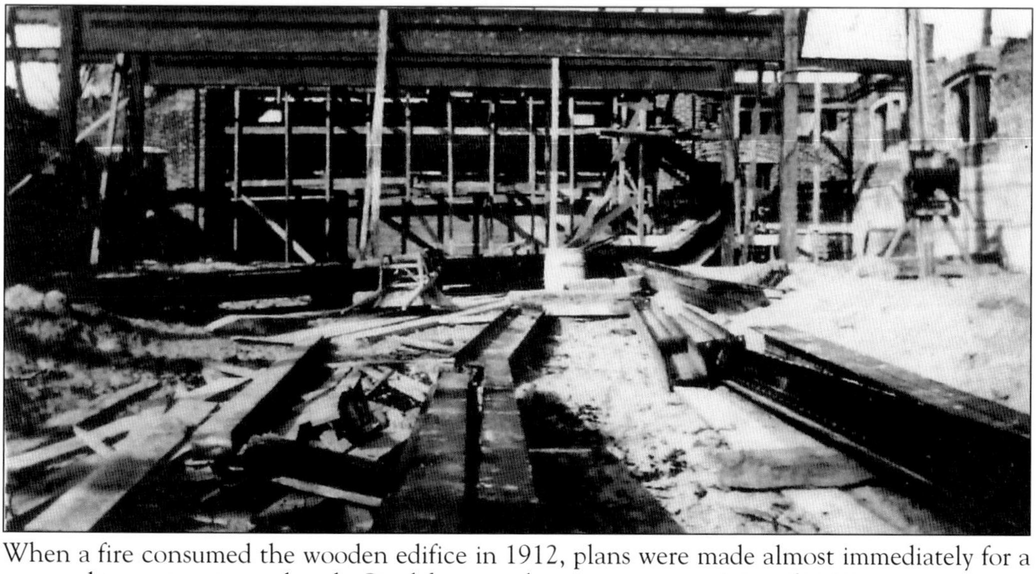

When a fire consumed the wooden edifice in 1912, plans were made almost immediately for a new and imposing stone church. Steel framework was going up in May of 1913.

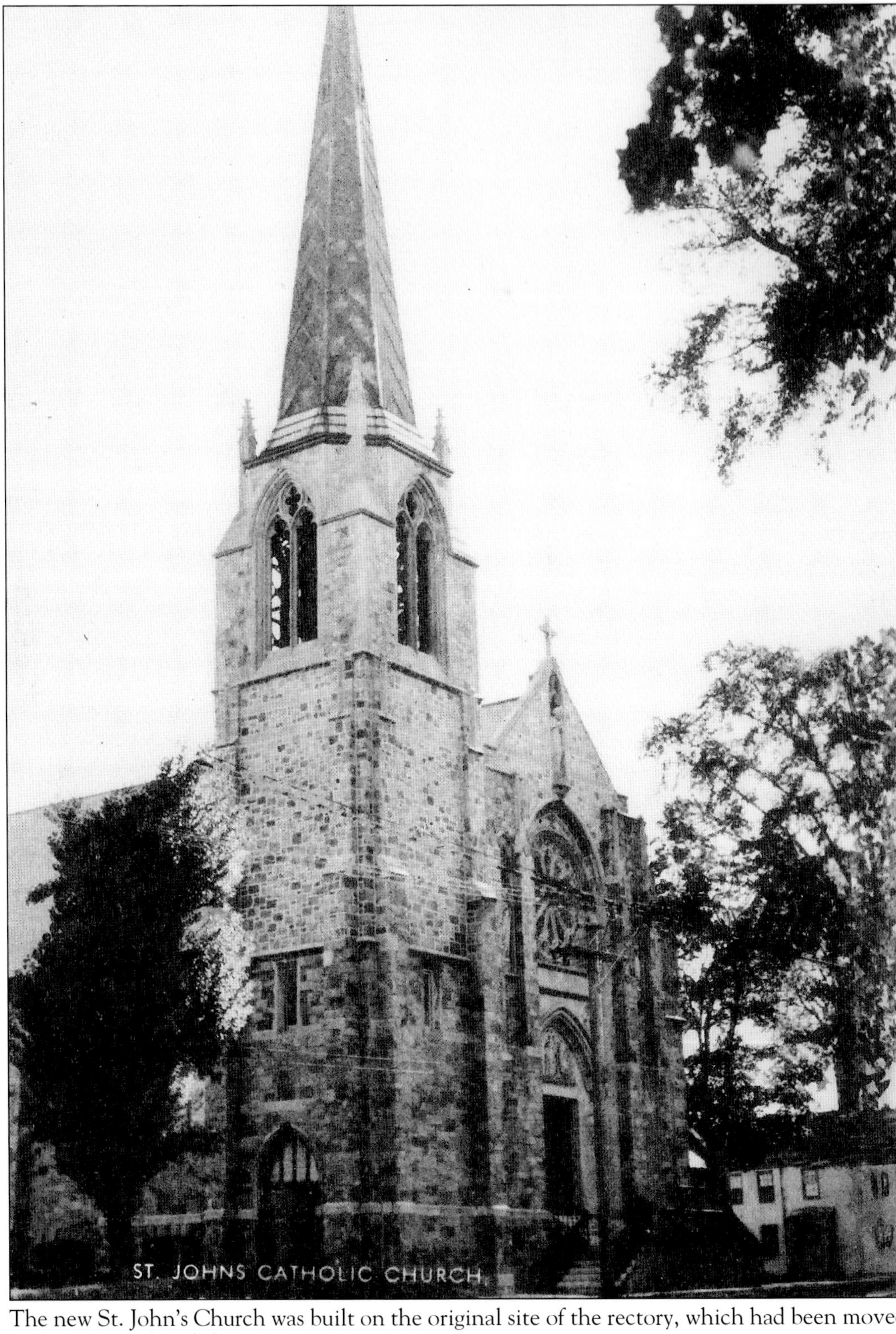

The new St. John's Church was built on the original site of the rectory, which had been moved to the former church lot.

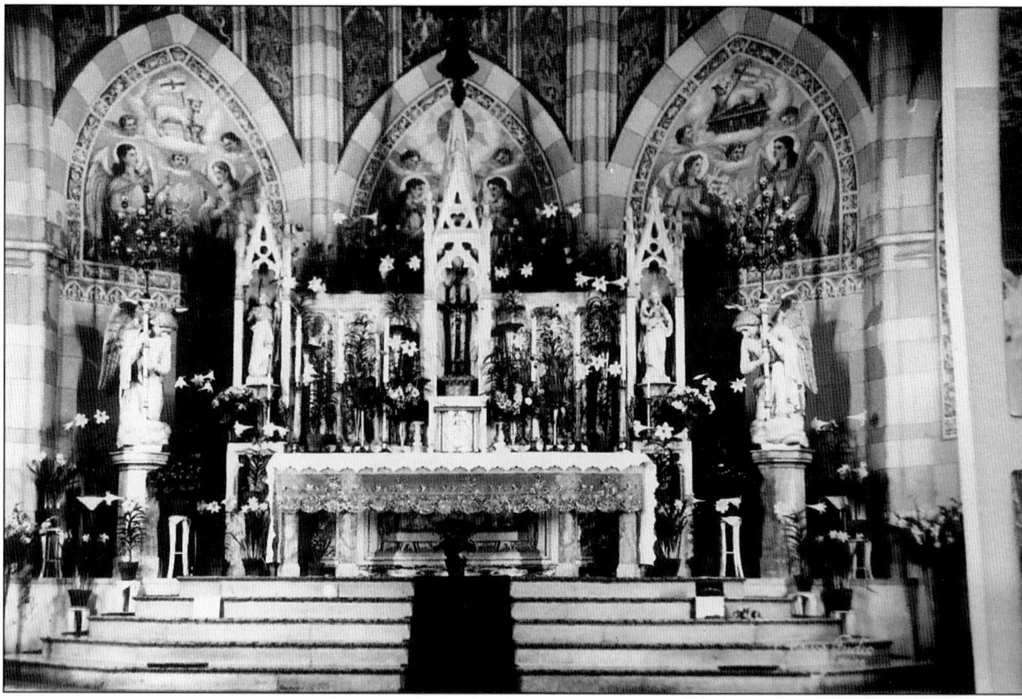

Completion took some fifteen years, both because early energies were diverted to the concurrent construction of a new parochial school and because St. John's interior was especially elaborate.

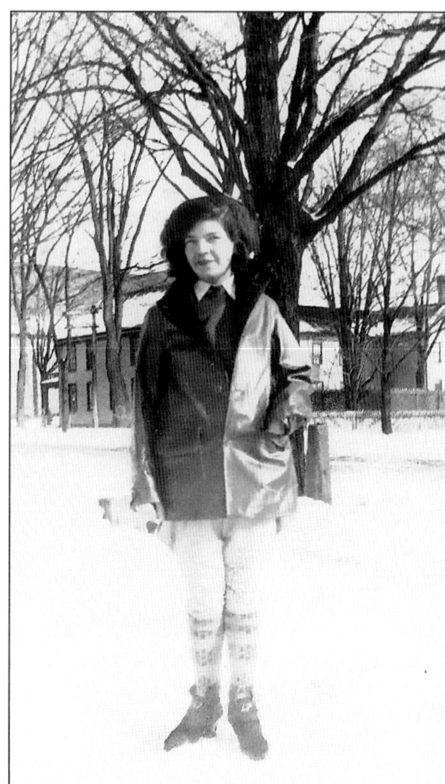

The parochial school was taught by Ursuline nuns, who occupied the former Captain P.C. Merryman home on Pleasant Street, shown here behind "Laura" Black.

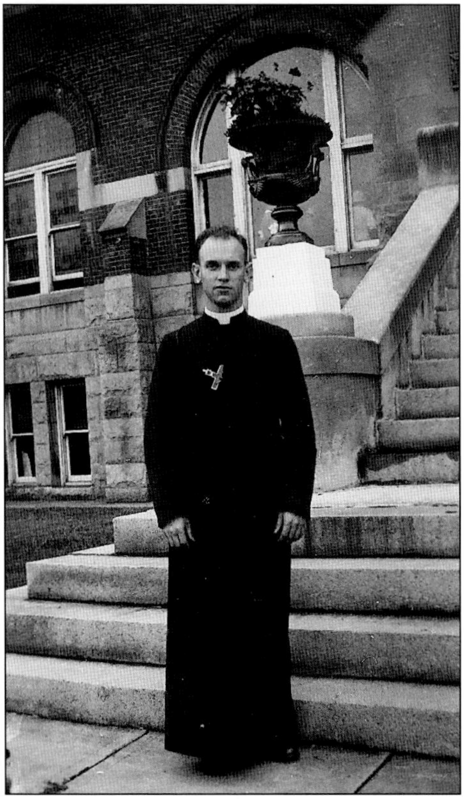

Joseph Lamarre, of Topsham, the third local youth to become a priest in the Marist order, later devoted his life to missionary work in the Solomon Islands.

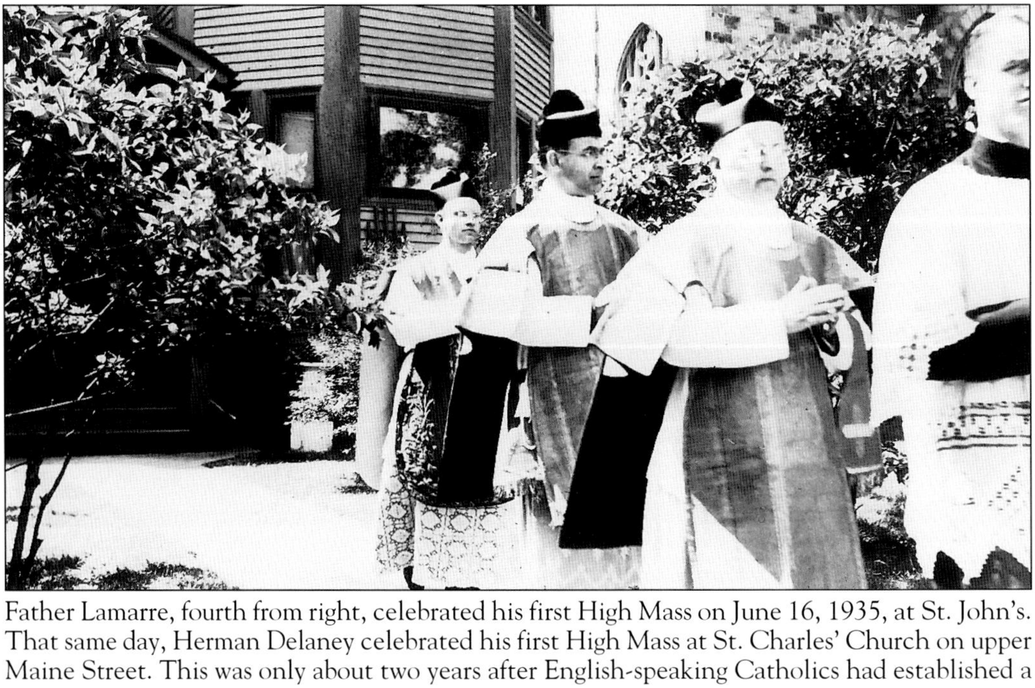

Father Lamarre, fourth from right, celebrated his first High Mass on June 16, 1935, at St. John's. That same day, Herman Delaney celebrated his first High Mass at St. Charles' Church on upper Maine Street. This was only about two years after English-speaking Catholics had established a separate congregation.

Thirteen

Bowdoin

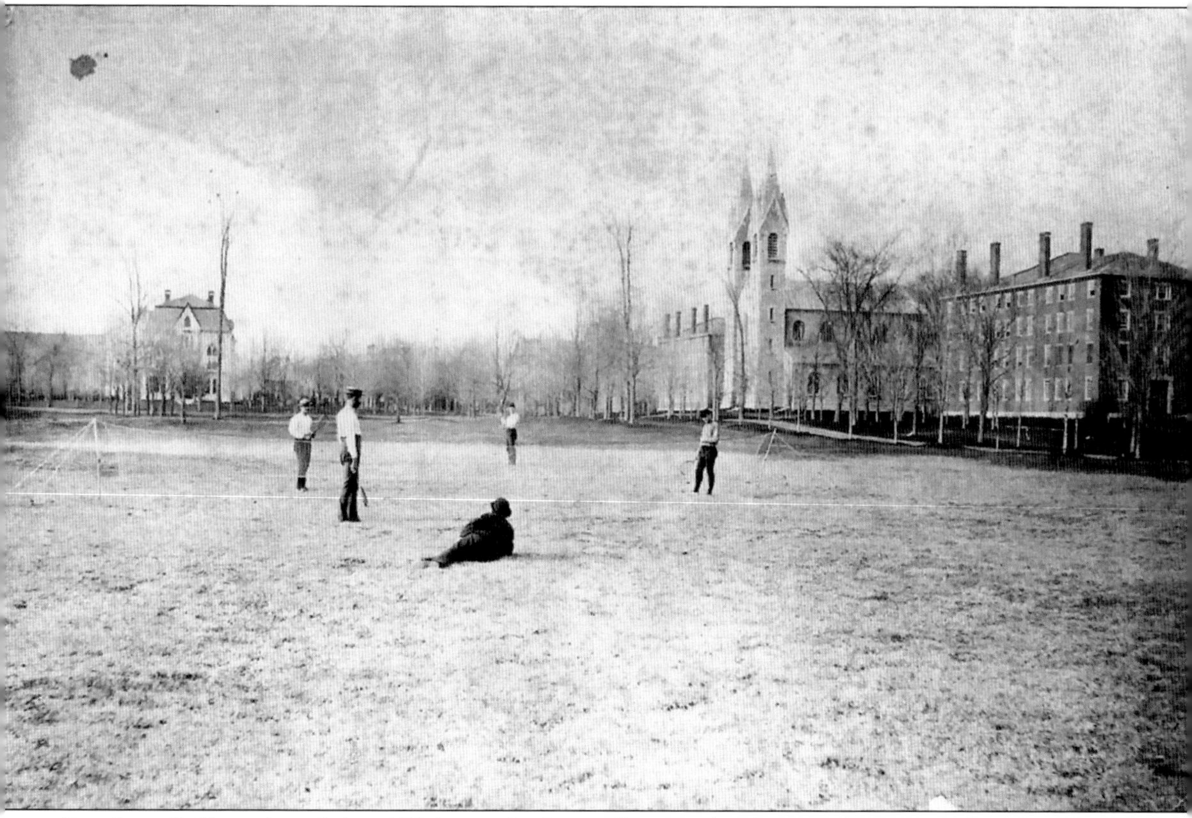

Bowdoin College, founded in 1794, was the first college in the district of Maine. A lawn tennis game of 1887 or 1888 shows how open the college green was then. In the left background are the First Parish Church (1846) and Memorial Hall (1882). Clearly seen on the other side, right to left, are Appleton Hall (1843), the Chapel (1855), and Maine Hall (1837). Winthrop Hall (1822), Adams Hall, and Massachusetts Hall (1802) can barely be seen through the trees.

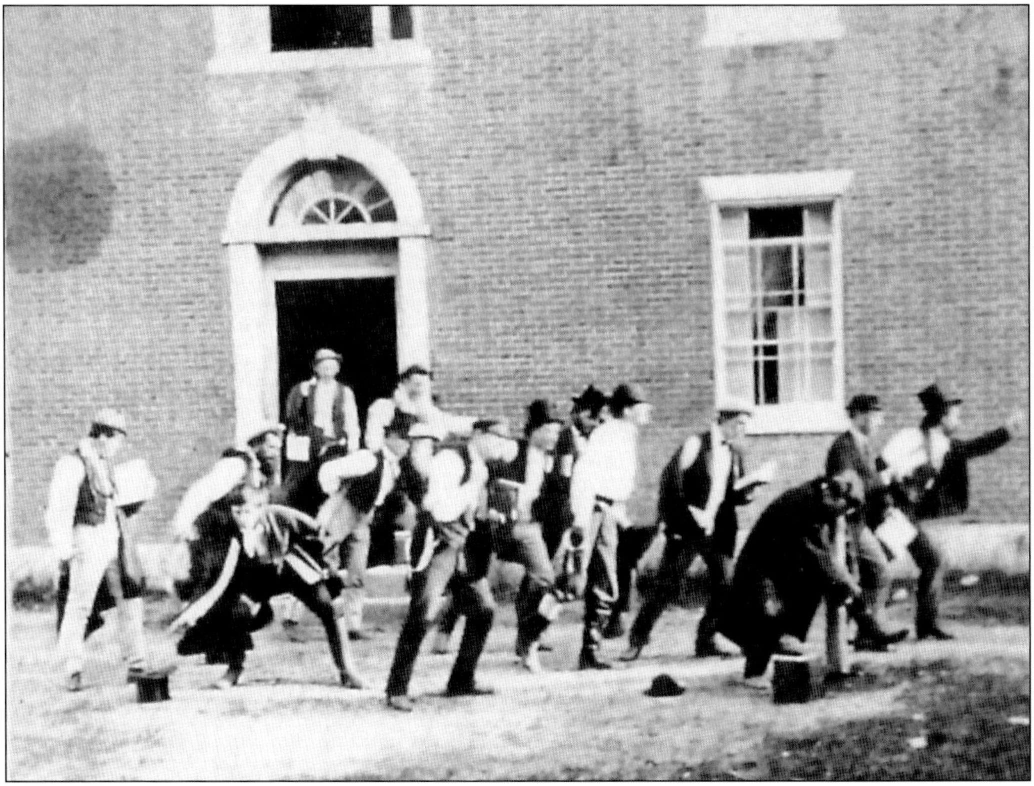

A group of 1870s-era students appear to be staging theatrics by a door to Winthrop residence hall.

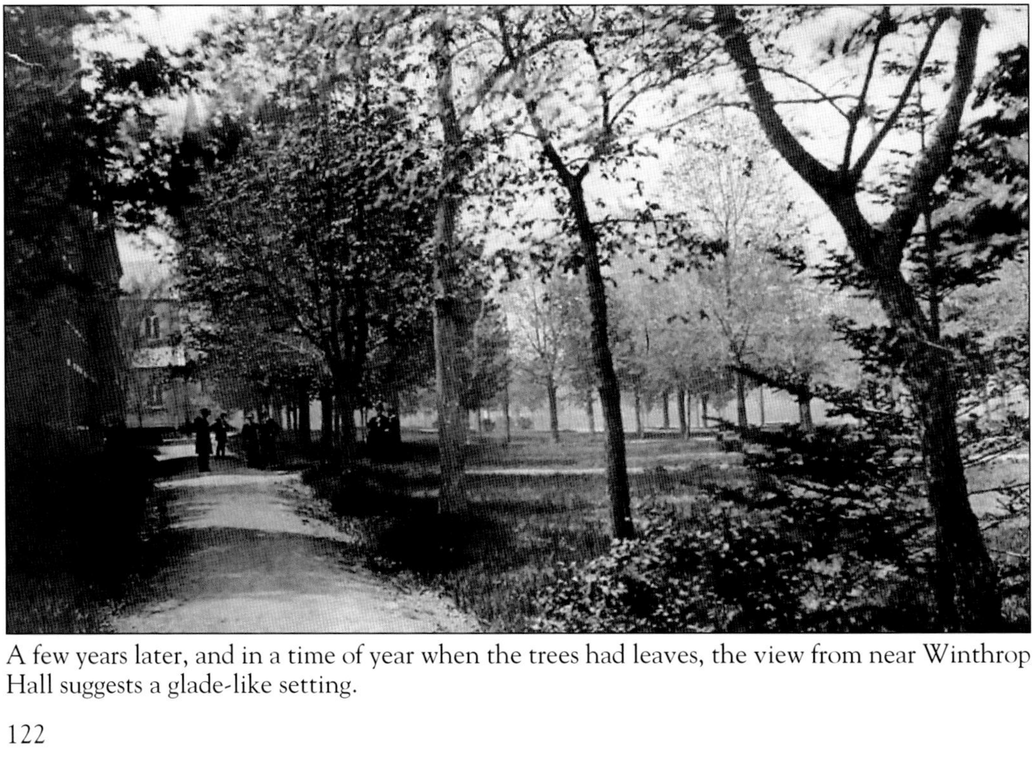

A few years later, and in a time of year when the trees had leaves, the view from near Winthrop Hall suggests a glade-like setting.

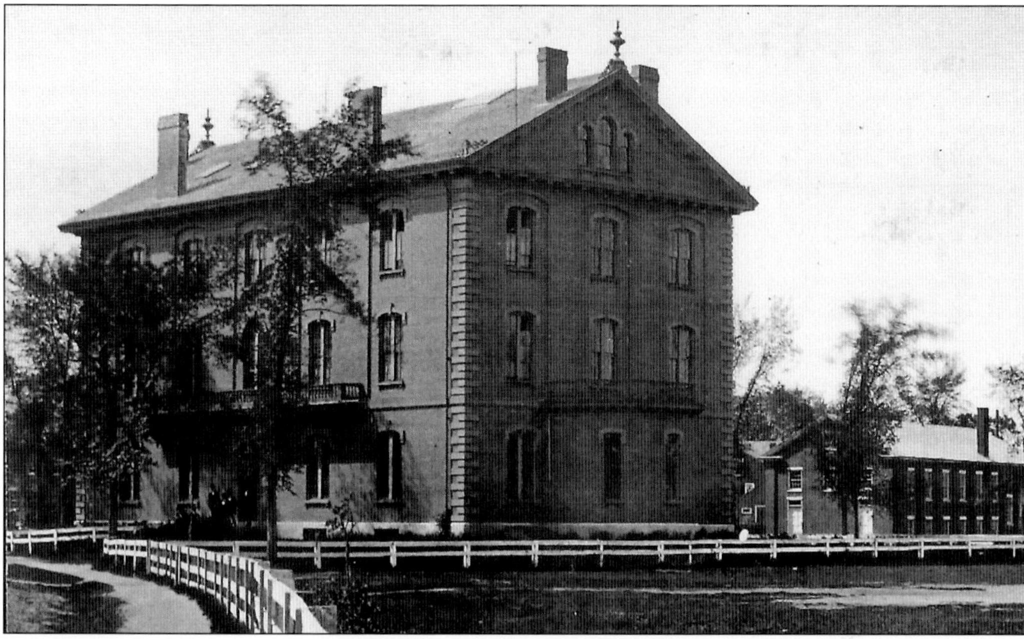

In 1861 Seth Adams Hall was built on a corner of the Delta to hold the Medical School of Maine, located at Bowdoin. Many men educated there served as local doctors. The building to the left was erected as a Commons and became the carpentry shop by the 1890s, but housed the chemistry labs at the time of the photo.

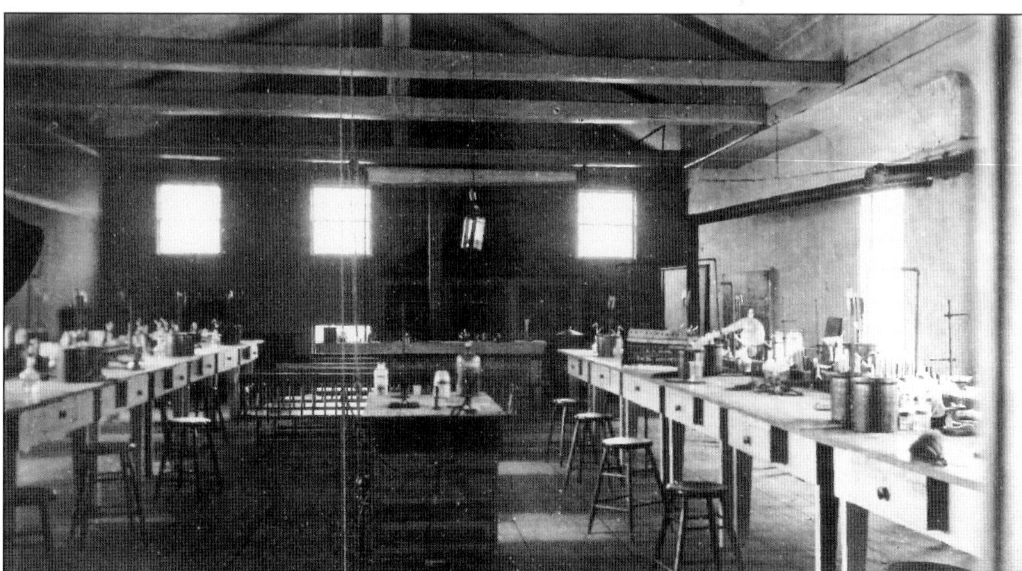

A college laboratory in the rear of the old Commons appears quite spartan.

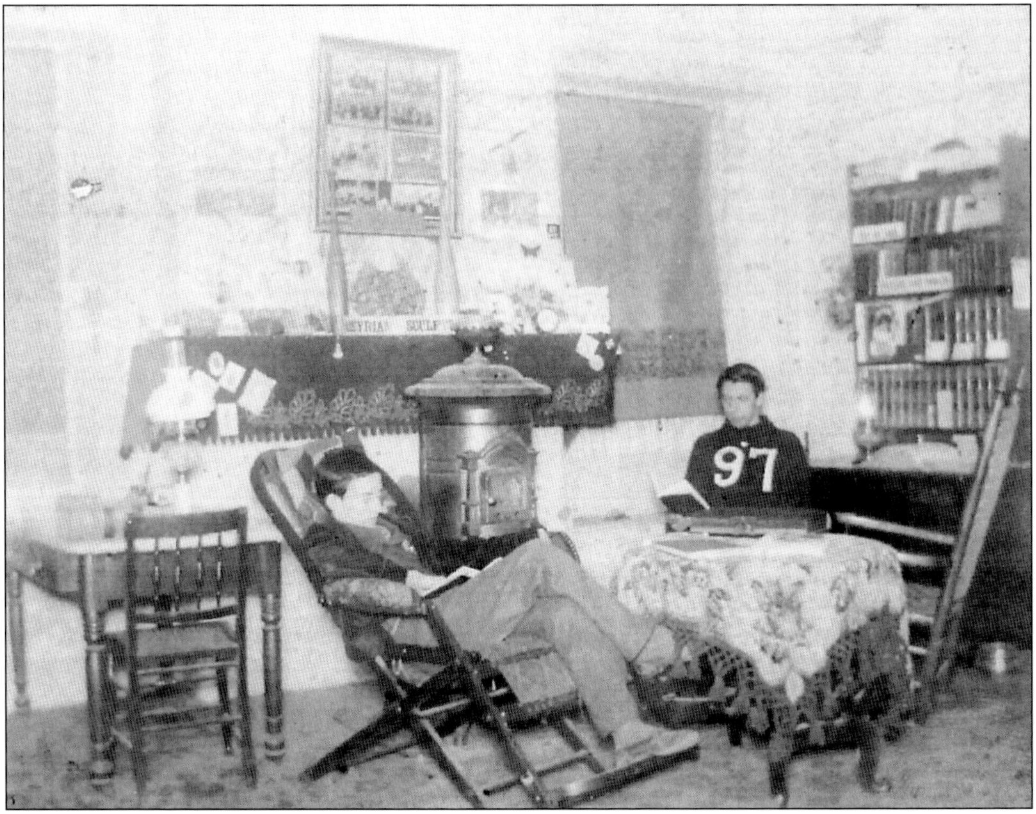

Room 20, North Winthrop Hall, in December of 1894 housed sophomores J.W. Hewett and R.W. Smith. Study rooms were heated by individual stoves set in front of what had been fireplaces.

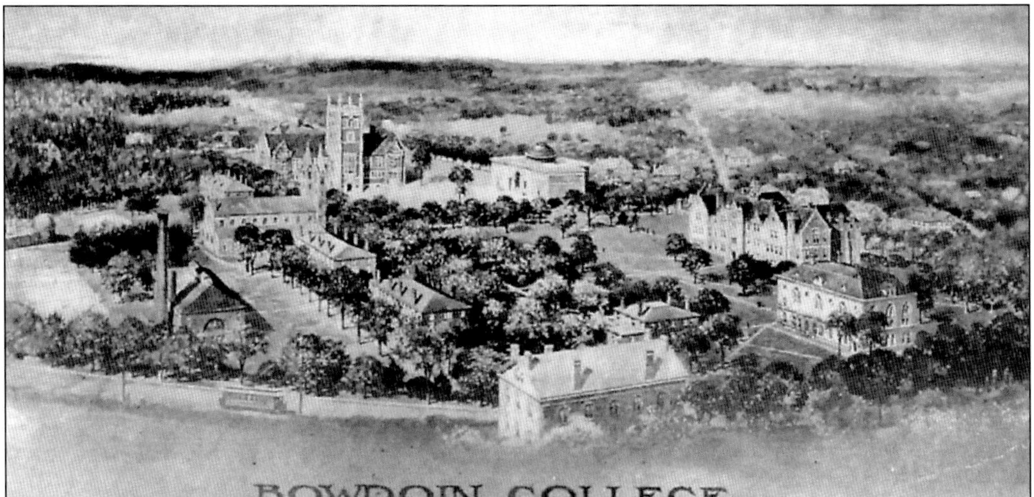

By 1910, a birds-eye sketch of the campus showed three new structures. The Searles Science Building of 1894 was on the right with the Walker Art Gallery, also built in 1894, beyond it; both near Maine Street Hubbard Hall (the new library of 1903) was erected at the end of the green. The trolley is on the section of Harpswell Street discontinued in 1948.

Fourteen

At Home

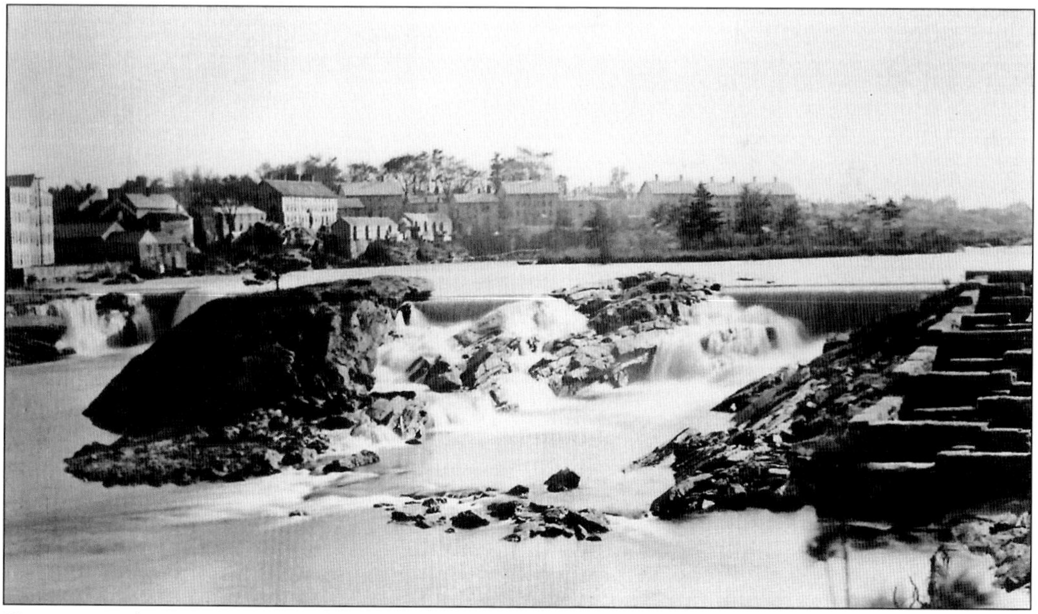

Housing in the two towns took many forms. Tenements erected along Mill and Cabot Streets by the Cabot Mill were variously described as "enough to make a Christian swear" by a crusading editor and as especially clean and shiny by a deliveryman. Brunswick in general lacked good sewerage and water supply, but the crowded conditions in the tenements exacerbated all problems.

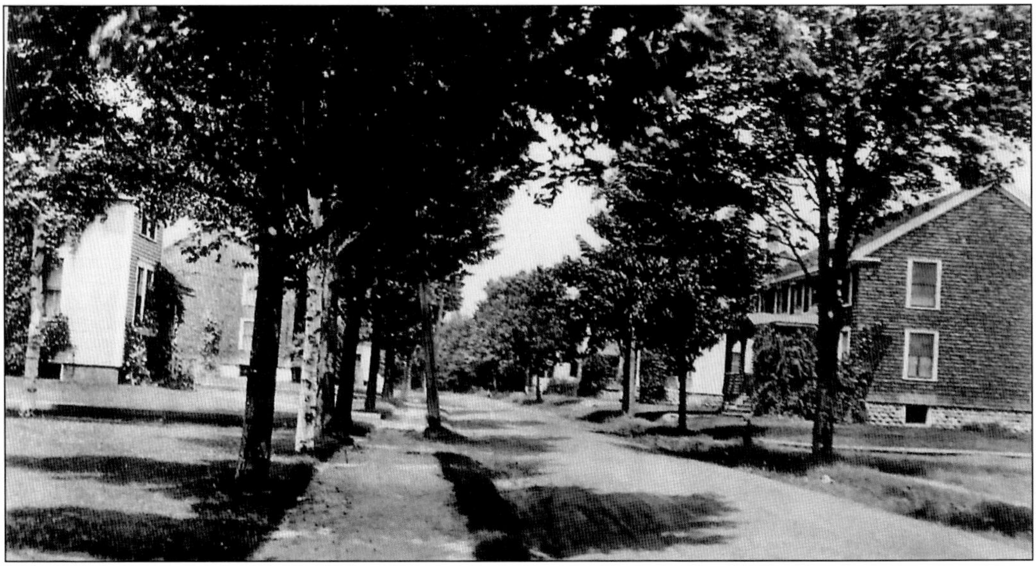

Pejepscot had more space for the mill houses. Some company housing, like the homes above, were of a good size.

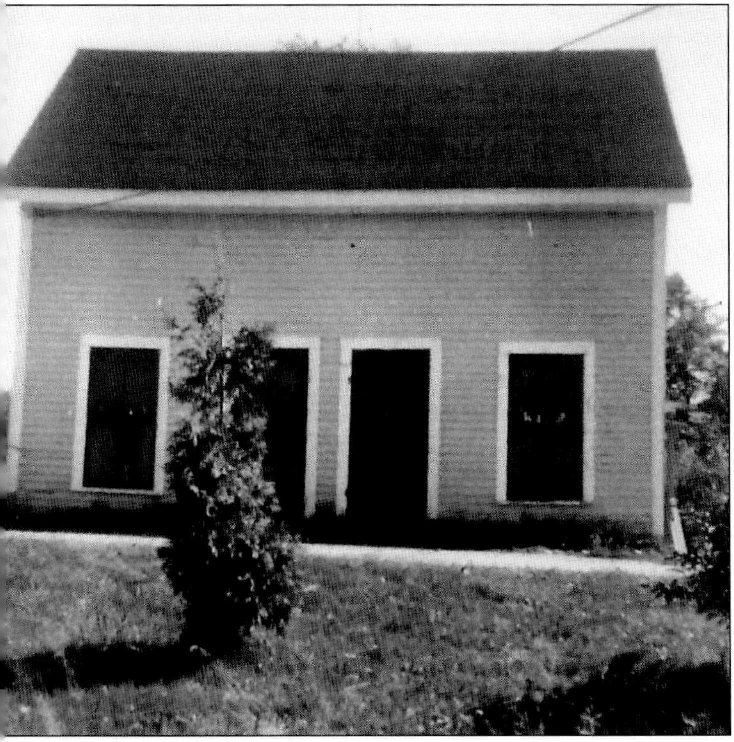

The mill housing also included two-family homes with three rooms per family. Advantages included a low rent of $4.50 per month and space for a garden. Families raised eight or ten children in these quarters, and some took in boarders, too.

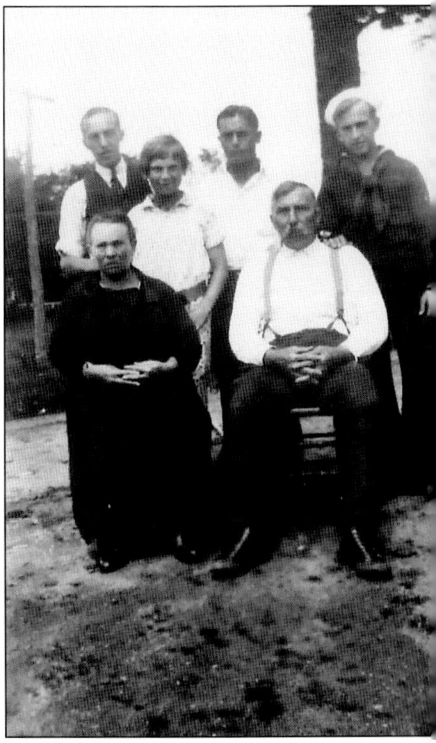

Residents of half of such a house were Anna and Joseph Obrin, shown about 1930 with four of their children: Joe, Susie, John, and Mike (wearing John's uniform).

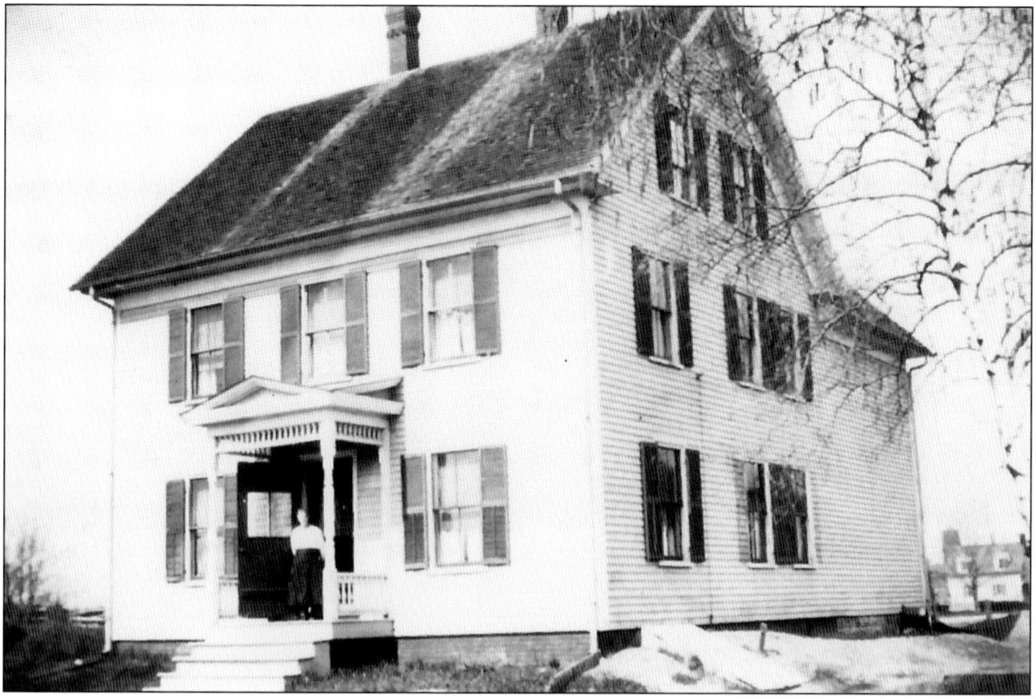

Many families left the tenements and the mills behind. Hermine Bouchard Morin (in doorway) lost her millworker father in a flood-related accident. She married a railroad man and they settled in this house on Prospect Street, Topsham Heights, an area also home to the millworkers for whom the "swinging bridge" was built.

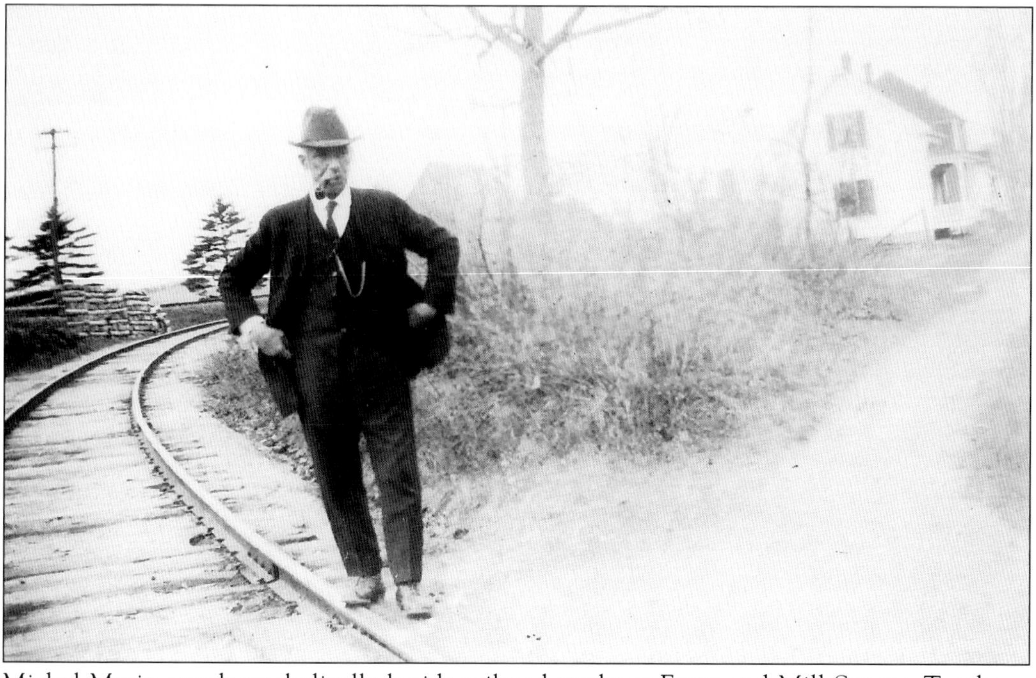

Michel Morin stands symbolically beside railroad tracks at Front and Mill Streets, Topsham, not far from his home. The tracks served the power station at the Topsham end of the falls.

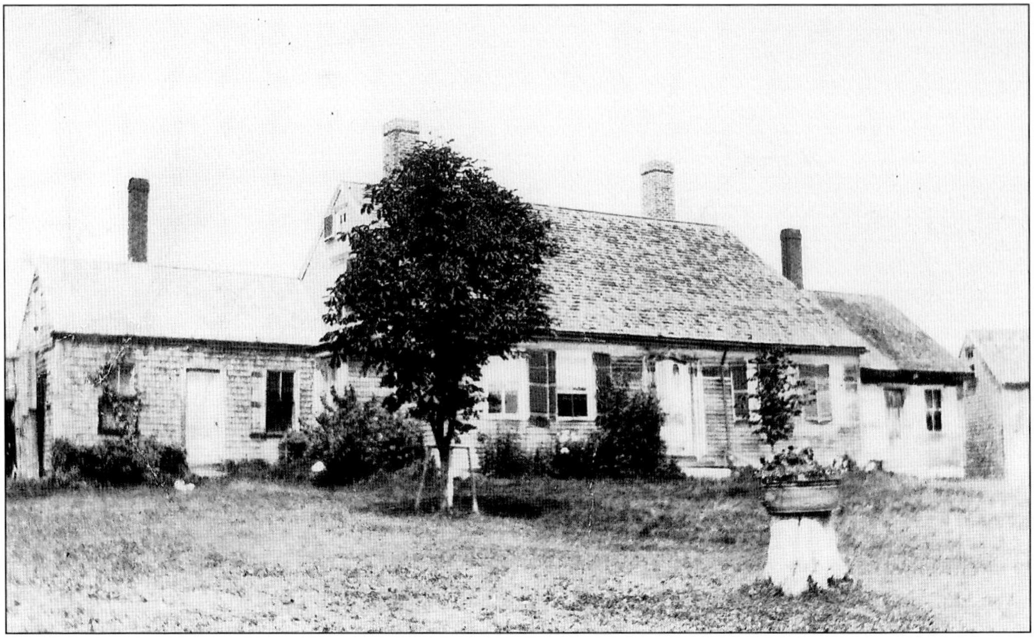

A farmhouse in Topsham, near the Bowdoinham line, had more extensive outbuildings than can be seen here.

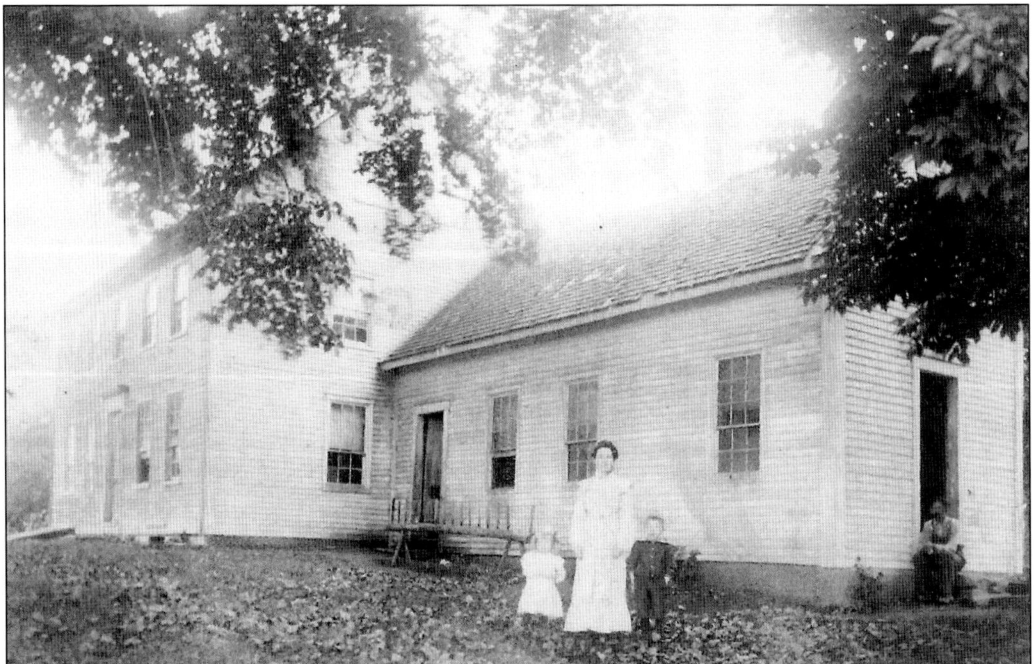

A few miles closer to the village, Florence, Ina, Albion, and Maurice Luce posed before their larger farmhouse, *c.* 1903.

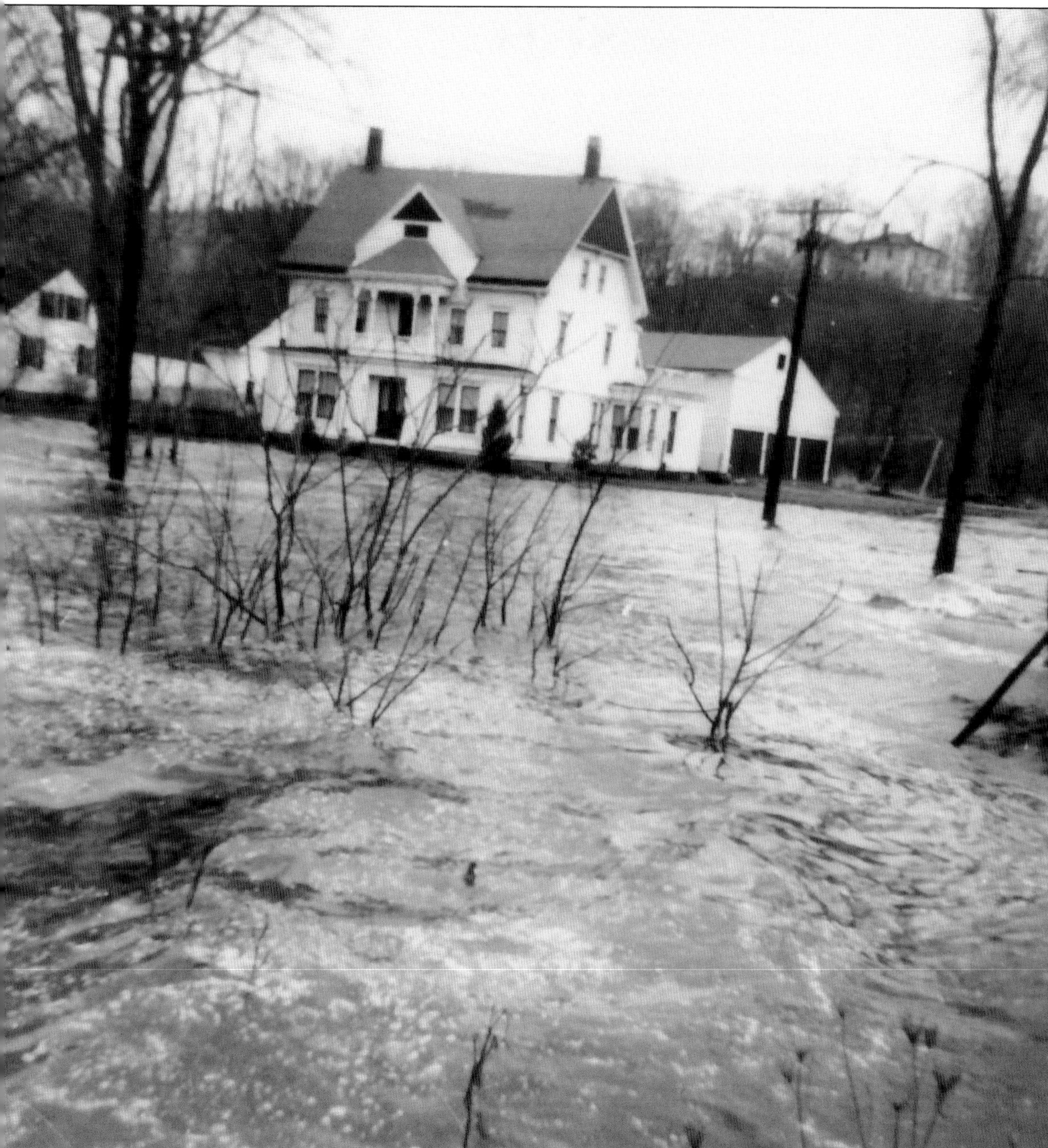

In the late nineteenth century, a few homes on Topsham's Summer Street were replaced or remodelled. Flood waters came close in 1953.

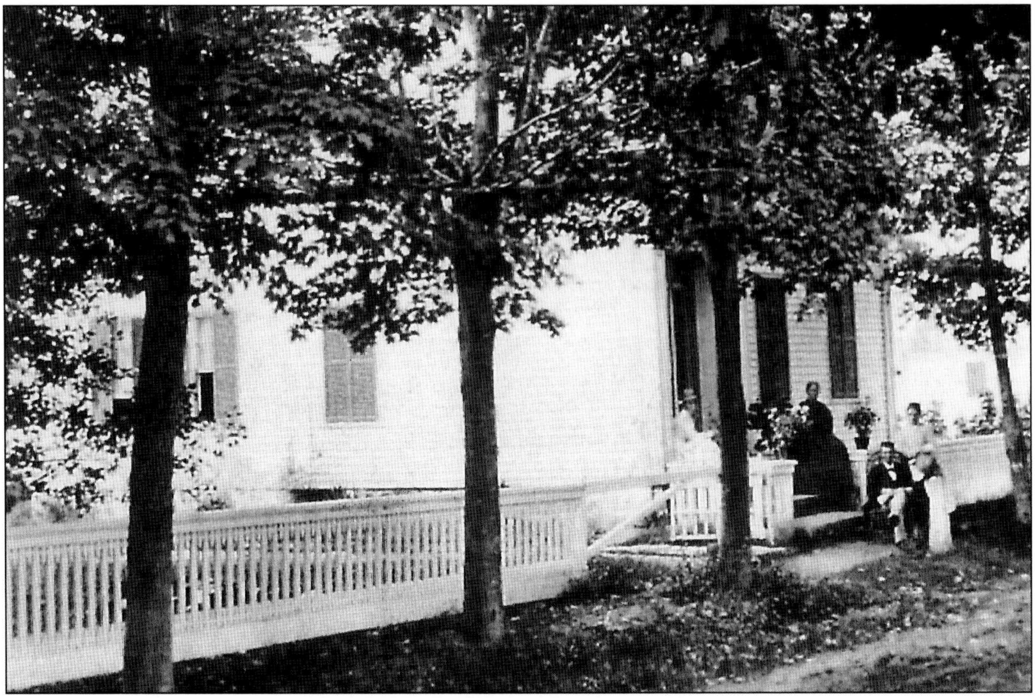

Brunswick town homes came in different sizes, like these unidentified houses "caught" by a local photographer in the 1870s. Four individuals on one front step appear to have a good yard with a garden beyond the fence, even if the house is fairly small.

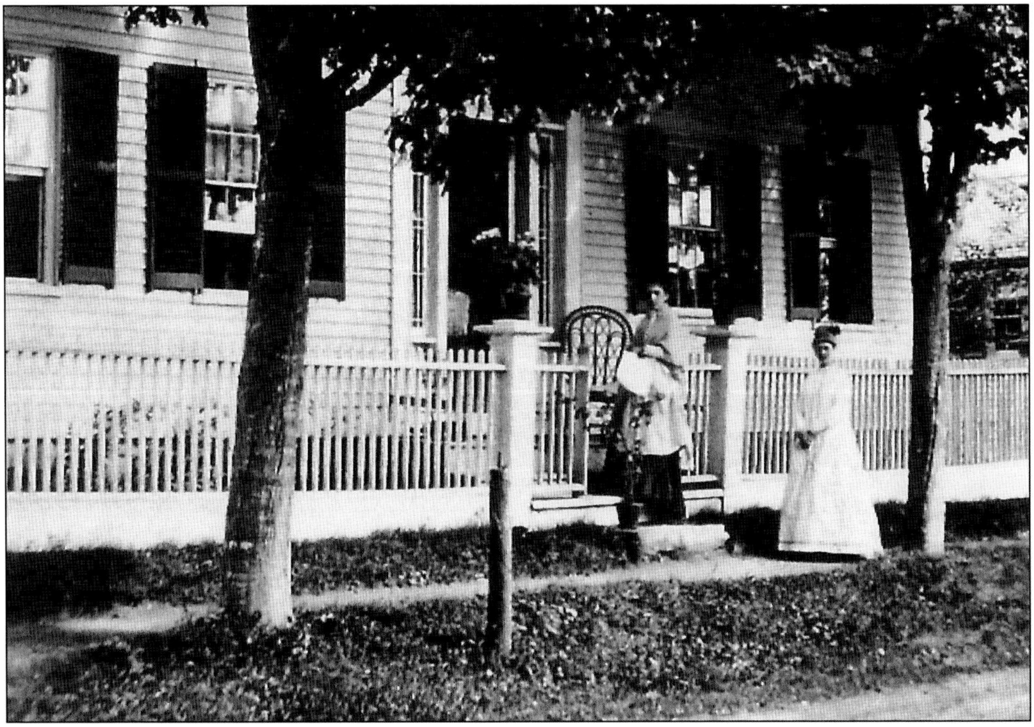

A somewhat larger residence apparently had but two female occupants.

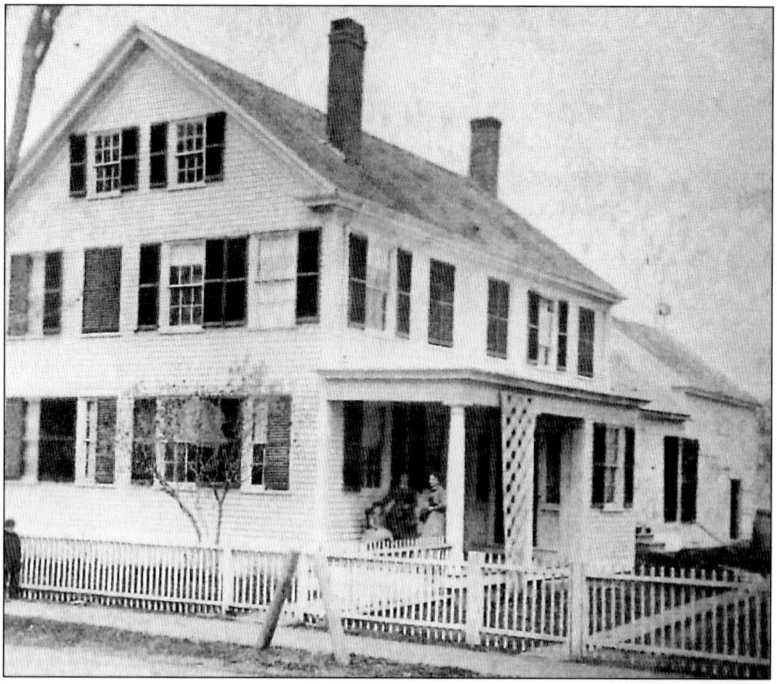

The Benjamin Furbish house on O'Brien (later Cumberland) Street was one of the moderately large homes—comfortable, but not grand—which lined the village streets.

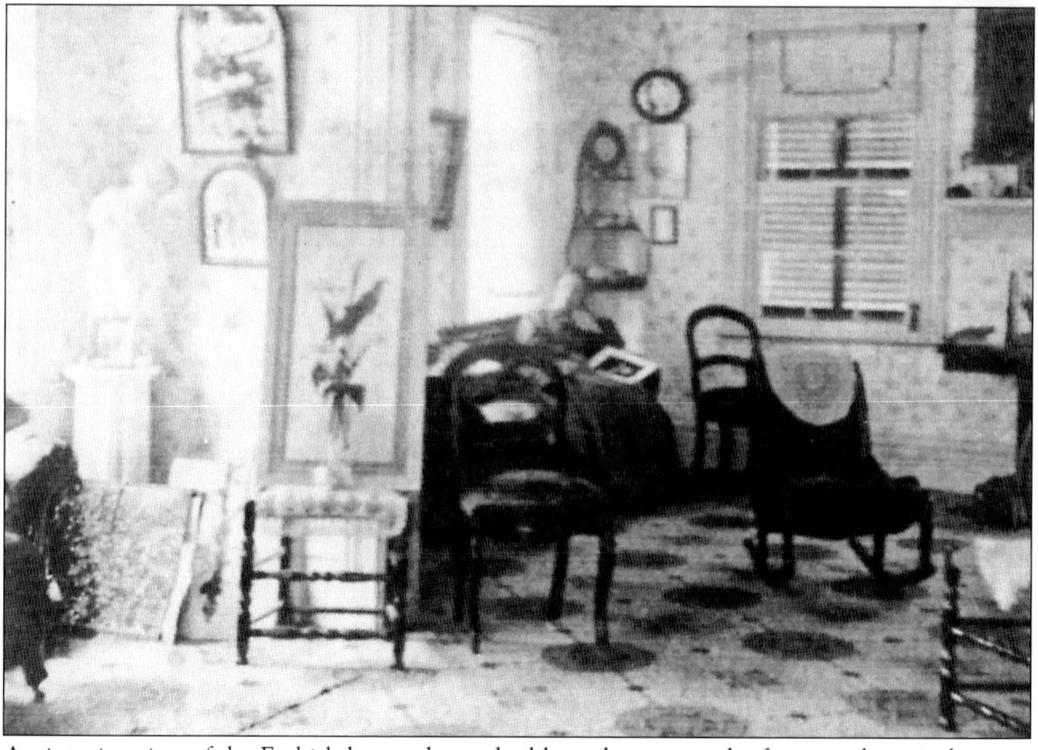

An interior view of the Furbish house shows double parlors across the front, with typical corner blocks in the woodwork. Note the wall-to-wall carpeting and the many types of art work on display. One suspects that the prominently displayed floral pictures were by the daughter of the house.

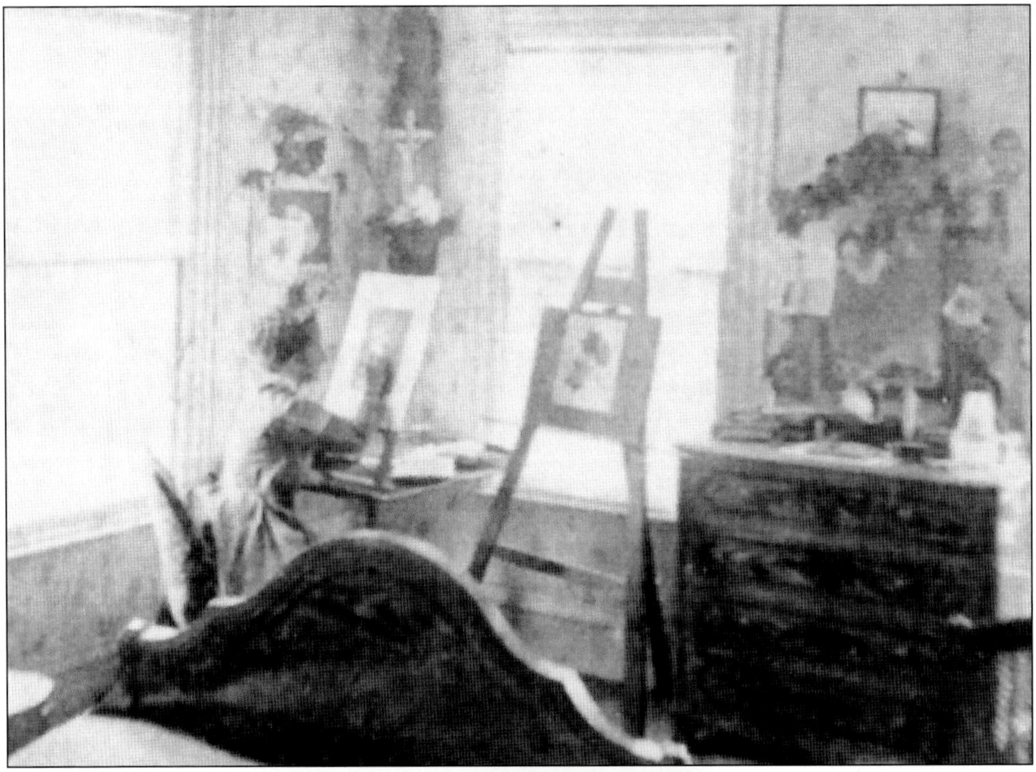

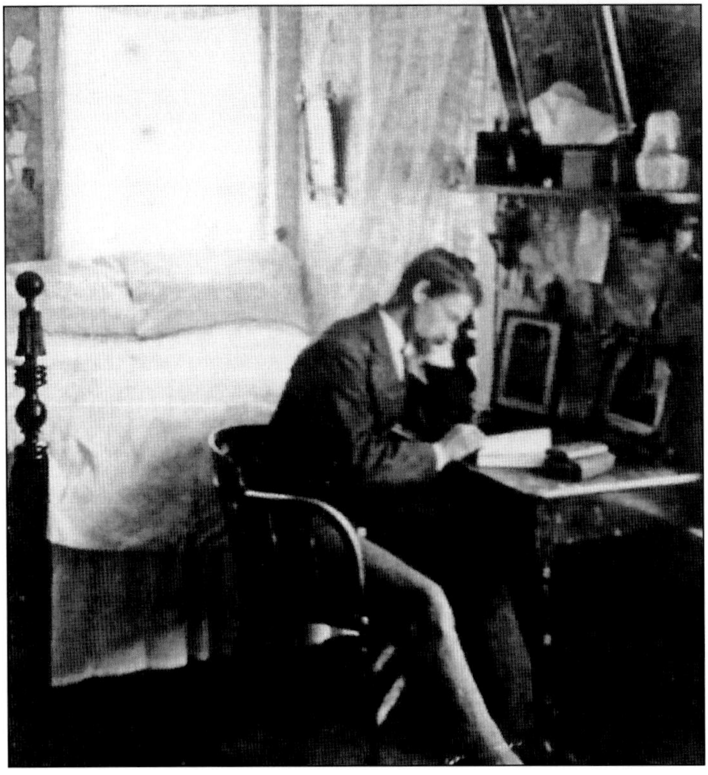

Kate Furbish, shown here at her easel, was a botanist who made paintings of her discoveries; one of these, the rare "Furbish lousewort," has been credited with preventing the construction of a hydroelectric dam in northern Maine. The painted bedroom set was in vogue at the time.

Frank (or was it John?) Furbish had heavier, more masculine, furniture in his room.

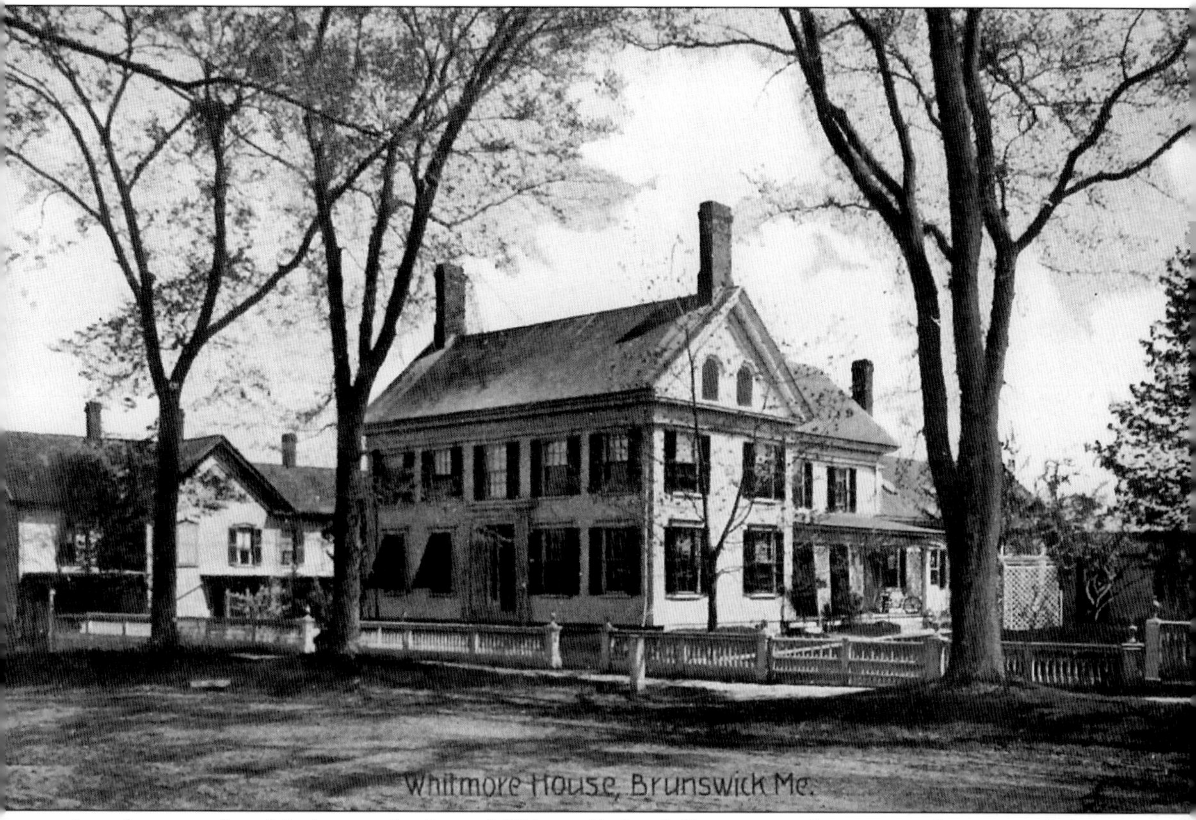

Another comfortable house, built in 1804 on Federal Street, was known at the turn of the century as the Whitmore House, after a former owner. However, when it became an inn during the twentieth century, it was given the name of an earlier tenant, Harriet Beecher Stowe, who wrote *Uncle Tom's Cabin* while living there.

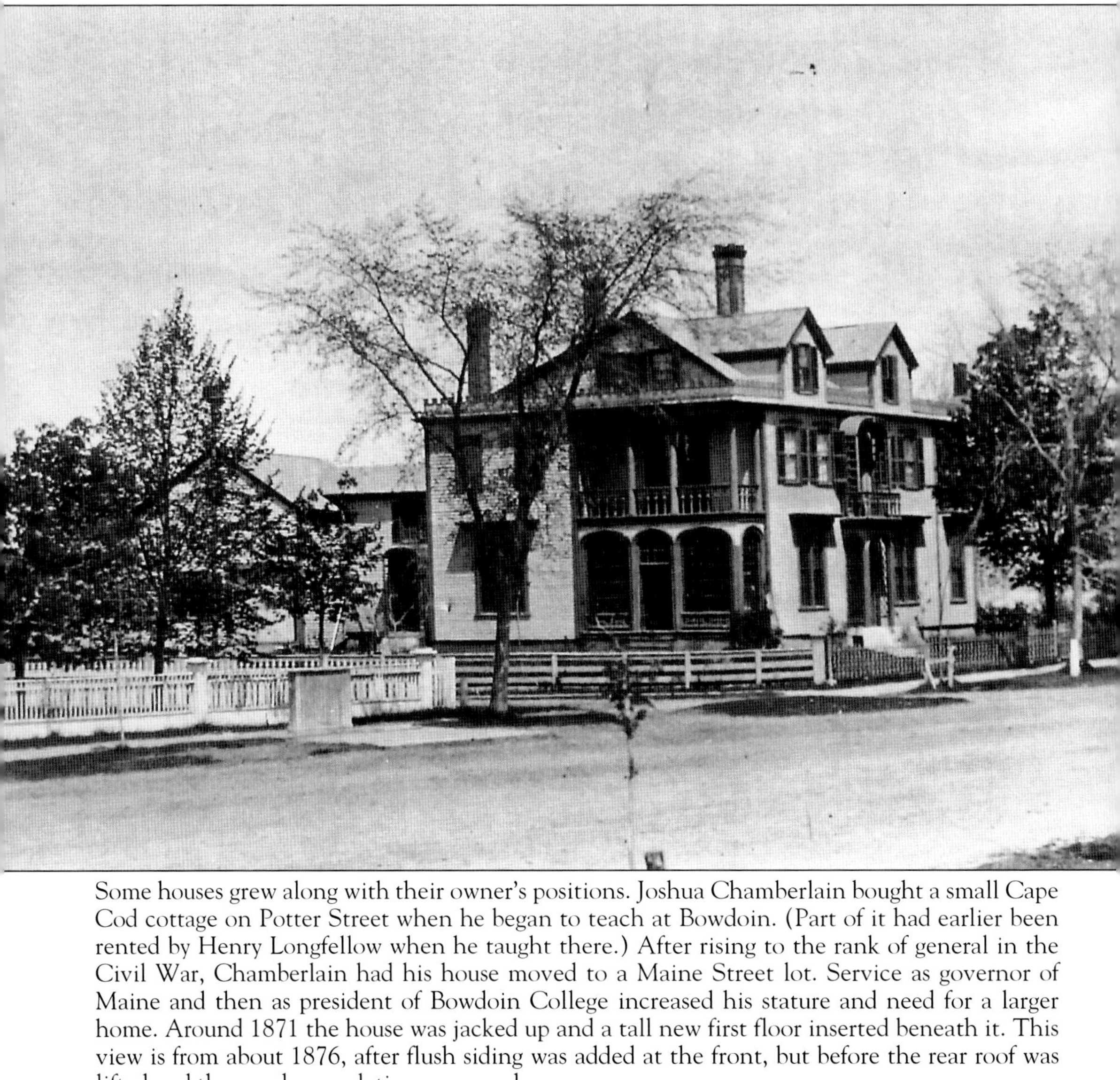

Some houses grew along with their owner's positions. Joshua Chamberlain bought a small Cape Cod cottage on Potter Street when he began to teach at Bowdoin. (Part of it had earlier been rented by Henry Longfellow when he taught there.) After rising to the rank of general in the Civil War, Chamberlain had his house moved to a Maine Street lot. Service as governor of Maine and then as president of Bowdoin College increased his stature and need for a larger home. Around 1871 the house was jacked up and a tall new first floor inserted beneath it. This view is from about 1876, after flush siding was added at the front, but before the rear roof was lifted and the porch crenelations removed.

Fifteen

The Younger Generation

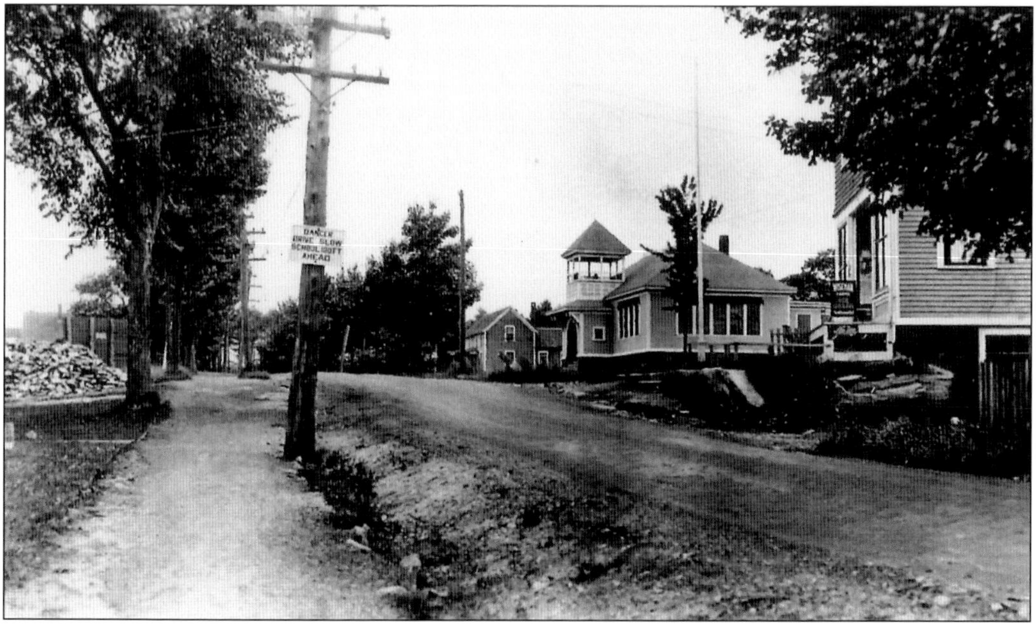

The growth of Pejepscot as a village with numerous children led to the closing of two small nearby schools and the construction in 1899 of a bigger schoolhouse there. The school, with another room added, stands near the village store (in the foreground).

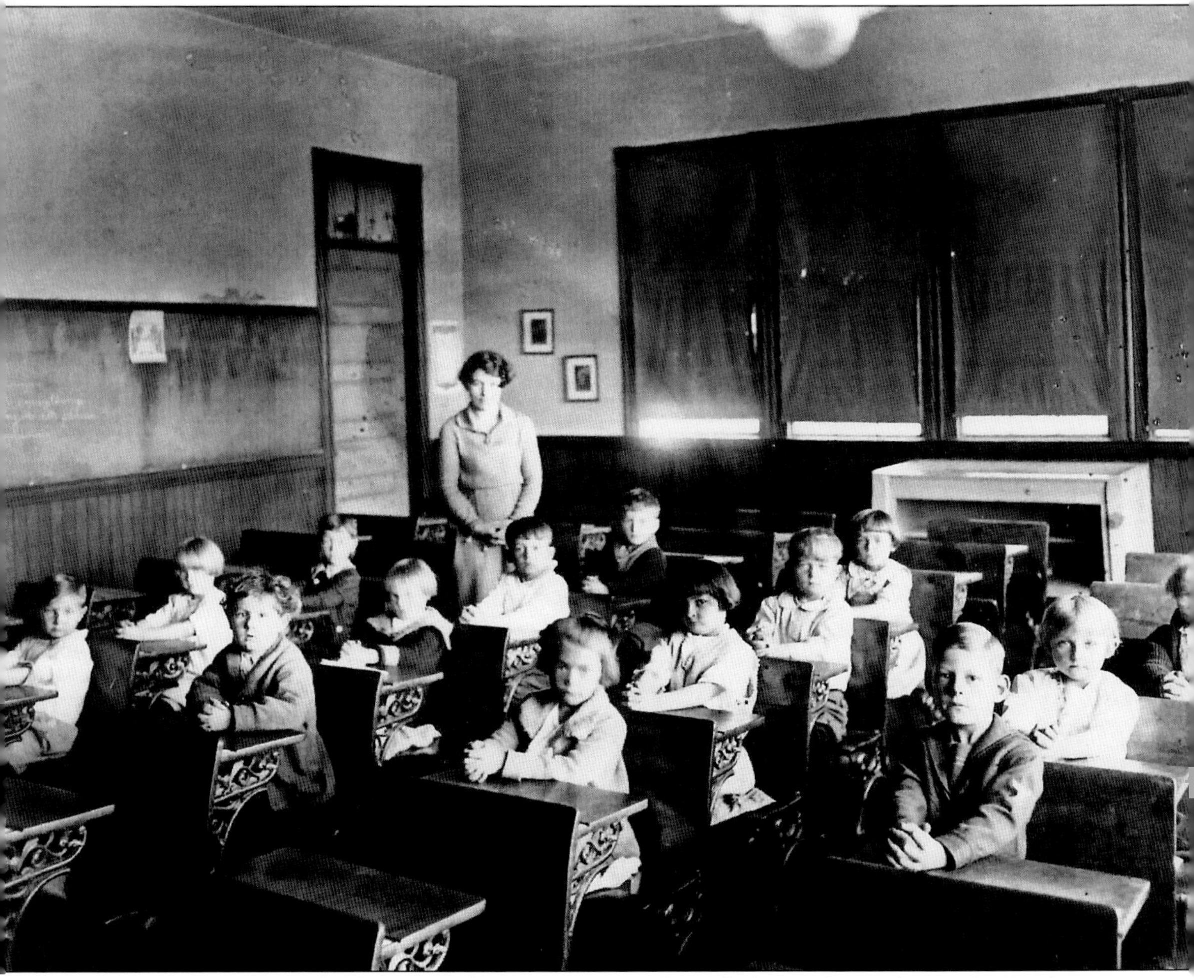

Pejepscot primary children pose for a portrait at their desks in the early 1920s. In the rear row are Arthur Vigeant, Ruth Ordway, Freddie Jones, and the teacher. Second and third in the next row are Mary Chonko and John Yambor. Second in the next row is Ruth Vigeant, with Lawrence Yambor and Josephine Tomko behind her. Closest to the camera are Junior Goodwin, Margaret Sheloske, and Mary Pagurko.

Opposite: An informal group of seventh and eighth grade girls at the Topsham Village School in the spring of 1925 includes Betty Patten on the right, with Rachel Patten next to her and Helen Sprague, second from left.

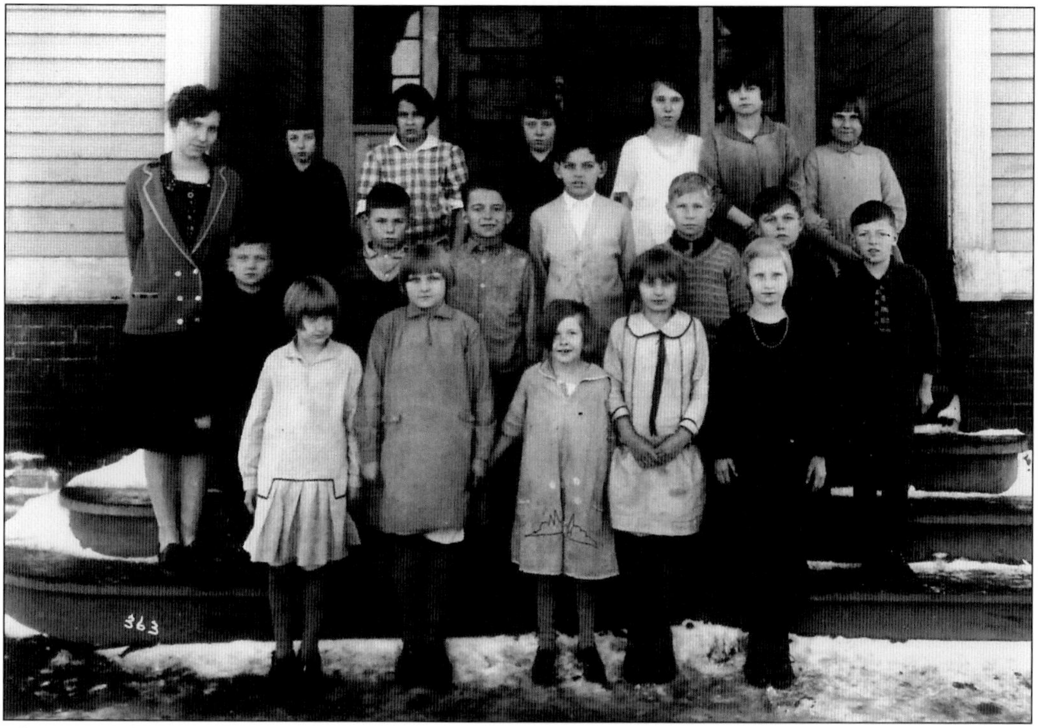

The upper three classes stand on the Pejepscot school steps in 1929-30 Front row: Ruth Ordway, Margaret Sheloske, Evelyn Atwood, Mary Pagurko, and Marguerite Noyes. Middle row: Mike Dobransky, George Yanok, John Yambor, Andrew Maynard, Earl Noyes, Lawrence Yambor, and Freddie Jones. Back row: Mrs. Roundie, Mary Atwood, Ruth Vigeant, Deborah Atwood, Elizabeth Yanok, Ella Hudak, and Susie Obrin.

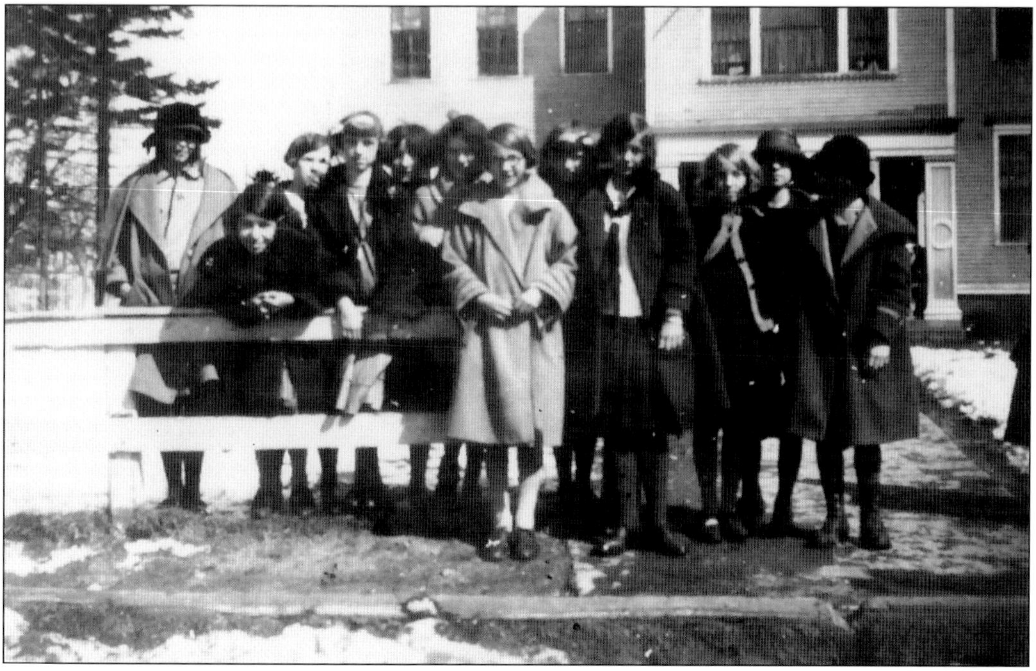

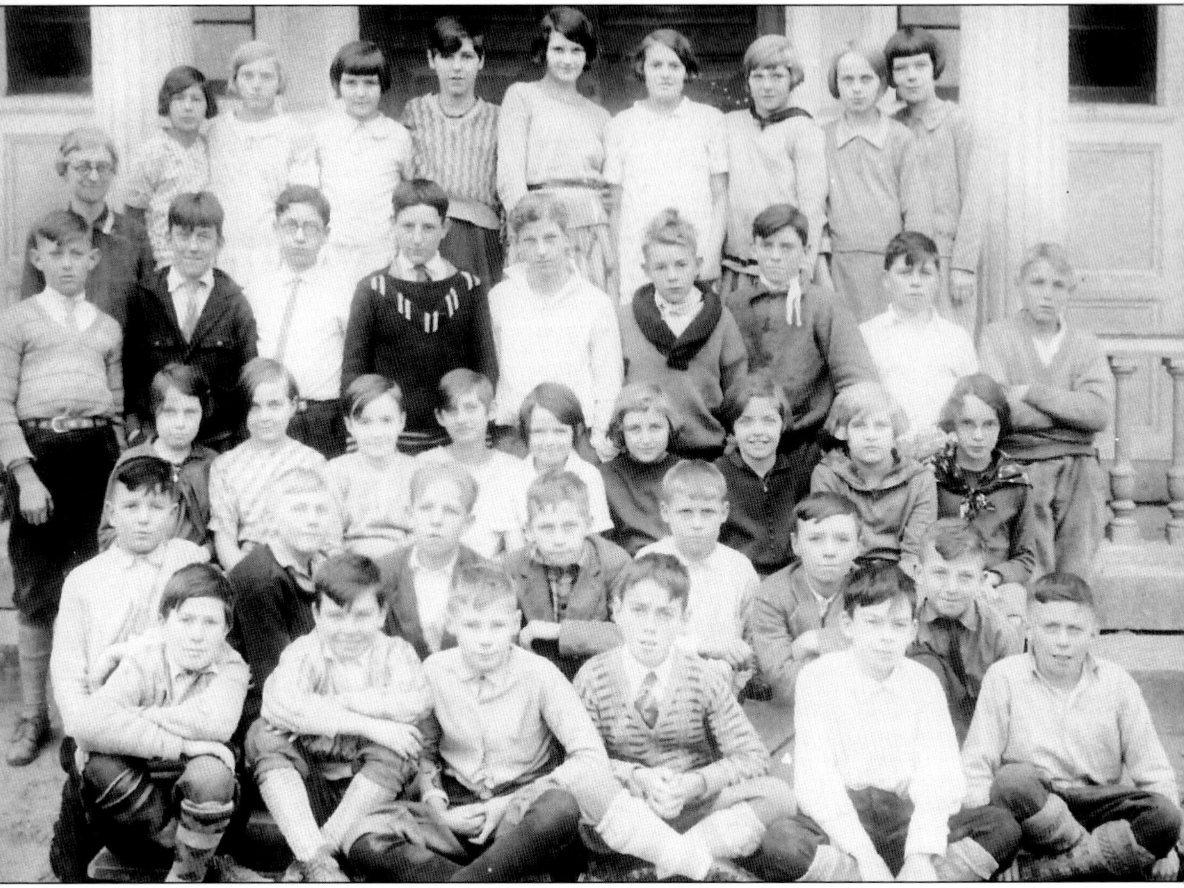

Whereas the names of children in the Pejepscot school in the 1920s testify to the ethnic diversity found there, students from the fifth and sixth grades of the Topsham Village School at about the same time included few who did not bear the "old" names. In the front row: Edward Hall, Merrill Harrington, Ernest Curtis, Elroy Haley, and William Cheetam. Second row: Linwood Stevens, Aubrey Thorne, Herman Douglas. Ralph White, Kenneth Wilson, Edward Fields, and William Clemons. Third row: Elizabeth Powers, Virginia Sprague, Josephine James, Betty White, Mary Scribner, Gertrude Cornish, Dorothy Carr, Etta McManus, and Dora Goud. Fourth row: Percy Hyde, Norman Marriner, Laurier Belanger, unknown (but remembered as French), Maxwell Everard, Dudley Olsen, John Ross, Maxwell Harrington, and Charles Johnson. Rear: Miss Edwards, Leona Elliott; Roberta Williams, Yvette Pickard, Josephine Douglas, Geraldine Hunter, Mary Hall, Barbara Rackley, Frances Merriman, and Ardell Morgan. The presence of only two with French surnames belies the numerous families of French extraction who had moved to town, most of whom sent their children across the river to the parochial school, where they would get religious training and continue to use the French language.

Sixteen

Other Activities

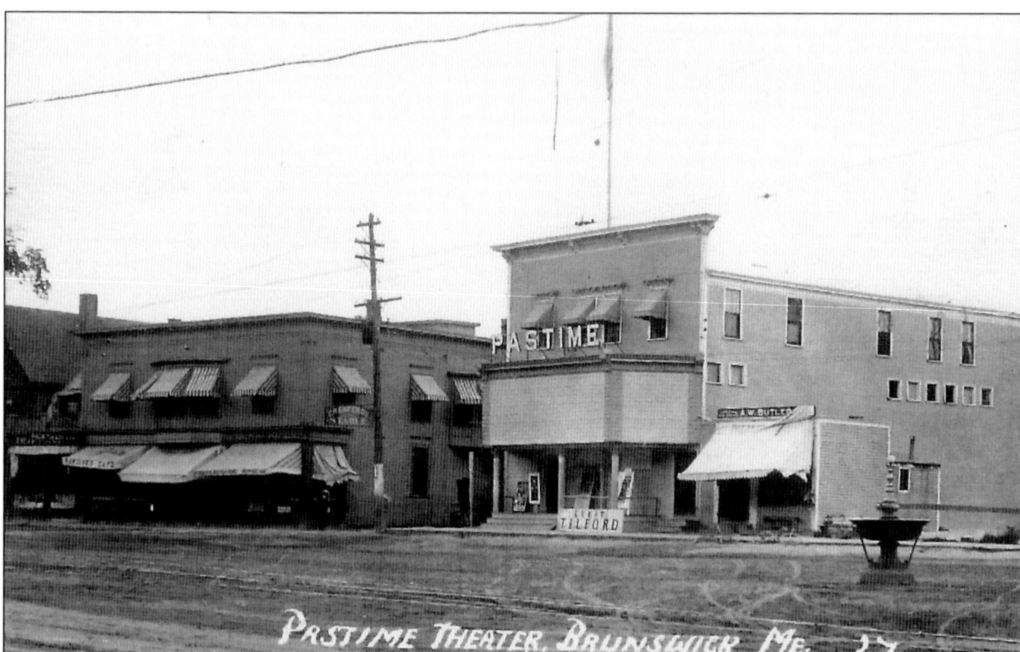

On March 3, 1908, Brunswick's first movie theater, the Pastime, opened on upper Maine Street. Offerings were continuous "Moving Pictures and Illustrated Songs" for three or four hours every afternoon or evening, costing 10 cents for adults or 5 cents for a child.

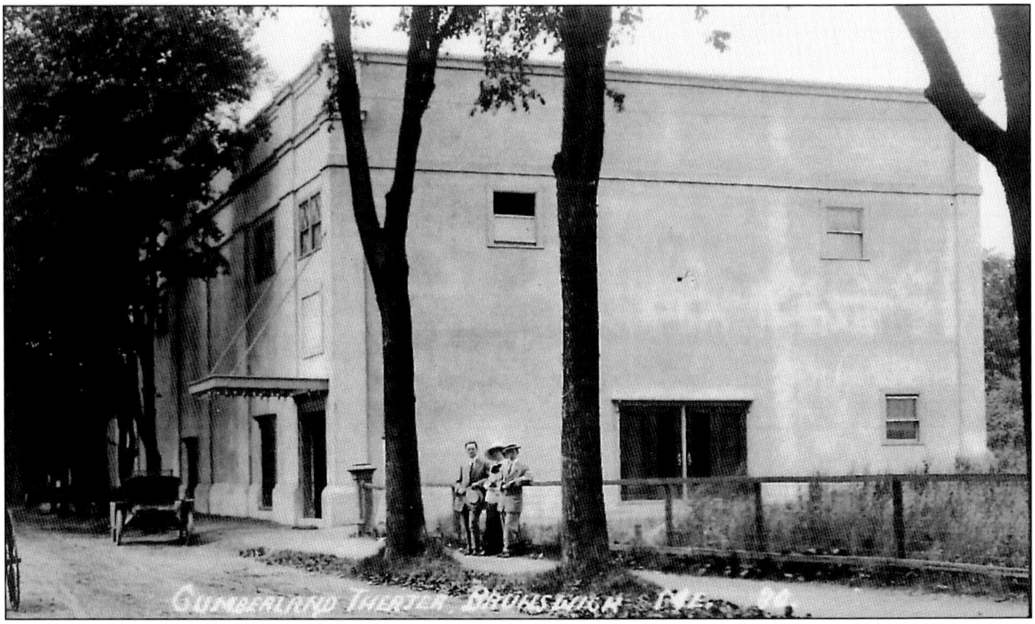

By 1915, the Pastime was showing the serialized "Exploits of Elaine" and had competition from the Cumberland Theater, on Cumberland Street, which offered serials and three- or five-reel dramas.

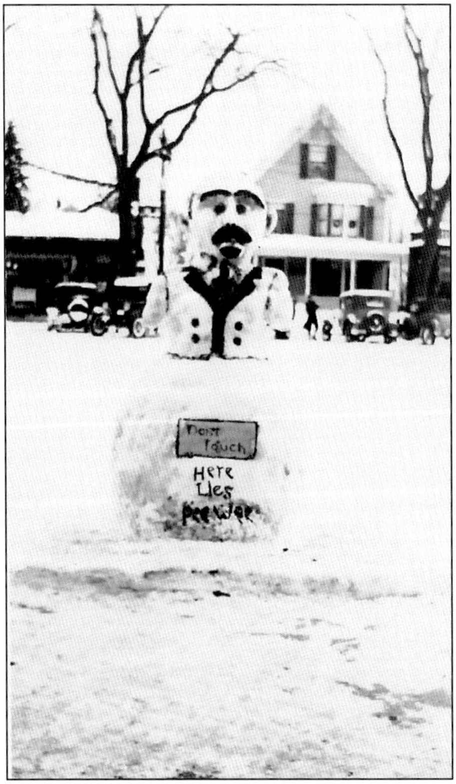

Recreation did not have to be costly: Nicholis Adami, employed at Kennebec Fruit, built an elaborate snowman, with parts colored by show-card ink, in front of the store for the New Year in 1922.

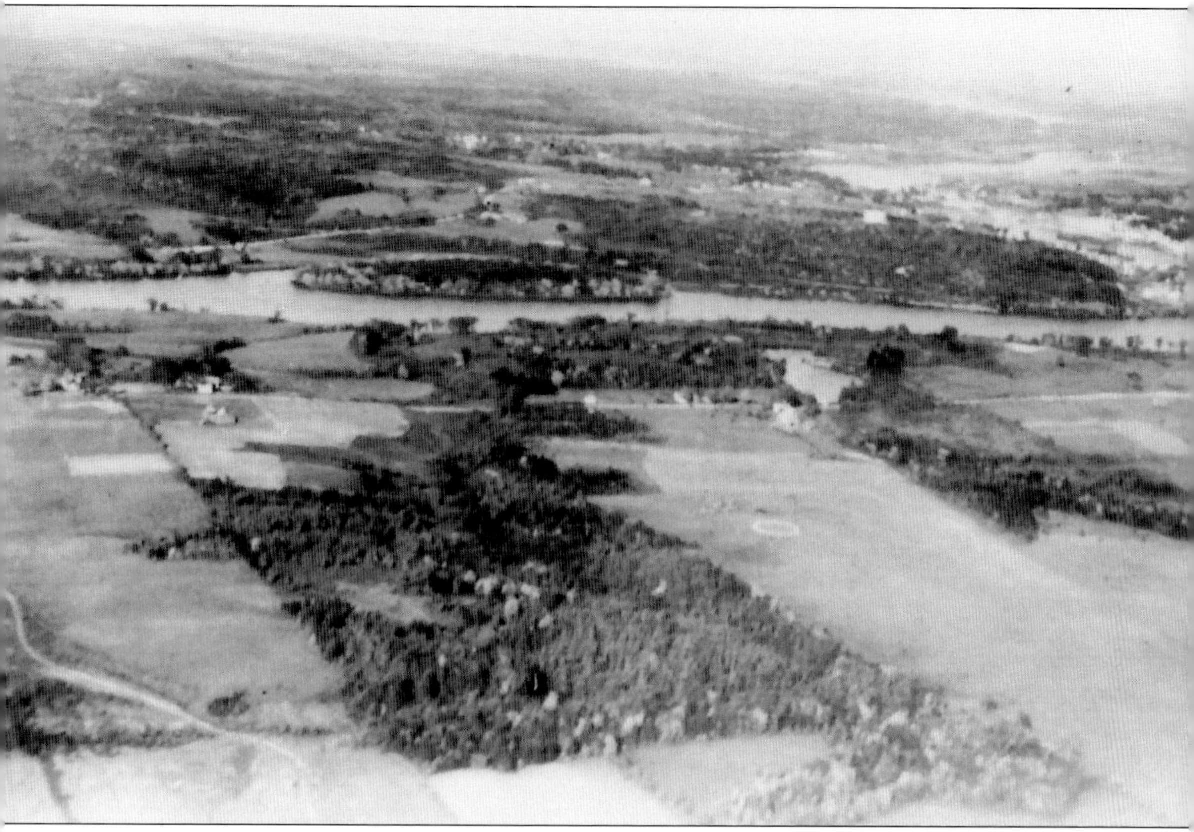

Later that year, an air-related event occurred on the River Road, Brunswick. Was this picture, dated July 5, 1922, snapped from a balloon which had taken off from the circle shown on the field across the road from Coffin's Pond, or was someone about to parachute into the field?

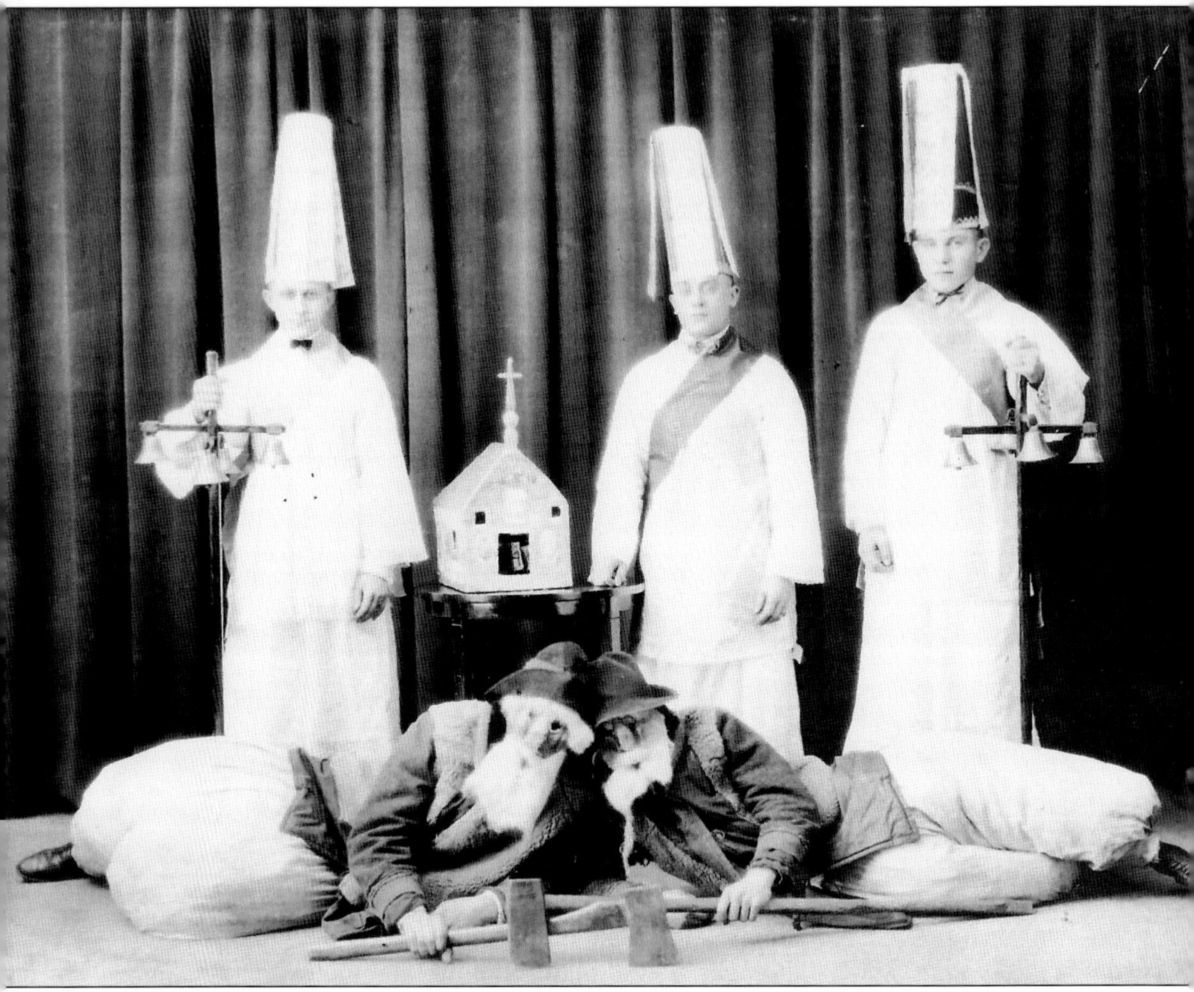

At Christmas time, Slovak homes in Pejepscot were visited by robed figures, some carrying a lighted miniature church bells and singing traditional songs. Others, called "gubas," were masked and in sheepskin jackets above full trousers stuffed with hay. Small children, as well as nearly grown girls, found them frightening, especially after the concluding song, hinting for "something liquid," meant they were given drinks at a number of houses! The "gubas" in the 1920s picture were Henry and John Pagurko; behind them were Joe Pagurko, John Obrin, and John Volovcik.

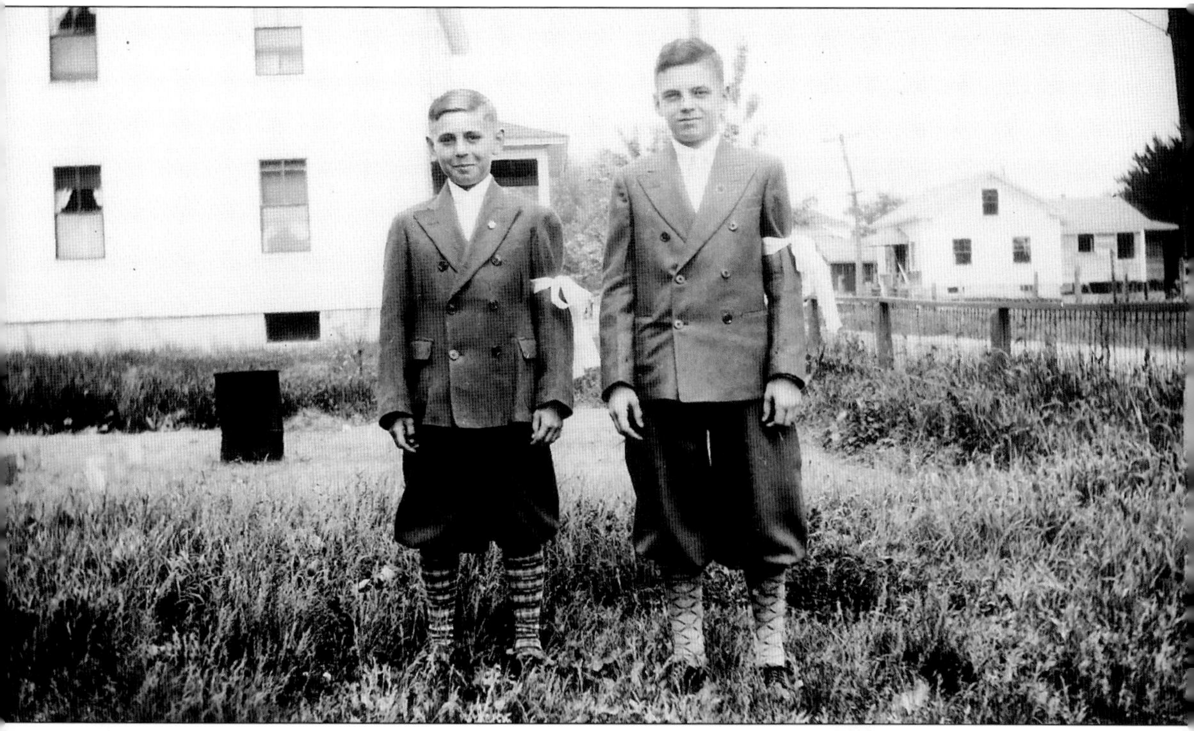

Romaine Savoi and Romeo Cloutier of Topsham posed for pictures after their first communion in the 1940s.

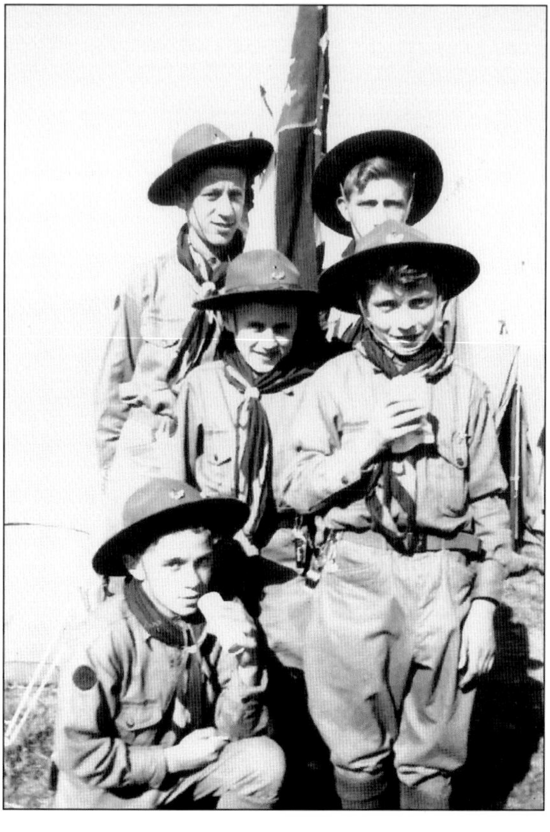

Scouting provided after-school activity for many young people: Marcel Menard (left rear) was scoutmaster for a troop from St. John's School who camped on the Bowdoin Delta in July of 1939.

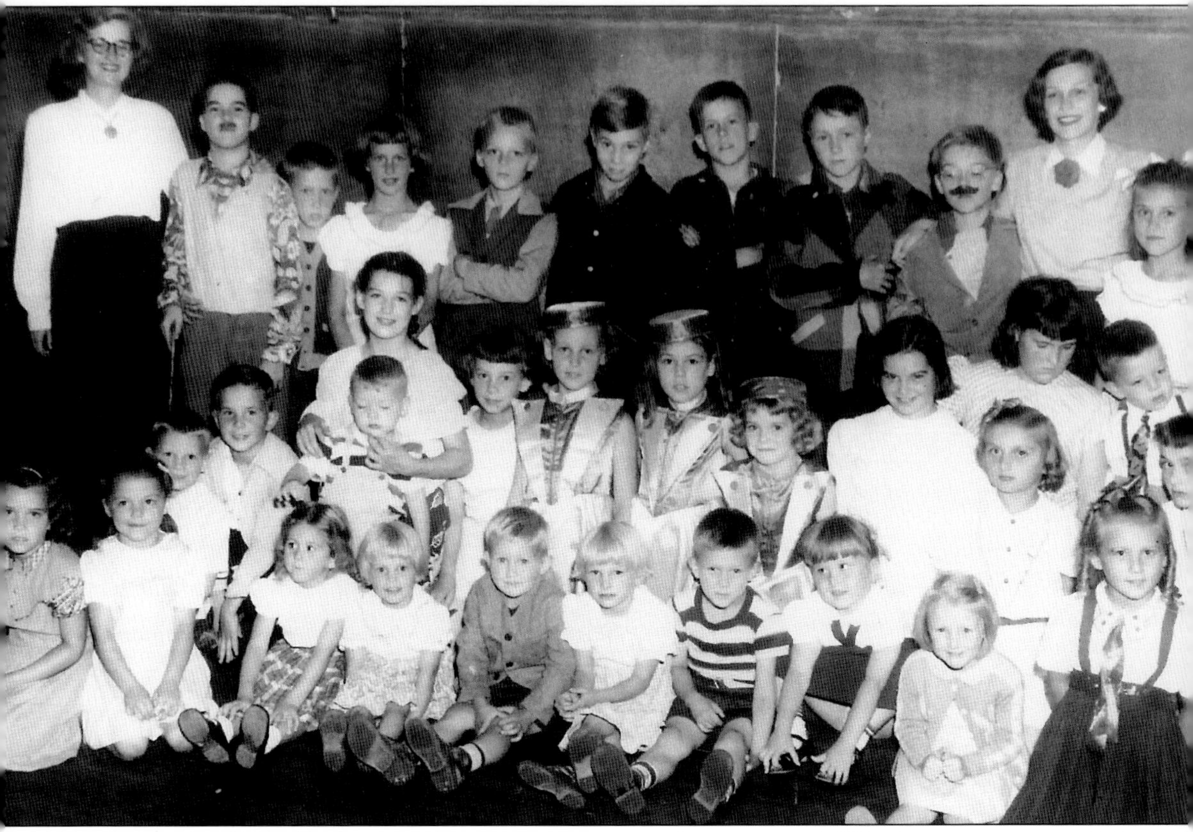

On the last day of a summer playground program in Pejepscot in 1951, the participants, of all ages, arrived in costumes—or moustaches perhaps sad to see summer fun ending, but looking eagerly forward. Although much would be different in the area by the time they became adults, much had also changed in the area in the previous century. They would adapt.